EVIL AND THE RESPONSE OF WORLD RELIGION

EVIL AND THE RESPONSE OF WORLD RELIGION

Edited by
William Cenkner

PARAGON HOUSE
St. Paul, Minnesota

First Edition, 1997
Published in the United States by

Paragon House
2700 University Ave. W.
St. Paul, Minnesota   55114

Cover Art: Art Resource, NY, *Cain and Abel*, Titian.

Library of Congress Cataloging-in-Publication Data

Evil and the response of world religion / edited by William
Cenkner.
  -- 1st ed.
      p. 256   cm.   -- (IRFWP Congress series : 1)
   Includes bibliographical references.
   ISBN 1-55778-758-1 (hardcover).
   ISBN 1-55778-753-0 (pbk.).
   1. Good and evil.   2. Religions.   I. Cenkner, William, 1930-
II. Series.
BJ1401.E78   1997
291.2' 118--dc21   96-37024
                                                        CIP

Manufactured in the United States of America

Contents

CONTENTS

INTRODUCTION
By William Cenkner

I.

T he most widely read book on evil in modern times or possibly for all time, with over three million copies in several languages, is Harold Kushner's *When Bad Things Happen to Good People*.[1] Rabbi Kushner's book in itself was not responsible for igniting interest in the problem of evil, but he was responding to an interest that has confounded in a special way modern society. His book published in 1981 emerged from a generation that had possibly written more on evil than ever before in history. In 1993 Barry L. Whitney, a specialist in theodicy, published a 650-page bibliography on evil, covering the years from 1960 to 1990 with titles only in English or translated into the English language.[2] He selected what he calls the most relevant items, 1,500 of which he annotated and another 2,600 categorized by theme. Other than this body of literature, he estimates that tens of thousands of books on evil have been written during this period in other languages.

Although a significant body of this literature reflects the present conversations in philosophy, religion and theology, the conversation is not limited to this arena. As the outstanding nineteenth century Russian novelist, Feodor Dostoevski, demonstrated in *The Brothers Karamazov*, evil is a perennial subject in world literature. This continues with the modern novel, short story, and even poetry. The contemporary art world evidences the same interest, for example, Anselm Kiefer and his captivating work, "Zim-Zum." Social and cultural historians, such as Michel Foucault, and postmodern critics, such as Mark C. Taylor, focus upon evil in their most relevant reflections.[3] American television programming is dominated by stories about crime and pain, with the courtroom and the hospital emergency room serving as major stages of human experience. Whether the professional world is academe or entertainment, the same problem has captured the imagination: evil.

One could attribute this to the enormity of world tragedy in this century: wars, holocausts, oppression of peoples. One could also attribute it to the atheism or humanism of this age which can be traced to previous centuries. The technological revolution, a direct offspring of the age of science, has taken giant strides in a few decades, but neither technology nor science seem to have mitigated the presence of evil in the modern world. Technological power has reached a level of domination that is unparalleled in the history of the world as we know it.

David Ray Griffin, a contributor to this volume and a Christian theologian, writes that the power to sin matches the power to dominate.[4] He believes that the greater possibility for good leads to greater possibility for evil. As the arena for growth and the opportunity for good expand, the possibility for deviation and deformity in life, nature, and progress equally increase. Many commentators reflect a fundamental experience of society today; namely, overwhelming power or radical evil is more frequently taking charge of this world and of human life.

It would seem that evil is as problematic today as it was among the founders of the world's religions or the first philosophers of the ancient world. This book is based upon the premise that the wisdom traditions of religion can speak to the modern world. It also implicitly advances the notion that the religions of the world have as a primary task to address the problem of evil.[5] The women and men who live within a religious tradition today encounter the problematic of evil in their faith stance, their moral life, and even in their life of prayer, worship, and mysticism.[6]

II.

The essays in this book emerge from a conference on "The Reality of Evil and the Response of the World's Religions," held in Seoul, Korea, April 28 to May 2, 1994, sponsored by the Inter-Religious Federation for World Peace (IRFWP). Thomas G. Walsh commenting on the conference quoted two presidents of the sponsoring group:

> No religion fails to attend to aspects of the human condition which stand in contrast to goodness, enlightenment, or unity with the divine reality. Without an understanding of evil—its origin, its

essential nature, its characteristics, and its means of proliferation—
the pursuit of religious ideals is futile. As IRFWP President, Paulos
Mar Gregorios has said: "In our work for the unity of humanity,
we have to face the problem of evil, because evil is the great
obstacle to true unity." In the words of IRFWP President, Chung
Hwan Kwak, "Our premise is simply that world peace cannot be
properly pursued without some clear understanding of the true
nature of our problem, its roots and its means for self-
perpetuation." Recognition of the power, tenacity and, often
sovereignty of evil in our world is imperative for those committed
to world peace through interreligious dialogue.[7]

The conference included over sixty participants from many
nations, ethnic groups, and religions. Papers represented Jewish,
Christian, Islamic, traditional African and shamanic, Hindu,
Buddhist, Taoist, and Confucian perspectives. The essays in this
book are nineteen representative participants from this group.

Under the broader title the conference was organized into three
distinct discussions: (1) theoretical explanations of and responses
to evil; (2) practical responses to evil; (3) activist responses to evil.
The first discussion focused on theological and philosophical
reflections on evil. Religions and philosophies, East and West, have
responded through their shamans, prophets and wisdom figures
with insight, knowledge and analysis. Each religious or philosophical tradition, either corporately or among individual thinkers, has
something distinct to say. The second discussion considered the
particular manifestations of evil, such as war, racism, consumerism,
and family fragmentation. The purpose here was to identify causes
and possible solutions, drawing upon the wisdom of the traditions.
Finally, a third discussion centered on concrete actions already
taken to combat evil. Programs such as Amnesty International,
Habitat for Humanity, the United Nations programs, and other
efforts in public service, whether religiously sponsored or not, were
considered.

The essays in this book are concerned with the first and second
discussion, namely, the theoretical and practical explanations of
and responses to evil. In editing this book I have made neither the
distinction between the theoretical and the practical explanations
of nor the theoretical and practical responses to evil. Although I
am somewhat responsible for these distinctions as a convener of the

conference, I found in the experience of interreligious dialogue that these categories were not distinct and discrete in many religious and philosophical traditions. If each tradition is to speak with its own voice, it needs to stand within its own context. For this reason I have arranged the essays according to area and geographic contexts and conclude with essays from the contemporary period that have clear pancultural implications.

III.

Part One introduces responses to evil from the religions of the book, that is, religions emerging out of the Middle East and the biblical traditions, Judaism, Christianity, and Islam. In Chapter 1, Gene G. James examines the creation story in the Hebrew Torah narrated by the priestly author, the P account, who gives special attention to prohibitions against the taking of life, eating meat, and other dietary restrictions. Evil is understood as an ever present tendency to chaos, a tendency within the creation stories, and within creation and human nature itself. Modifications and actual mitigation of the commandment against killing and meat eating is in recognition of this human weakness and tendency.

Sheldon R. Isenberg describes the evolving aspects of the problem of evil, beginning with the Hebrew scriptures, moving to rabbinic Judaism, and culminating with the Kabbalah, the major tradition of Jewish mysticism. Multiple insights emerged in this development: power to overcome evil, human responsibility for suffering, corporate suffering, and unfair distribution of suffering. The Kabbalah, however, revealed the process from broken harmony to the healing relationships with and between the human, cosmic, and divine communities.

David J. Goldberg, in Chapter 3, focuses upon the medieval Jewish philosophers of Abraham Ibn Daud, Moses Maimonides, and again the Kabbalist tradition. He continues with modern Jewish process theologians and the Holocaust but concludes with the insight of the Christian thinker John Hick who draws upon the poet Keats' notion of "The vale of Soul-making." According to Goldberg, soul-making, a theme that is repeated in several of the essays in this book, connects a contemporary response to evil with medieval Jewish thought.

Two essays speak directly from the Christian biblical tradition, both drawing upon the Christian symbol of the cross of Jesus as a source for a theological response to evil. Jane Mary Zwerner stipulates that suffering is the experience of moral or natural evil as meaningless or hopeless. Following Irenaean theodicy, she proposes that the transformation of the human person from mere material existence to moral and spiritual life is essentially linked to suffering. Within a Christian framework, we are called to accept the suffering and redemptive death of Jesus on the cross as a paradigm of communal solidarity.

Mary Ann Stenger, however, focuses on the ambiguity of the symbol of the cross throughout Christian history. Just as there is paradox in Jesus as the divine incarnate, so also there is paradox in the symbolic understanding of the cross. The cross can be a symbol of liberation from injustice and violence; it has also been used not infrequently to legitimate violence and injustice against women and those caught within slavery. For this reason the symbol of the cross must be in conjunction with the resurrection for a fully liberating image.

Two essays, Chapters 6 and 7, speak for and out of the Islamic tradition. The first by Muhammad Al-Ghazali is based solidly upon the *Qur'an* which points to the innate duality within human nature, a simultaneous capacity for good and evil. Since the root of evil is human intentionality, there is need for constant vigilance in order to reform and rectify such inherent evil tendencies. Yet personal well-being is not the goal of human growth and development but justice in the full course of social life. Islamic justice is to establish and actualize the harmony and balance at all levels of relationship with human beings and all God's creatures.

Riffat Hassan in her essay attempts to establish a feminist theology not only to liberate Muslim women but also Muslim men. Cognizant of the inequality of women in Islamic social history, she establishes from textual analysis of the *Qur'an* gender equality. She shows that misreading and misinterpretation of Qur'anic passages have been used to deny equality and justice to Muslim women. According to her analysis, woman and man are equal creatures of a just and merciful God whose pleasure it is for them to live together in harmony and justice.

Part Two of this book introduces responses to the problem of evil from Asian traditions, Buddhism and Hinduism in particular. Beginning with Theravada Buddhism in Chapter 8, Medagama Vajiragnana, drawing upon early Buddhist texts, articulates a traditional perspective by locating evil in ignorance, a typical Indian response, and in anything opposed to the attainment of enlightenment. Although evil is symbolized in the notion of Mara, not as some external force or demonic individual but as nature itself. He not only interprets Mara according to early Buddhist scriptures but also relates understandings from pre-Buddhist folklore. The pre-Buddhist Mara legends, however, are given Buddhist interpretation in early Buddhism and accordingly captured more readily the imagination of believers than reflective understandings of evil.

Three essays speak within the context of the Hindu tradition. Stephen Kaplan in Chapter 10 writes from the perspective of India's classical Advaita Vedanta and the medieval thought of Sankara who posited three different levels of meaning in dealing with the reality of evil: first, from a metaphysical level, the level of the highest truth, a level of nonduality in which no evil exists; secondly, from a phenomenological level where evil is the result of rebirth and the law of *karma*; and finally, from an epistemological level, where individuality and duality persist, evil is the result of ignorance. Kaplan draws upon the modern philosophy of K. C. Bhatacharyya for further insight into a Vendantic understanding of evil. He concludes by making a holographic analogy in order to exemplify how an Advaitin can maintain that evil does not exist while at the same time say it is a datum of experience.

William Cenkner in another essay from the Hindu tradition contextualizes the classical ways of dealing with evil and suffering from the early ritual responses to the more reflective and meditative disciplines and the high devotional and altruistic activity of the *Bhagavad Gita*. Modern opinion from the middle of the nineteenth century to the present is then highlighted with special attention to Rabindranath Tagore and Sarvepalli Radhakrishnan. Both of these figures placed their responses to evil concretely in the created world, not in an abstract metaphysical realm but in the realm of political and social reality.

Francis Xavier D'Sa, in the final essay from Indian life, reflects from the methodological framework of Raimundo Panikkar's triadic view of reality in examining the response to evil in the

Bhagavad Gita. At the very least this is an attempt at comparative theology in which Christian trinitarian thought gives definition to both evil and its response within Hinduism. Similar patterns of reality and similar insights are perceived in the *Gita* utilizing a triadic grid.

Part Three presents two essays from African traditional religion, specifically the Yoruba culture of Nigeria. In Chapter 13 E. O. Oyelade describes the beliefs of Yoruba society in relation to evil by drawing upon the wisdom oracle of Ifa and typical proverbs reflecting life-views. By distinguishing different types of evil as physical, moral, inflicted, and predestined, he demonstrates the equally different responses of the Yoruba people. They will, for example, have recourse to the tribal medicine man, the tribal king, and even traditional sacrifice.

Wande Abimbola, relying upon the Ifa literary corpus of sacred oral texts, identifies and examines the dynamic tension between evil and good in Yoruba understanding. The Yorubas seek a balance through a symbolic system of codes in communicating with an elaborate pantheon of supernatural powers. Again, sacrifice is frequently the principle of resolution leading to the restoration of good order. Quoting from the Ifa sacred literature, he demonstrates that the conflict between good and evil is in fact the perduring tension between the gods/powers and the anti-gods.

The final section of this book, Part Four, consists of contemporary responses, most from Western perspectives but each possessing significant global implications. For example, Peter C. Phan selects the liberation theology of the Latin American Christian, Gustavo Gutierrez, who deals explicitly with the problem of evil to address the exploitation and oppression of suffering peoples throughout the world. Gutierrez recasts the problem in terms of orthopraxis and in demonstrating how the suffering figure of Job eventually realizes God's preferential love for the oppressed and disenfranchised. By introducing the language of prophecy and the language of contemplation, Gutierrez includes worship, prayer, and mysticism as integral to the struggle for justice.

In Chapter 17 Anthony J. Guerra articulates the source and response to evil in the thought of Rev. Sun Myung Moon and the practices of the Unification Church, a new religious movement begun in Korea but now spread throughout the world. For Unificationists the original fault of Adam and Eve through sexual sin prevented the establishment of the true family. Thus Rev. Moon's movement intends to restore a God-centered perfected family by creating a new history of families united to reform world society. The marriage ceremony, arranged marriages, especially cross-cultural unions, and mass weddings raise up marriage and family life as primordial sacraments in the modern world.

M. Darrol Bryant points to ecological evil as the critical source of evil in the present, and caring for the earth, particularly within interfaith dialogue, as an immediate and viable response. He shows how mastery over nature, control of it, technological interventions, and the creation of an industrial technological culture have all led to a crisis that ignores nature as a living system. Such mastery is hostile to religious cosmologies and world spiritual traditions. He ultimately calls for the religions to take responsibility for the problem and to inspire a critical analysis of the ecological situation.

The final two essays presume the modern conversation with process theology, a major voice in theodicy and the problem of evil today. David Ray Griffin, speaking as a Christian theologian, states that the whole point of a theodicy is to show that the evils of this world do not contradict the perfect goodness of the divine reality. He addresses in particular demonic evil, that is, evil diametrically opposed to divine power with such strength as to thwart divine purposes and divine creations. Drawing upon Alfred North Whitehead's distinction between God and creativity, he not only responds to the problem of evil in general but also to a nonmythical notion of demonic evil in particular. Concluding that religion should attempt to overcome evil in all its forms, he believes that religion should serve especially as an agency of the divine in overcoming demonic evil.

Paul Badham, concluding with Chapter 19, explores the possibility of a world theodicy in responding to the problem of evil that would embrace both nontheistic religions and even those traditions denying the existence of a human soul. John Hick's soul-making theodicy is the context within which he asks whether such a theodicy has anything to say to a religiously plural world. The viability of a soul-making theodicy is examined in Judaism, Islam, Buddhism, and Hinduism. The latter two traditions offer the greatest challenge to the author. Badham's approach points to a growing interest in doing global theology and the actual practice of comparative theology.

IV.

I wish to thank the publisher and the editor of *Dialogue & Alliance* for using those essays that in earlier drafts appeared in their journal.[8] Appreciation is also expressed to Dr. Thomas G. Walsh and Dr. Frank F. Kaufmann who organized and planned the Seoul conference that gave birth to this book. I am grateful to Paragon House for taking on this project. A word of special gratitude is extended to Mary Dancy who prepared the final manuscript for publication.

This book is dedicated to those men and women who promote and participate in interreligious projects whether in theoretical, practical or activist forums. May they experience in their lifetime the greater unity of the human family.

NOTES

1. Harold Kushner, *When Bad Things Happen to Good People* (New York: Avon Books, 1981).
2. Barry L. Whitney, *Theodicy: An Annotated Bibliography on the Problem of Evil 1960-1990* (New York and London: Garland Publishing, Inc., 1993).
3. See Mark C. Taylor, *Disfiguring: Art, Architecture, Religion* (Chicago and London: The University of Chicago Press, 1992). For Taylor's discussion of Anselm Kiefer, see pp. 290-307.
4. See Chapter 18 below, David Ray Griffin, "Divine Goodness and Demonic Evil."
5. See Chapter 17 below, M. Darrol Bryant, "Ecological Evil and Interfaith Dialogue: Caring for the Earth."
6. See Michael Stoeber, *Evil and the Mystics' God* (Toronto and London: University of Toronto and Macmillan Press, 1992).
7. Thomas G. Walsh, "Seoul Congress Focuses on the Human Problem," *IRFWP Newsletter*, Vol. 11, No. 1, Spring 1994, p. 3.
8. See *Dialogue & Alliance*, Vol. 8, No. 2, Fall-Winter 1994. The authors who published earlier drafts are: Wande Abimbola, Muhammad Al-Ghazali, William Cenkner, Francis Xavier D'Sa, David Goldberg, Anthony J. Guerra, Peter C. Phan. I also thank Villanova University Press for the article by Jane Mary Zwerner, whose article with revisions was published in an anthology on social ethics by that Press in 1996.

PART ONE

Response from the Religions of the Book

1

The Priestly Conceptions of Evil in the Torah

By Gene G. James

Modern biblical scholars identify four writers whose work forms the Torah, referring to them with the letters J, E, D and P. There is also a final editor or redactor referred to as R. The contribution of P is usually thought to be the last of the four writers. However, much of what he wrote constitutes the least interesting aspects of the Torah for modern readers, such as long discussions of sacrificial rituals, the making of priestly vestments, and dietary restrictions. Because of his concern with such matters, he is referred to as P, an abbreviation for priestly writer. The majority of the narratives in P are variations of stories in JE. Thorough exposition of his work would require an examination of both what he omits and adds to their stories. This study is restricted to demonstrate that implicit in P's work is a conception of evil which is of great importance for understanding his worldview and ritual practices. The most relevant sections of P's work in this regard are his creation and flood stories in the book of Genesis (1:1-2:3; 7:8-9, 11, 13-16a, 21, 24; 8:1-2a, 3b-5, 7, 13a, 14-19; 9:1-17), and the dietary prohibitions in Leviticus (11:1-47).[1]

Creation

Neither the idea of creation by spoken word nor that of bringing order to chaotic matter was unique to P. The former can be found in the Egyptian *Memphite Theology*, the original text of which is dated by scholars to the Old Kingdom and, therefore, composed at least fifteen hundred years before P. In this account Ptah not only creates both the other gods and the world by command, he is also described at the completion of his work as satisfied with it and resting from his labor. The idea of creation by command is also found in the "Story of Ra and the Serpent" in which Ra the sun god says: "There was no Heaven and no Earth, There was no Dry Land and no Reptiles in Egypt. Then I spoke and living creatures appeared."[2] The idea of a god bringing order to chaotic matter is present in numerous Near Eastern creation stories, but the one with which the P story is most frequently compared is the Babylonian "Enuma Elish" story, itself modeled on an older Sumerian story. The similarities include a wind or breath from God which stills the waters, the heavens and the earth formed from preexisting material, the presence of subordinate gods (indicated in P by the use of the plural word Elohim for God and the remark, "let us make humans in our image," Genesis 1:26). Similarities also occur with the word Tiamat, the goddess from whose dead body the heavens and earth were made in "Enuma Elish," and the word *tehom*, the deep from which they are made in the P story.

There are of course differences as well as similarities. For example, in "Enuma Elish" the chaotic waters are personified in the form of a primordial couple, Apsu (fresh water) and Tiamat (salt water). They give birth to the heavenly court of gods, after which Tiamat overpowers Apsu and takes a new mate, Kingu, one of her own offspring. Frightened by Tiamat's violent behavior, the other gods agree to make Marduk their chief if he can slay Tiamat, which he does by inflating her with his breath or wind and then piercing her with lightning. He then kills Kingu and proceeds to make heaven and earth from Tiamat's body, and human beings from Kingu's.

Scholars who stress the uniqueness of P's account find great significance in the fact that watery chaos is personified in "Enuma Elish" and not in P. More important, in my opinion, is the fact that water symbolizes both an element essential to life and one when out of control in the form of floods posed the greatest threat to human existence known to the civilizations of the Near East. From this perspective, the most significant feature of both stories is that of a god who controls the destructive aspects of nature, bringing about the order on which human life depends. The fact that water is personified in "Enuma Elish" but not in P, is relatively insignificant, especially since at other places in the Bible the chaotic waters are personified. (See for example: Ps. 74:13, 104:9, 148:6; Job 26:12; Isaiah 27:1, 51:9.)

Scholars who stress the uniqueness of P also find importance in the fact that in P God creates by command. But, as pointed out above, this is not unique to P. Nor is spoken command the means God uses to overcome the primordial chaotic waters in P. In both "Enuma Elish" and the P story, the waters are stilled by the wind or breath of god. It is only after God has subdued the waters in this way that God brings other things into existence by command in the P story.

Theologians often attribute the doctrine of *creatio ex nihilo* to the P creation story. However, the primordial waters are clearly said to exist before Elohim creates anything in the P story. The idea of *creatio ex nihilo* is therefore not present. The central point of the story is that God brought order to preexisting, chaotic material symbolized by water and keeps it from returning to chaos. This idea is also stressed in some of the Psalms and in Job. For example, God is described in Job as having "shut in the sea with doors when it burst out from the womb" and saying to it: "Thus far you shall come, and no farther. . . here shall your proud waves be stopped" (Job 38:8-11). Such language suggests that if God were to relax divine activity for a single instant, there would be a return to primeval chaos, an idea similar to that of continuous creation in medieval Christian thought, where creation is not a one-time event but an ongoing activity sustaining the universe and keeping it from reverting to chaos.

Underlying the P creation story is the idea of primordial chaos which is a permanent threat to human existence but kept at bay by the order that God has imposed on it. However, this doctrine is not unique to P but is found in most Near Eastern creation stories. What is unique to P is the detailed way he describes the order of creation, assigning the creation of the heavens, dry land, and the waters below the firmament, to different days of creation. Also unique is the way in which he divides the creation of living beings into three groups, each assigned to a different realm of creation, the birds to the heavens, animals and human beings to the dry land, and fish and sea monsters to the waters. Thus, according to P, three basic types of creatures were made to function within three quite different types of environments. This seems to be part of what P means in saying that each creature was created according to its kind. This remark may also refer to more specific differences of anatomy and behavior that bring about adaptation to more specialized environments.

Other features unique to P are God telling all living creatures to be fruitful and multiply, and God giving them only plants and fruit for food. According to P, then, it was God's plan that all living beings should be vegetarian. This presupposes that all life is holy, that is, set apart as belonging to God only. It also presupposes that since God alone gives life, God alone can legitimately take it away. Thus, although there are no explicit prohibitions in the P creation story analogous to the one in the J story in which Yahweh forbids Adam to eat from the tree of good and evil, prohibitions against killing and eating meat may be deduced from the fact that only plants and fruit were given to creatures for their food.

An additional positive command is given to humans, now said to be created in the image of the gods, the latter also not an idea unique to P but found in earlier Egyptian thought.[3] The command is that human beings are to subdue the earth and exercise dominion over the animals. The Hebrew word translated as subdue is *kabash*, and the one translated as exercise dominion is *radah*. According to W. Lee Humphreys, the original meaning of both words is that of treading or stamping upon something, for example, upon grapes.[4] However, both words are used in the Bible primarily in a military sense to convey the ideas of forceful conquest and domination. This has led some people to interpret the command to subdue the earth and exercise dominion over the animals as giving humanity the right to use the earth and its creatures any way they wish. If one takes this commandment in conjunction with the immediately preceding text in which prohibitions against killing and eating other creatures are implied, it is unlikely that such license was intended. Given this context, and P's overall worldview, the commandment is more plausibly interpreted to mean that humans should maintain the order God has bestowed on the world, an order in which life is sacred. This would not rule out domestication of animals and their use in agriculture, nor would it prohibit modifying the earth in ways necessary to carry on agriculture. But it would hardly sanction doing whatever one wishes to the earth and other species. It instead lends support to doctrines of animal rights and preservation of the environment. To put the matter in terms of contemporary debate, the commandment enjoins stewardship, not exploitation of animals and the environment.

Disobedience, Destruction, and a New Beginning

The primary duties of humans in the P account are to refrain from violence by not killing or eating meat. According to P the flood occurs because humans did not abide by these prohibitions. Violence became so widespread that God resolved to destroy all living creatures and the earth itself. But the mind of God changed, and God decided to spare two of all living creatures along with Noah and his family, who apparently, unlike the rest of humanity, had kept the prohibitions against taking life and eating meat. After instructing Noah to build an ark and take two of all living creatures aboard, God opened the windows of the heavens and relaxed control over the springs of the earth, allowing torrents of chaotic waters from the deep to flood.

When Noah and the other creatures emerged from the ark, God once again told them to be fruitful and multiply as at the time of creation. This command represents a completely opposite judgment regarding the desirability of population growth to the one found in the "Atrahasis Story," the ancient Sumerian story on which the later Babylonian "Gilgamesh Epic" was modeled. For in the Atrahasis story the gods send a flood to destroy humans precisely because they have grown too numerous and noisy. The opposed judgments may be seen as reflecting the difference between a Hebrew author who belonged to a small group of people, who throughout most of their history were dominated by larger groups and hoped to grow in number in order to make their existence more secure, and an earlier author living in a more crowded urban environment.

God also stated that never again will the order of creation be threatened with destruction by allowing it to return to chaos. Humans are thereby assured that basic order will reign in the universe, that day will continue to follow night and season follow season. This promise is made not only to human creatures, but to all creatures, and God sets the rainbow in the heavens as a sign of the promise.

Noah took only two of each kind of animal aboard the ark in the P story because he was a vegetarian who obeyed the law not to kill and would therefore not be eating or sacrificing any of them. This is one of the major differences between the P and the J accounts of the flood, for in the J account Noah is instructed to take two of all unclean animals, but seven of the clean. Also at the conclusion of the flood in the J account, Noah sacrifices animals in gratitude for having been saved.

Reflecting on human conduct God concludes that the human heart is evil from youth, that is, the murderous and carnivorous nature of human beings cannot be eradicated. Knowing that Noah's descendants will resort to eating meat, God therefore institutes a new command, less stringent than the old one. Humans may now kill and eat animals, but only if they do not consume the blood which is the sign of life and hence belongs to God alone (Gen. 9:3-4). Thus, according to P, eating meat is a concession to the evil nature of humanity. Although eating meat is now allowed, the human situation after the flood represents a decline from the previous period, and the long lifespans achieved by human beings before the flood are no longer possible. Thus, in the lists taken from the "Book of Generations," human lifespans become progressively shorter after the flood.

Holiness

Like JE, P also describes a covenant with Abraham in which he is promised numerous descendants whom God will aid in conquering the land of Canaan. In P the covenant with Abraham and his descendants is interpreted as one in which God has set aside the Israelites from all other people, thereby making them holy. For the word translated as holy means that which is separate, in particular that which is set aside by or for God. The sign of the covenant which sets Abraham and his descendants apart from other people is circumcision. This criterion, it should be noted, also conveniently excluded females as incapable of holiness and therefore unqualified for the priesthood. Since, according to Jeremiah, many of the people living in proximity to the Israelites (including the Egyptians, Edomites, Ammonites, and Moabites) also practiced circumcision, the criterion was no doubt more useful in excluding women from the priesthood than in setting the Israelites apart from their neighbors (Jer. 9:25).[5] The covenant with Abraham is reaffirmed at various points in P's subsequent account of the Israelites, especially at Sinai where an injunction to keep the Sabbath is added.

People who are set apart by God to become holy are required to live by different rules than other people. The majority of P's work is concerned with specifying three basic types of rules: rules governing the conduct of sacrifices and rituals, dietary rules, and rules governing moral behavior. P goes into greatest detail regarding ritualistic rules. He also stresses that only Aaronic priests can properly interpret and apply such rules, and that exact conformity is required, a point made in a dramatic way when two of Aaron's sons are consumed by fire that shoots out from the altar because they perform a sacrifice in an improper manner (Lev. 10:1). However, it is the dietary rules that are of greatest relevance for understanding P's world view and the concept of evil implicit in it.

For modern scholars the dietary rules have been among the most puzzling features of the Bible. Most have held that there are no rational principles of selection underlying the rules that certain animals should not be eaten, that perhaps some were prohibited for health reasons, some because of their repulsive appearance, and others because they played some role in Canaanite rituals. However, at no point does P state that any of the animals are prohibited for these reasons. To the contrary, he introduces each rule as a requirement of holiness.

To understand the dietary prohibitions one must begin with the order imposed on the world in P's account of creation. As pointed out above, creation is there divided into three realms, dry land, the heavens, and the waters below the firmament, with different creatures assigned to different realms. The dietary prohibitions presuppose this scheme, assuming in addition that each creature ought to remain in the realm to which it was assigned. The animals appropriate to dry land are those that have four feet with a divided hoof and chew the cud. Those appropriate to the heavens are birds with feathers and wings; those appropriate to the waters are fish with scales and fins. There is also an appropriate form of locomotion for each realm: walking for land animals, flying for birds, and swimming for fish.

The criteria for land animals, having four feet with divided hooves and chewing the cud, identifies only herbivores. The paradigm cases of animals satisfying these criteria are domestic grazing animals such as goats, sheep and cows. Although pigs have divided hooves, they are ruled out because they do not chew the cud, that is, they are not herbivorous ruminants, but are omnivores that on occasion eat meat. The rabbit, on the other hand, is a herbivore but does not have a divided hoof, so it too is ruled out. Animals that do not have hooves but rather have claws to seize prey are also ruled out. So are all animals that have more than four feet such as the centipede; and those that crawl instead of walking, such as insects and reptiles. All the birds that are ruled out are either without proper locomotion such as the ostrich that cannot fly, or spend a great deal of time outside their proper element (the heavens) such as the heron, or are predatory such as eagles and owls. The birds that spend a great deal of time outside of their proper element are also predatory so they would also be eliminated. Bats are ruled out because they lack feathers. Shell fish, likewise, do not have scales and fail to exhibit the proper motion, swimming. Eels are ruled out because they lack scales. Animals that hop or leap pose a problem since their form of locomotion is neither a form of walking nor flying in the full sense of the word. P apparently felt that the movement of grasshoppers is nearer that of walking than flying and classified them as clean. The D writer disagreed and classified them as unclean (Deut. 14:19).

Provided blood was not consumed, killing and eating animals was allowed after the flood. The dietary restrictions narrow the range of animals that can be killed and eaten. The fact that it seems to be primarily predatory and carnivorous animals that are judged to be unclean should not be surprising, given P's belief that they were not included in the original plan of creation.[6] The necessity to maintain the original order of creation is central to P's worldview. The duty to be holy requires most of all that the categories of creation be kept separate and unmixed. Creatures that do not fit into any of the categories mentioned by P in his creation account are considered to be hybrids that bring about disorder in creation. They represent a return to the chaos that God banished in bringing order to the world. Consequently, P offers a number of rules to prevent such inappropriate mixing. Cattle must not be allowed to breed with other species; fields must not be sown with two kinds of seeds; an ass and an ox must not be hitched to the same plough; a garment cannot be made from two kinds of cloth.

Cleanliness and holiness are closely related features of P's worldview. To be clean animals must conform in every way to their kind. They must be perfect specimens that are not in any way defective. Animals that are disabled, mutilated, or have any discharge or disease are not to be sacrificed or eaten. Priests who conduct the sacrifices must also be free of all defects, such as open sores, malformed limbs or crushed testicles. Leaven was apparently forbidden in bread to be used in sacrifices because it is an agent that introduces changes in flour. On the other hand, the use of salt on meat sacrifices seems to have been mandatory because it tends to preserve it in its original state. The underlying idea is that any thing to be sacrificed should be as close as possible to the original form in which it came from God. All bodily discharges, whether those of animals or humans, were looked upon as a form of uncleanness. Such discharges represent a loss of form or breakdown of the organism. Sickness and death are thought of in the same way, especially death which represents the total breakdown of the organism. Thus the chief priest, who more than anyone else must be holy, is forbidden to even go near the corpse of an unclean animal or human being.

Morality

Morality is not a category separate from holiness, but means simply respect for cleanliness and proper order in human conduct. Killing is ruled out, except for slaying clean animals to eat and to perform prescribed sacrifices. Some actions such as having sex with a menstruating woman is ruled out because P believes it to be unclean. Actions such as bestiality, cross dressing, homosexuality, and racially mixed marriages are ruled out on grounds similar to those forbidding different species to breed. They are unholy because they are cases of inappropriate mixing. If any instances of uncleanliness or unholiness do occur, they must be immediately atoned for through blood sacrifice. Actions such as lying and stealing are presumably forbidden because they introduce disorder into society. Morality also demands proper respect for Aaronic priests, mandatory sacrifices, and observing holy days, that is, days set aside by or for God. As in the case of sacrificial and dietary rules, strict adherence to moral rules is required. For God as portrayed by P is described as a jealous God, punishing children of the third and fourth generation for the iniquities of their parents (Ex. 20:5).

Evil

The reason given for the flood in the P account is that God concluded that all flesh had become corrupt, presumably because both animals and humans had abandoned a vegetarian diet and were killing and eating others. Tendencies leading to hybrids and inappropriate mixing were also present. Just as creation in general is constantly threatened by chaos, so too there is a similar tendency toward chaos within creation itself. The chaos which constantly threatens creation in general may be described as external evil and that which is found within creation itself as internal evil. Internal evil is not limited to the tendency of animate life toward hybrids and inappropriate mixing, but internal evil is found in the human heart as well, resulting in violent and disorderly behavior that is contrary to God's intentions. The commandment that one be holy is a demand that one purify oneself, prevent inappropriate mixing, and control the evil tendencies of one's heart, just as God controls the external disorder that threatens the universe. Since the tendency toward disorder is a universal and constant feature of creation, there is no story in P analogous to the J story of Adam and Eve that attempts to trace the existence of evil to a particular incident. Evil is instead intrinsic to creation and human nature. It is God's recognition of the latter that causes God to modify the original commandments prohibiting killing and eating meat. Evil as thus understood is not synonymous with the punishment that God metes out to humans for failure to attain holiness. It is rather an active force which requires continuous resistance on the part of both God and humans. The question of how such cosmic evil against God's will can exist is not raised. P does not engage in direct discussion of evil. The account given here seeks to make explicit what P took for granted.

Conclusion

The themes of creation by spoken word, humans created in the image of the gods, and order imposed on preexisting chaotic material are not unique to P but are found in earlier Middle Eastern creation stories. However, the concept of God imposing order on chaotic material is central in understanding P's world view. Especially important and unique to P is the detailed way in which he describes creation, assigning different creatures to the heavens, the earth and the waters. Each type of creature has unique characteristics and modes of behavior adapted to a particular kind of life. All living creatures were told by God at creation to be fruitful and multiply and were given only plants and fruits as food. Humans were given an additional commandment to subdue the earth and establish dominion over animals. Although the primary meaning of *kabash* and *radah*, in which this commandment was formulated is forceful domination, it is unlikely that the commandment was intended to sanction whatever one wishes to do to the earth and to animals. Given P's overall worldview and the context immediately preceding the commandment, it is more probable that humans are commanded to maintain the order God bestowed on creation, by refraining from taking life, eating meat, and preventing inappropriate mixing of species. Thus, instead of sanctioning violence, the commandment calls for respect for all living beings and the preservation of nature. However, this does not rule out domestication of animals and modification of nature in ways necessary for agriculture. The commandment is also later modified to allow the use of animals in sacrifice and eating. This modification is presented as a concession apparently to eradicate murderous and carnivorous tendencies in human nature. A still later set of commandments, the holiness code, limits the type of animals that can be sacrificed or eaten. This code requires the Israelites to distinguish themselves from other people by practicing circumcision, observing certain holy days, and forbidding various types of mixing. The code also establishes a totally male Aaronic priesthood.

The rules regarding sacrifices, prevention of inappropriate mixing, and dietary prohibitions presuppose that the order of creation is retained in close agreement with original creation. Morality is not a separate category for P but is merely the avoidance of inappropriate mixing and maintaining of proper order in human behavior. P's worldview is one in which everything is highly ordered and subject to rigid rules. Even P's style reflects this exaggerated sense of order. He assumes that there is a proper way of stating everything, and one should not deviate from this way.

Implicit, therefore, in P's worldview is a conception of evil as the breakdown of order. Tendencies to evil are found both without and within creation. External evil is represented by chaos which continually threatens the order of creation and is held back only by God's constant activity. Internal evil includes both tendencies within creation which give rise to hybrids and inappropriate mixing, and those that result in inappropriate human behavior. Holiness requires that one prevent inappropriate mixing and control the evil tendencies of one's heart in the same way God controls the external disorder that threatens the universe.

Evil is thus an ever present tendency for creation to return to chaos. How can such evil, which requires constant activity on the part of both God and humans to hold it in check, exist? Perhaps P thought that the primordial material from which God fashioned the world, was not merely lacking order but inherently opposed to it. If so, his view of evil would be much closer to Neoplatonic dualism than it is usually thought to be. If P did think of the primordial material in this way, it would explain both why God has to struggle to keep creation from reverting to chaos and why human nature possesses an eradicable tendency toward violence. Assuming this to be P's view, then not only was God not conceived as creating the world from nothing, but God was also conceived as limited in power. The attempt of subsequent theologians to read the doctrines of *creatio ex nihilo* and the omnipotence of God into P's account is therefore mistaken. However, since P's conception of evil was an implicit rather than explicit feature of his worldview, he does not address the issues raised here. Attempts to raise and answer such issues in systematic fashion came long after P's time.

NOTES

1. Because of limited space it is assumed that the reader is familiar with these accounts and no exposition of them is given. For the same reason little attempt is made to compare P's treatment of these matters with JE's. Finally, since the probability is overwhelming that P was male, masculine pronouns have been used to refer to him.
2. *Story of Ra and the Serpent*, in *Old Testament Parallels*, ed., Victor H. Matthews and Don C. Benjamin (Mahwah, N.J.: Paulist Press, 1991), p. 29. The other creation and flood stories referred to in this article are also available in this work.
3. See John A. Wilson in Henri and H.A. Frankfort, John A. Wilson, Thorkild Jacobsen, *Before Philosophy* (New York: Penguin Books, 1974), p. 64.
4. See W. Lee Humphreys, "Pitfalls and Promises of Biblical Texts as a Basis for a Theology of Nature," in *A New Ethic For a New Earth*, ed. Glenn C. Stone, (New York: Friendship Press in association with the National Council of Churches, 1971).
5. Jeremiah's reference to the practice of circumcision among the Israelite's neighbors is pointed out by Robert B. Coote and David Robert Ord in their book *In the Beginning* (Minneapolis: Fortress Press, 1991), p. 68, a work I did not discover until this paper was being edited for publication.
6. My discussion of the dietary prohibitions is greatly indebted to Mary Douglas' discussion in Chapter 3 of *Purity and Danger* (London: Penguin Books, 1966) and Jean Soler's in "The Semiotics of Food in the Bible," in *Food and Drink in History*, ed., Robert Forster and Orest Ranum (Baltimore: Johns Hopkins University Press, 1979). The primary difference between my interpretation and Douglas' is that she claims that the predatory habits of animals played no role in the formation of the restrictions, whereas I follow Soler in arguing that avoidance of predatory animals is the most fundamental principle involved in their formulation.

2

From Myth to Psyche to Mystic Psychology:
The Evolution of the Problem of Evil in Judaism

By Sheldon R. Isenberg

M ystics and philosophers from many traditions have recognized that whatever it is we mean by or call God, God is beyond human description. Hence all descriptions of God are, in a significant sense, human projections. But that doesn't mean that they are therefore fictional. It does mean that as we struggle with our images, our feelings, our beliefs about God, we are also exposing the depths of our awareness of whatever it is which transcends us, whatever it is of which we are a part. Hence theology and theodicy are expressive of our human awareness of the greater whole of which we are a part.

Ideas about God, transcendence, and evil have changed in response to changing life situations. We have created the possibility of utterly destroying the planet, a possibility that Jewish and Christian imagination had relegated to God alone. This is a unique situation that has already stretched traditional theologies and theodicies, often beyond the breaking point. Certainly one result of the Holocaust has been that Jews have plunged into theological crisis. The old images and beliefs do not satisfy the vast majority.

The evolution of this millennia-old tradition requires that we move into a new phase of conversation about God and evil. However, the nature of Jewish conversation is that it always backs up before going forward, looking at the lines drawn in the past to see what directions are given for the future. Rarely does it reach agreement on those lines, but it never stops including the voices of the past. The process is called *midrash*. What follows is an outline of a story about the evolution of Jewish moral consciousness.

Jewish conversation always begins from the Bible. Although the Bible contains texts which originated over a period of a thousand years or so, nevertheless we can characterize a majority perspective on God and evil along with a strong minority dissent. The Bible construes a moral universe: victories and defeats, bumper crops and droughts, health and disease, happiness and misery result from God's evaluative judgment of human actions. Sacred myth and legend, prophecy and prophetic readings of history reveal the hidden, divinely directed moral connections. Disasters, long life and disease demonstrate God's pleasure and displeasure at human actions.

The fundamental story is told in the book of Genesis: What exists is the good, just God and the good world God created. God deserves our goodness, which means that we follow God's revealed will, what will come to be called *torah* (the teaching, the way). In response, God grants rewards of a long, healthy, prosperous life; God punishes disobedience with a short, unhappy, unhealthy life. Especially responsible are the descendants of Abraham and Sarah, the Jews, with whom God has covenanted. After God saved them from the slavery of Egypt, according to the story, they pledged again at Sinai and received detailed expectations for their behavior. Their collective fate is determined by the divinely established complex of rewards and punishments.

What we now consider natural calamities and historical-political disasters such as war, are interpreted as acts of God who responds to the Jews' adherence to their covenant with God. Droughts, floods, plagues, infertility of flocks and women are understood as the effects of divine curses which reflect back the inner twistings of disobedience, the rejection of covenant obligations. According to Yahweh's prophets, when the nation was conquered by Assyria and Babylonia, it was not because of inadequate defenses or leaders, but because they were sinful and impure. They didn't care for the poor, they neglected widows and orphans, and were unfaithful to God in their rituals.

The underlying myth is a personalized version of the impersonal Indian *karma* system. The same God who creates the world defines good and evil. Morality is defined by the will of the creator. The very structure and functioning of creation responds to divine moral judgment. Its description is revealed in the fabric of personal and corporate events. When human actions contravene divine rules, there are predictable results.

At this stage of thinking about God and morality, the male-oriented Bible projects God relating to humans basically as a great father/king. There are some mothering images, but they are relatively rare. The laws derive their authority from what Peter Berger calls a sacred canopy. That is, the laws that men make are spoken in the name of God. The source of moral judgment is externalized. From this widely shared perspective, the human experience of good and evil is childlike, subject to the will of a perfect, eternal parent.[1]

To be sure, with the exception of later apocalypticism, Judaism does not present people as helpless sufferers. Not only are they responsible for their own suffering, they also have the power of repentance to change themselves and their fate. As a just, compassionate father, the God who punishes also forgives and redeems.

This theological construction remained basic until the modern period: God is the cosmic father, the just judge, the ideal king who sets clear, fair rules. Belief in God's justice is so strong that God can be held accountable to God's own standards. For instance, the patriarch Abraham accuses God of injustice when God reveals the intent to destroy a wicked city even if there are good people present. Moses must persuade God not to destroy the people saved from slavery. Psalms and prophets claim that God ought to have already saved the people according to God's own sense of justice. There is an added level of abstraction that generalizes God's goodness into principles independent of God's words and acts. Moreover, affirming God's justice, these protests also call it into question. Seeded in the affirmation is real doubt which finds simultaneous, subversive expression.

Deconstruction of the Fundamental Construction

Many narratives in Genesis directly and indirectly subvert the biblical construction. Woven into the Bible's beginnings is the myth of the primordial human act of disobedience which foreshadows the whole history of human transgressions. However, the consequences of this primordial disobedience are not easily classified. There are curses that result from Adam and Eve's primal disobedience: sexual desire that leads to the painful labor of childbirth and the hard, sweaty labor necessary for physical survival. But as curses they are ambiguous: sex and food bring pleasure, children provide the blessings so crucial to the fulfillment of the covenant to come. The forbidden fruit consumed was the knowledge of good and evil—the knowledge revealed by the holy text itself.

The result of divine disobedience is, after all, life as we know it—perhaps not an unmixed blessing, but certainly not an unmixed curse. The first willful act bore witness to the first act of will, of conscious separation from the cosmic parent, a rite of passage. The second great act of willfulness results in the first death by fratricide. In general, the legendary biblical heroes are presented as mixtures of virtue and sin. The divine covenant is carried on from generation to generation by means which include noble actions as well as trickery and deception; even through Jacob's cheating Esau of their father's blessing, God's will for inheriting the covenant is fulfilled.

More subversive is the skeptical wisdom literature, particularly the books of Job and Qohelet. Here too ambiguity reigns. The narrative framework of the book of Job tells of a God-fearing, virtuous man visited with horrendous misfortunes as a result of a cruel bet between God and Satan which involves testing Job's faithfulness to God. Thus, from the beginning, the text delivers a strong message about the arbitrariness of misfortunes, directly undercutting the naive moralism of the majority perspective. Job's response to his situation is outrage. The key issue in wisdom literature is understanding: Job wants to understand his situation. He is convinced that his plight arises from a misunderstanding.

The core poetry presents a cycle of dialogues between Job and the comforters (all ignorant of the bet) who reassure him that, although he may be suffering, he should not despair, for his suffering is neither meaningless nor arbitrary. Since God is just, all knowing and omnipotent, Job is surely being punished for something. Thus, they argue, repentance is his best and only recourse. But Job stubbornly insists on a hearing before the divine Judge, for he is certain that once his situation is brought to divine attention, the errors will be rectified.

Job is heard; God's response is stunningly ambiguous. God

repudiates Job's comforters, the representatives of the simplistic constructivist argument. Job is not being punished; however, God continues, mere creatures should not expect to understand fully the intentions and acts of the creator. To read all suffering as punishment is to believe arrogantly that humans can comprehend God's mind. The fundamental biblical constructivist premise is subverted, not destroyed, as it is transformed from mechanical clarity to mystery. The paternalistic metaphor expands as the father-God tells the child: you are too young, too small to understand—and you always will be. This is the response of a parent being pressed by a child to justify what the parent cannot justify. We cannot explain all suffering, but that doesn't mean that it is ultimately inexplicable.

After this great revelation, the story reverses once again: Job receives back his health, wealth and more children. He has passed the test with honors. Another message now emerges, affirming divine control of human fate, denying the power of Job's subversion, while framing and reversing the message of what precedes: for now we are reminded that suffering can be a test. The text, however, is silent about justifying the deaths of Job's earlier family.

God, for Job, is the cosmic father whose power is absolute, but who also may appear arbitrary. There is no reliable instruction manual for life to guarantee reward for good behavior or punishment for bad. Yet the final step of denial is not taken, the assertion that the world is lawless, that no one is in charge. The book of Ecclesiastes, with little argument, even more radically disconnects the moral mechanism. All life is trivial, without surplus meaning. Since the cycles of life and death, joy and sorrow, pleasure and pain are eternally repetitive, there are no deeper messages to be construed. These subversive messages of Job and Qohelet accompany the fundamental biblical perspective throughout the millennia.

The deconstructive impulse arises from awareness that suffering often seems not to be fairly distributed. The rabbis will have available the belief in an afterlife for the appropriate balance to be made for unwarranted suffering. They will also continue to develop the conception found in the first chapter of Job that suffering may be a test of steadfastness. In each case what appears to be evil is not evil at all, for justified suffering and suffering as a test can hardly be considered evil. The appearances are saved; God is still the good father. Yet Job knows nothing of an afterlife, and none of his complaints find a direct response. In addition, great suffering on the part of others was used as part of Job's test. The flaws in the biblical constructivist mode remain constantly in view.

Apocalyptic Dualism

During the period when traditional Judaism develops from biblical Judaism, another understanding of corporate suffering arises. There arose a belief in an approaching cataclysmic battle between the super-terrestrial and terrestrial forces of the good God and the human and demonic forces of an evil realm. This develops as a response to Jewish experiences of defeat and persecution. In the apocalyptic myth, whose biblical expression is to be found in the second half of the book of Daniel, the persecuted community constitutes God's forces on earth. In the language of the apocalyptic Dead Sea Scrolls, they are children of light. Their enemies are God's enemies, the children of darkness, who are controlled by the demonic realm of evil.

Evil is totally externalized. Both good and evil have their origin in a supra-human realm. Membership as a child of light is predetermined as is all of history. What humans do or do not do is irrelevant to the process except insofar as their actions are predetermined. The father-God is good, his family is good—all others are evil. While the myth appears dangerously dualistic, the revelation, the apocalypse, comforts the beleaguered community with the secret knowledge that although they may appear to be suffering defeat, the real war between God and Satan or Belial has already been won. In the end the forces of evil never really had a chance. The father is the great emperor who can defeat all comers. Being on his side is enough and all is preordained.

Evil and the Rabbis

There is another developmental stage when we begin to take responsibility for our own governance, or at least recognize that people—in this case, men who are rabbis—are making the rules. No longer are judgments of right and wrong identified solely with obedience and disobedience to a supra-human parent. In a famous Talmudic story two rabbis are struggling over a point of law. One invokes miracle after miracle to prove that God approves of his position. Even a heavenly voice affirms his view. Citing the Torah itself, the second rabbi wins the argument with the words, "It is no longer in the heavens."

According to the ideology of the rabbis, their function is to spin out in their dialectic the details of God's revelation. Their systematic, highly rational deliberations, they claimed, had the force of the written Torah. The rabbis' legal dialectic was a species of revelation. There would be no more direct, prophetic revelations, for God had given over his rule-making responsibility to humanity in the form of the collective wisdom of this male, intellectual-spiritual elite. Thus, the rabbis took a crucial step toward acknowledging that people create their own laws and thus define for themselves good and evil. Yet the rabbis' self-understanding was nested in the earlier mythic structure: their rabbinic reasoning could not bring them to a direct contradiction of written Torah, and, as before, suffering was viewed as God's way of punishing infractions of the rabbis' Torah.

Rabbinic explanations of suffering or evil emphasize that no suffering is undeserved and no sin ultimately remains unpunished. They went to extraordinary lengths to affirm God's justice. They even search diligently to find some small failure to fulfill a *mitzvah*, a divine commandment, to justify the suffering of the heroic martyr, Rabbi Akiva. Akiva was tortured and killed by the Romans for refusing to give up his devotion to Torah, the Torah revealed to Moses on Mt. Sinai and the Torah which he was helping create as a rabbi.

Reward and punishment, in this life or the next, constitute the cornerstone of the rabbinic moral-legal calculus. Their sense of the rational, consistent ordering of a just reality required that punishments and rewards follow human actions regularly. Punishment, however, is not only a reflexive response to a past act, but also may lead to redemption in the future. God is often portrayed as a just father who punishes his children to turn them to better behavior. Not that the rabbis believed that desire for reward or fear of punishment constituted admirable motivations for fulfilling *mitzvot*. *Torah lishmah*, fulfilling God's will for its own sake and not for the sake of a reward, was far more preferable.

The rabbis tighten the underlying biblical mythic structure. The God who is king and father must be perfect in distributing judgment. There are no arguments with God about judgment. It is the rabbi's duty to legislate and God's duty to arrange life events to respond. For the rabbis nothing that happens to a person or the people can truly be evil. It all must fit within the calculus. Suffering was punishment or test or would be balanced out in the world to come.

Despite the permission to express serious doubts implied by the inclusion of Job and Qohelet in the Bible, the rabbis seem to have internally suppressed such speculation. The rabbis were relatively free with their speculations about theological matters. But there were boundaries. For instance, the denial of God was considered an unjustifiable belief. Similarly, the denial that God is the ultimate judge in the final judgment of one's deeds during embodied life, was the worst of sins. Such a belief would rule one out of a share in the life-to-come that was otherwise the automatic right of every Jew.

The rabbis living in worldly defeat, in exile from their holy land, would not openly admit the least doubt about the moral functioning of the universe. They had to believe that evil would eventually be punished and the good rewarded, if not during this life then after leaving the body or in the world-to-come. In their rational consistency, they had to believe that in some way the Jews had left themselves open to suffering, that they could not be suffering unjustly. This is the position that finally became untenable for the vast majority of Jews in light of the Holocaust.

Of course they questioned and doubted, but their most serious doubts were put in the mouths of apostates or Godless pagans. *Ha-kofer ha-iggar*, "the denier of the root (or essence)," is the term of opprobrium reserved for one who denies that God observes or responds to what people do. One may not deny God's existence but, as the Epicurean, simply believe that God doesn't care, i.e., that "there is no Judge, and there is no judgment" (Urbach 28). Although this view parallels the basic message of the skeptical wisdom canonized in Qohelet, the rabbis ruled it out of court.

Justice, however, is only one divine attribute; God could be a stern father, but God was also forgiving and loving. God's attribute of justice was balanced with that of mercy. Therefore, forgiveness is always available given a genuine turning of act and intent away from the path of sin, *teshuvah*. For two thousand years traditional Jews have in their daily prayers blessed the God who forgives and redeems their sins. The most holy days in the Jewish calendar occur during the ten days of Teshuvah which begin with Rosh Hashanah

(New Year) and end with Yom Kippur (Day of Atonement). The annual drama includes time for self-examination and to ask for forgiveness from fellow humans and God and ends with the divine judgment that sets conditions of life to be contended with during the coming year. In the *Siddur*, the prayerbook, we get the sense that life is a test and that God sets our fate for the coming year based on our behavior in the past. However, there is little belief exhibited in the improvement of the world in which we are embodied.

There is a sense in which theology is always anthropology. What we say about God reveals, sometimes very subtly and indirectly, what we believe about ourselves. For the rabbis, just as God can be torn between the divine attributes of justice and mercy about whether to create a troublesome world filled with troublesome people, so too are humans torn between contradictory desires. While dual apocalyptic anthropology designates people as either children of light or children of darkness, the rabbinic cosmos unifies and internalizes in humanity all the qualities of being, including good and bad.

The Evil Inclination

In the legal segments of the Bible we find no speculations about internal motivations for going against God's will. Although the narratives provide far more complex understandings of human behavior, still we find little in the way of subtle, complex examination of the psyche. Even when God asks Abraham to sacrifice his own son, the text makes no attempt to expose the tensions of the inner workings of their thoughts and emotions. The rabbis, however, did speculate about the inner workings that result in good and bad behavior. With an acute awareness of our inner struggle to do the right thing, and of how easily we are seduced away, they taught that we are created with a will that is not naturally unified, but rather is split between the inclination toward good and the inclination to sin, towards evil.

The rabbis believed that only humans (and the supra-human denizens of demonic realms) are capable of evil. However, the rabbis were sensitive to a key question of theodicy. If God created us with the evil inclination, didn't God bear some responsibility for the results? The rabbis' commitment to preserving God's goodness was absolute. So, they reasoned, God creates us with an evil inclination (*yetzer*) for good reasons. In fact, some speculated that it is not really intrinsically evil, but rather serves a divine purpose. Were it not for the evil inclination humans would not build a house, take a wife, or have children. One rabbi even suggested that the evil inclination (*yetzer*) rejoices when someone can resist its temptations.

For the rabbis, ambivalence about whether such an evil impulse is really evil is also entangled with their powerfully ambivalent views on sexuality and women. The rabbis constituted an intellectual male elite who, as they legislated, were continuing God's revelatory function. Israel, the bearer of Torah, exists to serve Torah; the rabbis, in their scholarly and legislative functions, recreated Torah, which already existed before the world was created for whose fulfillment the world was created. Thus the rabbis believed that their preoccupation with Torah was an activity sustaining all of creation. This view gives cosmic significance to their intra-personal struggle with the evil inclination which pits the desire to be connected with God through study against the distractions of their passions. It is not that the passions are *per se* evil; when the good impulse rules the evil inclination, then both are united in doing God's will.

The rabbis believed that no one can prevail over the evil inclination (*yetzer*) alone. Although God created it, he also gave them Torah as an antidote. Only with God's help can one resist the innate attraction to evil. The purity and intensity of the rabbi's relationship with Torah is threatened by the intensity of his passions, especially sexual desire. On the one hand, men were commanded to procreate and to give their wives sexual gratification. On the other, the intense desires and pleasures associated with these commanded activities were experienced as interference with the desire to serve God wholly, especially through thorough occupation with Torah. This internal male struggle was projected on the female who was often objectified as a source of temptation and seduction.[2] To be holy, to be a *tzaddik*, was to conquer one's passions—a victory that you could never be sure you had won as long as you drew breath.

The function of the evil impulse cannot, however, be truly evil since the good God created it. The perspective on human evil is ultimately, in theologian John Hick's categories, Irenaean. Even evil serves God's purposes, for it is there to be overcome with the help of Torah. Ultimately it is the evil impulse which drives people toward as well as away from Torah.

The underlying myth informing Jewish views of evil manifests a duality between an unflawed God and a flawed creation. If God is imagined as separate from creation, as a father is from children, then the range of interactions is delimited. Judgments of good and evil will always involve an external standard set by another kind of being who is unflawed. There is a tension in the myth of a perfect father-king-God who authorizes earthly representatives, the rabbis, to legislate on God's behalf, and therefore to determine what is good and what is not.

Evil in the Zohar

Kabbalah, the major tradition of Jewish mysticism, responds to this dual tension with a profound recognition of a flawed God, which reveals another stage in understanding the biblical claim that humans are made in God's image. Humans are another way of God revealing God. The added dimension, the evolution in consciousness in Kabbalah, is the unification of what had previously remained utterly separate: God and creation. This was accomplished in Kabbalah in at least two ways. The monistic vision that all manifestation proceeds from the same unmanifest source, such that everything that exists is an aspect of God; and the teaching of the identity of macrocosm and microcosm, i.e., that humanity is a replica in miniature of God.

I will focus briefly on *Zohar*, the Book of Splendor, because it is the central text of Kabbalah from the 13th century. Like the medieval Jewish philosophers, Kabbalists recognized the potential for self-idolatry inherent in the anthropomorphic tendencies of biblical and rabbinic theology. Since idolatry is virtually the most cardinal of sins for Jews, the Kabbalists teach about a God so far beyond the capacity for the human consciousness to encompass as to be ultimately and totally unknowable, indescribable, inexpressible—in essence, unmanifest. The unmanifest source of all being is called *Eyn Sof*, the Infinite.

The Infinite emanates all there is. The Infinite, in one sense, is utterly transcendent, but all this complex, multi-leveled reality is in some sense God manifesting God. The Infinite (*En Sof*) manifests in stages as an interconnected system of divine potencies called *sefirot*, most commonly symbolized as the tree of life. The sefirotic tree of life is God manifesting in our universe; everything receives its being from *Eyn Sof* pouring through the complex connections on the power-net which is the immediate origin of all that we experience as existing. The radical gulf between creator and creation characteristic of biblical and traditional rabbinic cosmology is bridged. In one sense worlds separate humanity from the world of divine potencies (*sefirot*); in another sense the world is the divine potencies (*sefirot*) at this level.

Kabbalists disagreed with the neo-Platonic view of evil as absence of being, a view current in medieval Jewish philosophy. They did not accept the belief that distance from God on the chain of being implies proportionately less reality, so that evil was the utter absence of God. While for Maimonides and others evil designated radical unreality, lack of being, for Kabbalah the realm of evil, the other side, was too real, too much a matter of Jewish corporate and personal experience, to be denied its reality by attributing the human experience of evil merely to an intellectual deficiency.

Instead, in the daring mystical mythology of Kabbalah, evil is taken to originate within God as broken connections within the sefirotic system. The evil we experience is due to a break that prohibits the exchange between the divine energies, especially those designated love (*chesed*) and justice (*din*). The break results in suffering on all planes of being, for the power that limits and separates (*din*) operates without love. The result is that the connections of love cannot be made, and the interactions become negative, full of hatred and destructive.

The break in the divine potencies (*sefirot*), and therefore evil, originated with Adam's sin which is uniquely conceived by Kabbalah. Adam's sin was neither disobedience of an external rule, nor the result of an internal split will, but rather a fatal misperception. Adam could have seen the tree of life, i.e., the total connectedness of everything that exists as a divine system which unifies in a web of knowing, loving, compassionate relationship. Instead, he focused on only the dimension of manifestation, the tree of knowledge of good and evil. Thus he saw—and this is the fatal flaw—himself as separate.

That was the break; his awareness separated so that his own internal microcosmic tree was broken. The resonance of the broken harmony from his own consciousness resulted in a break in the divine sefirotic macrocosmic consciousness. Healing comes when we participate in a state of consciousness that realizes that in the depths of reality, all beings are participants in higher wholes. In Kabbalah evil results from breaking relationship, by not seeing, understanding and valuing the interdependent relationships without which nothing exists, including God. We break relationship as a result of intra-personal breaks: misperceptions, emotional disconnections, hatreds and so on. In that break, God-manifesting-as-Shekhinah joins the people in exile. God is not only lord and master, God is also mastered, if only temporarily.

In our evolution, we need to learn to play out all positions. At this moment in Jewish history, for instance, after Jews spent 2000 or so years learning about being powerless in the world, many Jews in modernity are learning from the experience of having relative freedom and power. We have experienced evil from one position, horribly culminating in the Holocaust; now we are working out the experience of having power over others. Those two roles, those polar positions, have yet to be put together in our consciousness. Situational evil has yet to be redeemed.[3]

When sefirotic energy becomes mixed with that of the demonic realm of evil, the break in relationship within God is commonly described as a temporary divorce between the masculine and feminine aspects of God. They are symbolized as the king and queen or the father and mother turning away from each other. At that moment the last Sefirah, Shekhinah who is the queen, is under the control of the demonic realm. On the Sabbath, according to Kabbalah, the powers of the realm of evil that keep them apart wane and king and queen rejoin and rejoice in ecstasy. Kabbalists believe that when they make love with their wives during the Sabbath, there is a special healing, a *tikkun*, that occurs between king and queen and therefore in the world. In fact husband and wife can experience themselves and each other as the divine *sefirot* Tiferet, the Holy One and Shekhinah in union.[4]

Healing the Break

The king and queen do not become each other; they connect across their differences. This is a crucial teaching of zoharic mysticism, that unification within God means connecting different powers, not isolating them and not homogenizing them. If this is true for the divine system, it must also be true for the microcosmic human systems. In one *Zohar* passage, Abraham who is the archetype of the energy of abounding love (*hesed*) is perfected by his willingness to sacrifice his son Isaac, who is the archetype of *din*, the energy of limitation (e.g., the ability to say no to a child). Merciful love must be tempered by a sense of limits. At the same time, Isaac, offering himself willingly as a sacrifice, is perfected by *hesed*. This dynamic of connecting potencies so that they are modified by each other illustrates the *Zohar's* conception of unification. The text asserts that each of the *sefirot* is completed by virtue of its uniting with other divine potencies (*sefirot*). Each is itself more than it had been by virtue of its connection with the energy of its apparent opposite.

There is a comprehensive model of relationship being projected here on God. For God is a number of relationships: husband/wife; father/mother; brother/sister; king/queen, etc. This is how Kabbalists projected their imagery of God, and also how they conceived their internal states. Through the connections they made, the inner healings, as well as the connections between them, the larger whole of which they were a part also healed. Another way of putting it is that all roles are ways of being human and as we interact with each other we have the potential of learning more and more about the possibilities, to more and more realize the whole.

The *Zohar* symbolizes the sefirotic system, i.e., God-manifest, in many ways: as a divine couple, a divine family, a tree rooted in *Eyn Sof* (the Infinite), a cosmic androgyne. For *Zohar* the primary identification of God is not as a single person over against humanity and the rest of creation. Nor does *Zohar* limit the alternatives to an impersonal principle or nothingness. Rather God is an organic system unfolding as the universe which encompasses all possible processes and relationships, including those disruptions and distortions which result in suffering and in evil. As part of what is unfolding, we live on our plane with a mixture of good and evil influences as we channel the continuing outpouring of that divine energy grid—or distort it. When we are able internally to heal ourselves as vessels for the divine flow, we reflect back healing to the all-encompassing divine system.

There is here a different kind of reciprocity than other voices in the Jewish conversation had imagined. The parent-child relationship has become something else, something more complex, with the power hierarchies far more ambiguous. We are prone to sin, the divine energies are prone to disruption. We heal the divine system and the harmonious, compassionate flow of being replaces the distorted painful emanations of the realm of evil. We can do that because we are of the same essence, we share the same structure.

This imagery seems to project a role reversal, an Oedipal-like desire for control over parents: a child will heal them, even restoring their sexuality with the child's own. At a deeper level, however, another image emerges. The healing of constituent parts are required for the healing of the whole. An implication, not expressed in the mystical myth, is that as humans we are capable of healing, of transcending the primordial struggle, of returning to or realizing our Eden-like state not in ignorance and innocence, but with all the wisdom of having traversed manifestation.

Another implication could not be drawn, I think, until this century. Men and women have not lived together within a pattern of complementary equality. Of course, Kabbalists lived within the traditional Jewish patriarchal, hierarchical social system; they could not themselves hear this particular teaching of the tree of life. The Kabbalistic insight that the process of healing the world must include a healing of male and female can be understood today as the necessity to heal the wounds that put male and female at odds with each other. If we cannot heal that relationship, we will not heal relationships between peoples and between species. All these healings are part of healing God. One way *Zohar* describes the healing, the *tikkun*, is as the right containing the left, the demonic realm is integrated with the *sefirot*, purified, redeemed, taking its appropriate place.

For the *Zohar*, this revision in conceiving God is a deep, esoteric truth, to be revealed to the rare adept. I believe that the power of a true symbol is that it continues to teach according to the changing needs of the generations who absorb it. The *sefirot* constitute that kind of symbol and, just as this vision of divinity has taught Christians since the Renaissance, it can teach others. We must gift with and receive from each other our highest symbols. And we must give freely, understanding that others may have different things to learn. It is no accident that we live in the only time in history when virtually all sacred texts and symbols are universally available; it is also the only time when we can learn together and from each other without having to become each other.

NOTES

1. In a very preliminary way I am attempting to trace this story of evolution through an extended metaphor of maturation within a family context. The total dependence of infancy gives way to a maturing internalization of and identification with an externally imposed sense of right and wrong which further develops into taking full responsibility for creating one's values, even if one chooses to remain within a traditional context. The final stage of spiritual maturity is not easy to describe, of course. It includes, however, a perspective that transcends the distinction between good and evil and between God and evil.

    In Jewish mysticism the transformation is described with a variety of metaphors: healing (*tikkun*), rescuing the sparks, the right side holding the left side, etc. The same consciousness—human and divine—whose misperceptions result in evil may be healed. In the family metaphor, all the roles of the family are understood to be contained within a single process. The evil results from a break in relationship and is not the fault of the child or the parent. Rather it is a property of the whole. From an evolutionary perspective, evil may be seen as those phenomena, the healing of which produces the next evolutionary stage. As humans we advance when we learn from our mistakes. That is, good and bad have to do with how we respond to our existential situation, how we learn.

2. The Bible already transmitted messages about Eve's blame and Adam's sin. Legal codes considered women special sources of ritual pollution which the rabbis later interpreted as evil, and in the wisdom literature the potential wise men are warned against the seductiveness of women. Yet these examples do not prepare the reader for the level of fear and mistrust expressed in the post-biblical literature.

3. This analysis is, of course, simplistic. Yet I am drawn to it, for it asserts that all of our experience has the potential to contribute to our evolution— although it need not. In the Holocaust there were many acts of heroism, many incidents that revealed nobility at the most surprising moments. Even today as the Holocaust affects our consciousness fifty years later, good and evil continue to collect around it. This is not to argue, of course, that any suffering is worth it. Rather, that the judgment of good and evil is a constant on-going process, relative to the evolution or disintegration of an individual, a community, a species, etc.

4. This phenomenon deserves close comparison with tantric practices.

3

Providence and the Problem of Evil in Jewish Thought

By David J. Goldberg

There is no more agonizing problem of belief than the existence of evil in a world allegedly created by a benevolent God. What makes the problem all the more acute for Judaism is that it cannot evade it by attributing evil to an ultimate source independent of God, for that would be a denial of monotheism. It cannot, for instance, countenance the dualistic doctrine of Zoroastrianism with its two deities, of light and darkness, from which the good and the evil respectively emanate. Indeed, the prophet of the Babylonian exile repudiated that notion when he said in God's name: "I am the Lord, and there is no other. I form light and create darkness, I make peace and create evil, I the Lord do all these things" (Isaiah 45:6f.).

All the biblical authors seem to have thought of goodness as intrinsic to the character of God. By contrast, God creates evil and tolerates its continued existence. God encourages humanity to fight it and destroy it if it can, but evil has no part in the divine being.

Speculation of why God does allow evil to exist is not, however, found in the Bible. Abstract speculations of this kind were foreign to ancient Hebraic thinking. The biblical authors were concerned with humanity and the kind of life it should lead. When the mystery of evil is discussed in the Books of Job and Ecclesiastes, for example, the argument centers around why the righteous suffer, not around the deeper problem of why there is suffering at all, or why the various manifestations of evil abound in God's creation.

Insofar as biblical authors address the dilemma of theodicy, their solution is usually to suggest a punitive or remedial purpose to evil. It is a demonstration of God's justice. The adversities of human life are to be seen as aspects of God's wider, educational concern for God's children. "Know then in your heart that, as a man disciplines his son, so the Lord your God disciplines you" (Deuteronomy 8:5). "For the Lord reproves him whom He loves, as a father the son in whom he delights" (Proverbs 3:12).

Suffering, therefore, is a form of divine chastisement, a token of God's beneficence rather than God's anger. It is this theory that is boldly challenged by the author of the Book of Job. Job is a righteous man who has suffered unjustly. The conventional, simplistic reward-and-punishment doctrine propounded so tenaciously by Job's friends is clearly an inadequate explanation for his suffering. But having advanced the argument with eloquent daring, the author of Job is then forced to concede that human ignorance precludes us from knowing the answer. Faith in God's ultimate purposes must suffice. That is the import of God's speech out of the whirlwind when God says to Job: "Where were you when I laid the foundations of the earth. . .?" (Job 38:4).

Rabbinic literature is similarly averse to speculation on the mystery of evil, while accepting unquestioningly the doctrine of divine providence; that whatever happens in this world happens by God's will. The Talmud expresses the belief in its most extreme form in the statement of Rabbi Chanina that "no man bruises the finger here below unless it has been so decreed for him above."[1] And rabbinic bafflement about solving the riddle of theodicy is candidly admitted by the second-century teacher who said: "It does not lie within our power to explain either the well-being of the wicked or the suffering of the righteous."[2]

It was not until medieval times that the metaphysical problem regarding the very existence of evil was discussed by Jewish thinkers. Abraham Ibn Daud (twelfth century, Spain) and Moses Maimonides (twelfth century, Egypt) are two representative philosophers who attempt to grapple with the questions posed by the apparent reality of evil, given the three basic propositions of theistic faith: that God is wholly good; that evil is real; that God is all-powerful.

The acceptance of all three propositions as true would seem to involve us in a contradiction. For if evil is real, then either God wishes to remove it (or not to have brought it into being) and cannot do so, in which case there are limits to God's power; or God can remove it (or need not have brought it into being) but does not choose to do so, in which case God cannot be wholly good. The only way out of the dilemma is to reject—or at least to qualify—one of these propositions.

No recognized Jewish thinker has ever sought to deny that God is wholly good. Even those medieval philosophers[3] (e.g., Bahya Ibn Pakudah and Joseph Albo) who hesitated to use attributes like good-ness of God, because of the anthropomorphism involved, conceded that at least this can be said of God: that God is not the opposite of good. It is surely a sound religious instinct which refuses to ascribe any evil to the nature of God. A being who desired evil in any ultimate sense would not be worthy of worship, as it would be morally inferior to the person it had created, who would banish evil if it had the power to do so.

The solution for Ibn Daud and Maimonides was to deny the reality of evil; that is, to reject the second proposition. Ibn Daud[4] declares that our reason tells us that God cannot produce evil, and this is taught by scripture and in the Jewish tradition generally. Reason tells us that this is so because for God, who is wholly good, to produce evil would be a contradiction in terms. Human beings are both good and evil at the same time because the good stems from one part of their character, the evil from another. But since God is not composite, it is logically impossible for the divine nature to embrace both good and evil.

Why, then, do we find evil in the universe? According to Ibn Daud, most types of evil that we can imagine are merely the absence of good. For example, poverty is the absence of wealth, darkness the absence of light, folly the absence of wisdom. It is not correct to say the God creates poverty or darkness or stupidity, any more than it would be correct to say that God has made no elephants in Spain! The absence of elephants in Spain is not something positive which God has to make. The only logical way of stating the proposition is to say that while God did indeed create elephants, God did not create them in Spain; that is, God is certainly responsible for the fact that there are no elephants in Spain, but this is not due to a no-elephant creating process but simply because the scope of God's elephant-creating did not extend to Spain. By analogy, God does not create evil—which is simply the absence of good—but God does refrain from bestowing certain good things on certain people; that is, God does not give wisdom to the fool.

Is not the absence of good in itself evil? To this Ibn Daud replies that when we ask God to make the imperfect perfect, we are asking for the world as we know it to be abolished. If plants were to be made more perfect by becoming animals, animals by becoming humans, humans by becoming like Moses, Moses by becoming like the angels, then there would be no gradations in creation. Whereas God's goodness wishes to benefit a varied multitude of creatures, and this is only possible in a world where there are imperfections as well as perfections.

Maimonides[5] follows more or less the same line of argument. All evils are privations. Therefore, God does not create evil but is responsible, rather, for the privation of the good, that is, God cannot be said to have created a blind man, but to have created a man to whom no sight was given.

It has to be said that neither of these attempted solutions is satisfactory. They are largely semantic games. To suggest that a person racked by a cruel disease which torments body and soul is simply being deprived by God of good health, is to come dangerously close to abuse of language. Such an artificial distinction does not contribute significantly to an understanding or acceptance of evil.

In defense of the medieval philosophers it could be argued that they shrank at ascribing evil in any positive sense to the all-good God. What they were doing, consciously or unconsciously, was to try to minimize in a number of ways the power and force of evil. They were trying to demonstrate that while we cannot deny the existence of evil in the universe, it is not quite as bad as we imagine at first glance. But they seem to have been unaware that any amount of evil, even an evil minimized and expressed negatively, is still a major obstacle to belief in a God who is wholly good.

Maimonides is not entirely oblivious of the difficulty. He argues that God cannot make a material universe without the properties of privation because—a view which goes back to Plato—matter must have this property in order to be matter.[6] To expect God to create matter which is not matter is to ask God to do the logically impossible.

Again we are back to Ibn Daud's thought that the world as we know it must have the nature it does have if it is to be an imaginable world at all. But what of moral evil? Maimonides replies that this, too, is the result of ignorance. If human beings knew the truth, there would be no wars or hatred or enmity. That is why the promise is held out that one day: "They shall not hurt nor destroy in all my holy mountain; for the earth shall be full of the knowledge of the Lord, as the waters cover the sea" (Isaiah 11:9).

Maimonides denies that there is more evil in the world than good. Most of the evils which befall humans are due to their wrong exercise of free will. The free will defense—that humanity has freedom to choose good or evil, blessing or curse, life or death—is central to Judaism's notion of the two inclinations, the *yetzer tov*, the good inclination, and the *yetzer hara*, the evil inclination, which constantly struggle for mastery of human nature. The kind of world we have is the only one, Maimonides would have said, that can serve as an arena for the emergence of moral worth.

In the Kabbalah, on the other hand, evil is treated as something positive. Indeed, the Kabbalistic doctrine of the "other side" (*sitra achra*), the demonic side of existence, comes very close to dualism, although the Kabbalists warn against this repeatedly. They give the illustration of a wild dog controlled by its master's chains even though appearing to enjoy a certain degree of freedom to bite. The Lurianic Kabbalah (named after its founder, Isaac Luria, 1534-1572) in particular, deals at length with the subject of evil. According to its theory of *tzimtzum* (self-contraction), God withdraws from the divine self into the divine self, to make room for the world. The light which pours into the empty space results in the "breaking of the vessels" and even after the reconstruction of the sefirotic realms some of the infinite light is spilled over, as it were, to form worlds in decreasing order. Eventually the over-spill nourishes the denizens of the "other side"—the *k'lipot*, shells or husks which surround the good, as the bark of a tree or the rind of a fruit, and which parasitically take nourishment from the good. Thus evil is the result of that cosmic catastrophe known as the "breaking of the vessels."

Some of the bolder Kabbalists tend to see this as a kind of

purging by God of the evil in God, which comes perilously close to the notion of a finite and limited God, but is their attempt to grapple with the problem of how the infinite can produce the finite. Since God needs to have creatures so that God can benefit them, God has to produce that which is not-God as the environment in which they can exist, and this not-God is bound to contain imperfections and evil. This is, in mythical terms, another statement of the free will defense. A human being can only become God-like by making the good its own through the exercise of free choice. This requires a world in which there is evil as well as good.

In general, modern Jewish theology—like modern science—tends to be relativist rather than absolutist in its assertions, reticent of dogmatic assumptions and suspicious of resolved solutions. Two factors in particular have contributed to this stance. One is post-Enlightenment knowledge of the natural sciences and therefore the workings of natural law. The rigid mechanical system of the Newtonian universe is queried nowadays by quantum physics and chaos theory in particular, which have revealed that chance and indeterminacy are real aspects of the fundamental nature of things. The contemporary theologian, aware of the proximate causalities of modern science, is far readier than was his medieval counterpart to question the scope of all-powerful in listing the attributes of God. The concept known as process theology, of a God who is not yet omnipotent and depends on human cooperation to become so; who is, indeed, in the process of becoming has its Jewish adherents, notably Levi Olan and Henry Slonimsky. Harking back to the Kabbalistic theory of *tzimtzum*, they posit a God who is limited by its own nature, infinite in some respects but finite in others, and dependent on co-partnership with humanity in the work of creation.

The second crucial factor is Jewish consciousness of the Holocaust, which though it may not have been objectively different in kind from all other historical episodes, has raised to new levels of sensitivity our perception of the brutality of which human beings are capable and of the agonies suffered in this world by the innocent. While the problem of why an all-good, all-powerful God can tolerate evil in creation has always been the most difficult question for a theist to face, the sheer scope and nakedness of the evil witnessed in the twentieth century has rendered banal all earlier attempts at an answer.

Both factors have, moreover, impressed on us in a new way the need to differentiate between natural and moral evils. Natural evils are not caused by human action and may not even affect human beings, since they include the cruelties observable in the animal world—Tennyson's "Nature, red in tooth and claw"—though those which do cause human suffering are flood, famine, earthquake, disease and death itself.

In the past such happenings were regarded as acts of God (as they are still termed in English law). Today we tend to look upon the casualties not as individuals singled out for suffering by divine decree, but as victims of an unfortunate conglomeration of circumstances within a system that operates according to general natural laws. What calls for explanation is not why particular calamities happen to particular people, but why they occur at all.

Here we can speculate that there must be death, so that the generations may succeed one another; that pain is nature's way of alerting us to bodily danger; that accidents are unavoidable in any logically possible world that is governed by universal laws, and do not automatically negate the benevolence of its Creator; that all these seeming evils serve at least the one good purpose of challenging human beings to learn to conquer or control them, and thus of stimulating progress; and that they assume a different complexion when viewed in the perspective of an evolving, rather than a static, universe. The moral evils or evils committed by humans—crime, war, oppression, persecution, torture, and genocide—present a different problem. It is much harder to assert nowadays, as did Maimonides, that there is more good than evil in the universe. Babies suffered cruel deaths in former ages, but were not hurled alive into gas chambers. The horrors of Hiroshima and the napalm bomb seem too monstrous for theodicy to cope with, so that the more subtle (or crude) the defense, the greater appears to be the affront.

For many believing Jews there is a strong distaste for even raising the issue. Guilty at having been spared when six million perished, and diffident about proposing any partial explanation for evil on such a cosmic scale, these Jews take refuge in the natural and commendable reticence which has ever frowned on *tzidduk ha-din* (justifying God's justice) when the suffering of others is involved. Nevertheless, a number of Jews have written on the Holocaust and its theological implications. From such writings several different attitudes emerge, but where there is consensus is in rejecting as an insult to the memory of the victims any solution which depends on the tidy biblical scheme of reward and punishment. Even in former times the measure for measure explanation had to contend with insuperable obstacles. How did it resolve the suffering of the innocent and the escape of the guilty? How did it understand the deaths of small children? Were all these apparent instances of evil manifestations of God's retributive justice, or, as some explanations would have it, punishment for sins committed in a previous existence?

After the destruction of the First Temple in 586 BCE, and again after the Second Temple was destroyed in 70 CE, there was a tendency for Jews to blame themselves, and say, in the words of the prayerbook, *mipne chata'einu*, "it was because of our sins" that these misfortunes came upon us. While admiring the pious humility of our ancestors, after the Holocaust such self-castigation is no longer intellectually or emotionally tenable. To suggest that the six million men, women and children in any sense deserved their fate seems to be sacrilegious. On the contrary, with a kind of spontaneous religious insight, the Jewish people refer to Holocaust victims by the term traditionally applied to martyrs, as *k'doshim*, "holy ones."

Many of the Jewish thinkers who have presumed to write on the subject in the aftermath of the Holocaust have come close to suggesting that in the particular circumstances it is irreligious to probe too deeply. Leviticus chapter 10, verse 3: "And Aaron was silent" (at the death of his two sons, that is, he accepted the divine decree) is a text hallowed by tradition.

For all that, and with the fullest appreciation of the need, on occasion, of a theology of silence, it can be argued that the would-be believer will not find repose in faith unless he can discover some inkling of how to reconcile moral evil with the intentions of a purposive mind. From this point of view, and despite existentialist shudders, the quest for a theodicy is still valid if God is to continue to be worshipped in any meaningful sense. One response has been to jettison the time-honored belief that such happenings are acts of God. How can they be, since they are by their very nature flagrant violations of the divine will? God does not command, but on the contrary, forbids the murderer to commit murder; therefore, God cannot be said to cause either the act or the suffering that results from it. However, God has created a universe in which such barbarities can and do happen. God allows them and does not prevent them. It is in this sense that God can be held responsible for humans' inhumanity to each other.

The most far-reaching and coherent treatment in recent years of this problem of theodicy comes not from a Jewish, but a Christian scholar, John Hick, in his *Evil and the God of Love*. To claim that investigation of the problem of evil is religiously improper, that it is ipso facto irreligious for one to seek to justify God, Hick responds:

> In this formulation of the difficulty the word "justify" seems to cause the trouble. But suppose we use instead the more neutral term "understand." Is it impious to try to understand God's dealings with mankind? . . .By what authority must we insist upon maintaining an unrelieved mystery and darkness concerning God's permission of evil? Surely this would be a dogmatism of the least defensible kind. It is, of course, permissible to hold, on the basis of an investigation of the issues, that there is in fact no theodicy, no legitimate way of thinking about the problem of evil that satisfies both mind and conscience; but in view of the fallibility of human reasoning it would be unwise to hold this with absolute confidence, and quite un-justifiable to forbid others from making their own attempts. It may be that what the theodicist is searching for does not exist. But, on the other hand, even if no complete theodicy is attainable, certain approaches to it may be less inadequate than others, and it may thus be possible to reach some modest degree of genuine illumination upon the subject and to discover helpful criteria by which to discriminate among speculations concerning it. If so, efforts in this direction need not be wasted.[7]

Hick's own approach, in a Christian context, is to side with Irenaeus (second century) rather than St. Augustine, who emphasizes the idea of the fall of the human and attributes the evil in the world to this. Irenaeus, on the other hand, sees the world with its hardships and its challenges as the appropriate arena for the emergence of those values which make human beings God-like in their struggle for the good and thus equip them for their role of enjoying God forever. Irenaeus is anticipating by several hundred years the famous phrase of the poet Keats that this world is not a vale of tears but "the vale of Soul-making." The myth of Genesis represents the natural condition of a human being as a finite creature remote from God; but this state is endemic to humanity and is not the result of any fall. Only in a world in which there has to be a struggle for the good, can human beings freely choose God.

Hick is thus presenting the classical free will defense, and its parallels in Jewish thought are numerous. Both Ibn Daud and Maimonides would have approved of Hick's argument. Basically, the free will defense considers what is the scope and extent of the affirmation that God is omnipotent. Is it really true to say that God can do anything? Can God, for example, create a stone which even God cannot lift up? Can God create another God? Can God will the divine nature out of existence? The answer to these questions will surely be in the negative, but is that not a limiting qualification of God's omnipotence?

As the medieval Jewish thinkers repeatedly insisted, God cannot do the absolutely or logically impossible, because this involves a contradiction in terms. For example, it is absurd to ask God to make five into ten without adding anything to the former, or to bring back the day gone by in its original condition. Thus, even God cannot give humanity free will and the opportunity of exercising it, of choosing good and rejecting evil, if the human is placed in a world where there is no evil and therefore no possibility of choice. Even if we accept that this world is to be a vale of soul-making, it cannot be at the same time a hedonistic paradise. We are still bound to ask why God should allow creatures to suffer pain when it is not necessary for their moral development: the sufferings of children and animals, and all those physical evils which seem pointless. The theist has to admit that it is a mystery impenetrable to the rationalizing human mind. But, the skeptic would retort, if we have to fall back on the idea of a mystery, this only means that the problem is insoluble. This is tantamount to saying that God must have a morally sufficient reason for allowing human suffering, but we do not know what it is. That is acknowledging that we do not know the answer to the problem of evil, and that there is, therefore, no theodicy.

The theist, defending his belief in a beneficient, voluntarily self-limiting creator, might tentatively respond as follows: that the apparently random element in nature is essential, for if it were always possible to discover the theological necessity of each kind of suffering, this would interfere with free choice. This does not mean, as the medieval philosophers would have proposed, that God sends the earthquakes, diseases and so forth with a didactic purpose, to provide opportunities for sympathy and help, but only that an environment in which such things are possible can serve as a vale of soul-making.

The contingencies of the world process are genuine and frequently perplexing. The existence of the whole process, with its contingencies, represents a divine creative act, the purpose of which is to make it possible for finite creatures to inhabit an autonomous world in which their creator is not automatically evident and in which, accordingly, their moral and spiritual capacities may freely develop. In and through and out of this religiously and morally ambiguous situation—which is human existence as we now experience it—and out of its continuation, variation and transformation beyond this present life, the infinite good described in Judaism and Christianity as the kingdom of God is finally to come.

The mystery and paradox for human reason lies in the fact that if we lived in a world in which rewards and punishments were justly apportioned to our deeds, our moral natures would never have an opportunity to develop; and if in that world the ultimate constructive use of evil was an established scientific fact, then the world would not function as a vale of soul-making.

Such a tentative rationalization, haltingly offered by the theist, affords no more than a glimpse through the darkness surrounding the problem of evil. The person of faith knows better than most that God hides the divine being. But for the person of faith, hard though it is to believe in God, it is harder still not to believe. Or, as the Chasidim were fond of saying, when you know that God is hidden, then God is hidden no longer.

NOTES

1. *The Babylonian Talmud* (London: The Soncino Press, 1948), Hullin/ Chullin, V.1, p. 32, 7b.
2. *The Babylonian Talmud* (London: The Soncino Press, 1935), Aboth/Avot, Ch. 4:15, p. 52. The translation here is slightly different.
3. Bahya Ibn Pakudah, *Sha-ar Ha-Yichud*, Chap. 4; Joseph Albo, *Ikkarim*, II, 23. Further references are not available.
4. Ibn Daud, Abraham ben David Halevi, *Emunak Ha Ramah En*, VI, 2, translated *The Exalted Faith* (Rutherford, NY: Fairleigh Dickinson University Press; London: Associated University Press, 1986).
5. Moses Maimonides, *The Guide to the Perplexed* (New York: Dover Publications, 1956), Part III, Ch. 10-12, pp. 265-71.
6. Issac Husik, *The History of Medieval Jewish Philosophy* (Philadelphia: Jewish Publishing Society of America, 1941), p. 288.
7. John Hick, *Evil and the God of Love* (San Francisco: Harper and Row, 1977).

4

The Discovery
of Christian Meaning
in Suffering:
Transformation and
Solidarity

By Jane Mary Zwerner

T heodicists from Augustine to Hick have placed the fall at the heart of their apologies for the existence of evil in God's creation. This strategy does seem logical since the creation account in scripture does assign sole responsibility for the world as we know it to the hands of God. But these theodicies and this strategy leave a well known residual body of problems concerning the existence of evil.

I find the Irenaean type of theodicy, especially Hick's soul-making thesis,[1] more promising than the Augustinian, though I shall leave the arguments to another time and place. But even that theodicy does not answer the question: Why, if evil has positive value,[2] should humans attempt to eliminate, prevent, or reduce evil? In Hick's context, the question would be framed as follows: If the world as we know it is the environment best suited to soul-making, why then should humans direct their efforts to changing it?

I believe that the most fruitful approach for answering this question does not begin with the fall, but with the cross. It is only through reflection upon and acceptance of Christ crucified that Christians can truly understand that the existence of an omniscient, omnipotent, and omnibenevolent divine being does not imply the absence of suffering. After a brief look at the symbol and truth of the cross I shall take a longer look at the dynamic of suffering in transfiguration reality, including its communal dimension; and finally, examine the phenomenon of transfiguration.

The Cross

The cross on which Jesus of Nazareth was crucified is both the reality and symbol of the personal experience of evil. I shall stipulate the definition of evil as any actions or states of affairs which intend and/or realize destructive effects for human persons, their relationships, and/or the natural environment. This stipulative definition presumes that there is a *telos* or natural end for human persons and natural objects. Actions or states of affairs which promote the realization of that *telos* are good, and those which frustrate or defeat that *telos* are evil. If those goods or evils are intended by rational agents, those are moral goods or evils; and if they are the effects of non-rational agents or events they are natural good or evils.[3]

I further stipulate that suffering is the experience of moral or natural evils as meaningless or hopeless. This stipulative definition implies that to experience evil is not necessarily to suffer evil. The Christian understanding of evil is somewhat paradoxical, because suffering has a positive element. Although the negative effects of evil are not denied, the experience of evil is also an occasion for a positive faith experience, in relation to an encounter with God.

The spiritual history of the community of faith, both in the history of the Hebrews and in the life of Christ, reveals that God is present to the people of faith in the midst of suffering. Even so, God very often does not reduce or eliminate that suffering. The human expectation that God should reduce or eliminate evil is cogent especially if one assumes that the purpose of creation is for creatures to be happy. The soul-making theodicy, however, posits as the highest good the transformation of human persons from *bios* (physical or material existence) to *zoe* (personal spiritual and moral life). That transformation or transfiguration is the *telos*, the *summum bonum* of creation, and the cross is the paradigmatic historical event and metaphor for that transfiguration.

The life of Christ is a vivid account of the positive value of evil and of transfiguration. In his earthly ministry Jesus did not eliminate all evils, did not cure every one in need, nor transform institutions and governments. He clearly stated and indicated that his mission was to accomplish the interior transformation or transfiguration of human persons. Those persons, by nature imperfect and sinful, are called by Jesus to receive the Holy Spirit and to be transfigured, to become the new man or new woman. This call to rebirth in the Spirit resonates in Hick's philosophical description of transcendence from *bios* to *zoe*. The mission of Christ is not to transform the vale but to transform persons.

As Hick explains, the ultimate value is not happiness or health, though these are certainly good things which we rightly enjoy. Rather, the ultimate purpose of human existence is to attain personal moral and spiritual life, to realize the likeness of God. The death of Christ on the cross and his resurrection demonstrate that transfiguration can occur, and perhaps must occur, within the context of suffering.

The history of the Hebrews reveals a similar story. Although they are the chosen ones of God, they are exiled, enslaved, dispossessed, dispersed, exterminated. Yet it is throughout these hardships and crises that God is ever present to them. The meaning of this narrative lies not in whether God removes or relieves these trials, but that God's people are transformed throughout their history into a community of faith. God is revealed to the faithful in these events.

One objection to this description of God's presence in human suffering is that God, in the Judeo-Christian tradition, is equally revealed in joyous and beautiful events; and that God should be revealed mostly or only in these joyous and beautiful events. Philosophers often object that only a limited God would require both the pleasant and the painful to accomplish holy purposes.[4] But this objection misses the mark for it originates in a misguided assumption, namely, that happiness is a life with a greater balance of pleasure than pain.

I agree that God created persons to be happy and to naturally prefer pleasure to pain. But happiness abides in the process of transfiguration—in the process as well as in the goal achieved—which requires both joy and sorrow. The happiness of transfiguration is qualitatively different than the happiness captured by the contrasting hedonistic notions of pleasure and pain. It is a happiness best described as peace, completion or joy, that is the rejoicing in heaven and earth when the human heart affirms its true mission. The peculiar mystery or paradox of Christian faith is that this peace or joy is experienced vividly in the midst of suffering or great pain.

This paradox is repulsive to many who are raised within the Christian tradition, especially if they also are influenced by the culture of some Western philosophies such as utilitarianism or pragmatism. This repulsion was recognized by the early followers of Jesus. In 1 Corinthians 1:18-25, St. Paul instructs:

> The message of the cross is complete absurdity to those who are headed for ruin, but to those who are experiencing salvation it is the power of God.
>
> Scripture says, "I will destroy the wisdom of the wise, and thwart the cleverness of the clever."
>
> Where is the wise man to be found? Where the scribe? Where is the master of worldly argument? Has not God turned the wisdom of this world into folly?
>
> Since in God's wisdom the world did not come to know him through 'wisdom,' it pleased God to save those who believe through the absurdity of the preaching of the gospel.
>
> Yes, Jews demand 'signs' and Greeks look for 'wisdom,' but we preach Christ crucified—a stumbling block to Jews, and an absurdity to Gentiles;
>
> But to those who are called, Jews and Gentiles alike, Christ the power of God and the wisdom of God. For God's folly is wiser than men, and his weakness more powerful than men.[5]

Paul acknowledges that what he is preaching is an absurdity and a stumbling block to those who are not experiencing salvation.

The passage explicitly reveals that the world does not come to God through wisdom as understood by the world. It is neither by signs and augurs nor by logic and discursive argumentation that one comes to know God. It is through believing in the absurdity of what the gospel preaches that one comes to know God. Christ crucified is precisely what the gospel preaches. Thus St. Paul's preaching might be recast as the following syllogism:

> Those who are saved are those who believe through the absurdity of the preaching of the gospel.

> The absurdity of the preaching of the gospel is the preaching of Christ crucified.

> Thus, those who are saved are those who believe in the preaching of Christ crucified.

Salvation demands belief in the crucifixion, not in the creation or the fall.

Now some may argue that claims about creation and the fall are part of a body of beliefs which include claims about crucifixion; and that a necessary condition of being a Christian is acceptance of the body of beliefs. That may well be, but I shall not argue for or against that here. Rather, I shall focus on St. Paul's acknowledgment that although the crucifixion will be construed by some as an absurdity and by others as a stumbling block, those who are saved will understand.

What, then, is the absurdity of the cross? It is essential to understanding the revelation of the cross that God did not rescue Jesus from crucifixion. The resurrection surely reveals the power of God, but so does the fact that Jesus suffered on the cross. Resurrection by an omnipotent God, however, is not an absurdity. The absurdity is the fact that Jesus had to suffer and die on the cross. The absurdity is that he who is the Savior is one who is brought low by worldly standards. The atonement interpretation of the crucifixion is certainly valid, and might explain why Jesus had to suffer and die on the cross. But the crucifixion as atonement cannot exhaust its meaning if we consider Mark 9:34-37:

> He summoned the crowd with his disciples and said to them: If a man wishes to come after me, he must deny his very self, take up his cross, and follow in my steps.

> Whoever would preserve his life will lose it, but whoever loses his life for my sake and the gospel's will preserve it.

> What profit does a man show who gains the whole world and destroys himself in the process?

> What can a man offer in exchange for his life?[6]

The exhortation is issued not only to his disciples, but also to the crowd with them. Thus, not only are Jesus and his disciples to experience the cross, but also every one who follows Jesus is called to the cross. Thus, the meaning of the crucifixion is essentially linked to experiencing salvation, and it is not exclusively dedicated to Jesus' atonement for our sins.

If the atonement interpretation were the whole story, and Jesus accomplished that, then the individual assumption of the cross would not be necessary. It is in the losing of self—the denial of self and of the world—that the power of God is revealed and the individual is saved. The cross represents both suffering and the denial of self. Suffering and self denial are linked because suffering is a response to evil. If one responds to evil as meaningless, or adopts an attitude of hopelessness, then one renounces divine providence, and that renunciation gives evidence to the legacy of original sin.

By denying one's self, one acknowledges the divine hand in all events. This is not to say that God causes or creates evil and so one should gladly accept it. It is to say that God, rather than ourselves, is our hope. Our reliance upon the power of God in all events, even in the face of evil, to make all things work for good is a simultaneous affirmation of God and the denial of self. To suffer evil, when suffering is the experience of evil as gratuitous, is to renounce God's power. The ultimate acceptance of God requires the ultimate denial of self: namely, the cross. It is in this sense that suffering is essential to salvation.

Suffering

I have stipulated that suffering is the response to evil as hopeless or meaningless, and it is in that sense a negative experience. But in Christian discourse suffering is the opportunity for God to be revealed as the hope and meaning of humankind. The revelation in suffering is our reliance upon God as the strength that allows us to persevere in the face of evil. The affairs and states of the world are the venue for experiencing evil, but God crafts the master plan. It is not necessary that specific instances of evil be instrumental in some aspect of God's plan. It is rather that in the face of evil we rely upon God to be with us, assuring us that God's love and wisdom transcend the moments of human existence. Our response to evil may not transform the evil into good, but our response to evil may transform us if we encounter the power of God in solidarity with us during that moment of our personal cross. In this sense suffering is almost paradoxical, for it is at once the negative experience of evil and, at the same time, the positive experience of God's power in our lives.

It is in the midst of desperation that humans often turn to God for the first time. Let us shift our discourse to the positive aspect of suffering, namely as an opportunity to acknowledge human dependence upon God and to deny the self-reliance of pride.

Suffering[7] instructs and transforms for it confronts persons with their limitations and dependencies upon God and other persons. Many insights, for example, patience, tolerance, compassion and mercy, are most truly revealed within the context of great personal loss. Does this mean, then, that we should seek to suffer or cease our efforts to decrease it? I think not. The value is not in the suffering *qua* suffering but in the experience of suffering as a transforming event. It is not good to experience pain or good to do without basic needs; suffering is not an end to seek for its own sake. Rather, the good which comes through suffering is the interior transformation of the human person who suffers. We should not seek to suffer but seek to suffer well. When suffering does present itself, we should endeavor to experience it not at the level of *bios* but at the level of *zoe*. The paradigmatic example of this experience is that of Christ on the cross.

The agony in the garden reveals that Jesus did fear his suffering but that he did not reject it. He accepted it in faith. This dual characteristic of Jesus' actions substantiates the claim made above that we should not seek to suffer, and that we might even seek to avoid it. But if our actions to eliminate or reduce suffering are not successful, we must search for God's revelation within that suffering, and interpret that experience within the context of transfiguration.

A persistent objection to God's goodness proceeds from the claim that the value of suffering may be established if one grants that certain lessons can be learned only by suffering. We could even grant that suffering is not a contrivance as Mill thought,[8] since it is "intrinsically impossible"[9] that one gain these lessons or virtues without suffering. Even so, the objection continues, God could manage these instructions without gratuitous suffering. I believe I have proven elsewhere[10] that it can never be shown that any instance of suffering is gratuitous.

Briefly, the assumption that what appears to be gratuitous is in fact gratuitous begs the question against the existence of God. It may be that there is some non-apparent purpose to suffering, namely, that God does exist and suffering serves God's purposes. The most reasonable position for both the theist and the non-theist, with respect to gratuitous suffering, is that we simply do not know whether any instance of suffering is gratuitous. The theist assumes that it is not, while the non-theist assumes that it is; both sides beg the question.

The cross illustrates that even apparently unmerited suffering, as a specific type of gratuitous suffering, can have positive value. Many non-theists would allow that merited suffering is consistent with the existence of God (as understood in the Judeo-Christian tradition), but object that it often seems that people who should not suffer do. Is there a more striking and poignant case of unmerited suffering than that of Jesus? The harsh injustice of Christ on the cross, the absurdity of his punishment at the hands of human executioners presents itself as intrinsic to his own transfiguration. It is a mystery that we cannot comprehend but an exemplary cause which instructs as to the transforming power of suffering.[11]

Given that some instances of suffering are positively valuable while others are questionable, we can return to the soul-making thesis: the purpose of this creation is transfiguration from mere physical or material life to moral and spiritual life. Transfiguration requires some formation which occurs only through suffering. Hence suffering is not incompatible with the existence of an omniscient, omnipotent, and omnibenevolent divine being. The life of Jesus of Nazareth, the Christ, and his death on the cross and his resurrection, are vivid and searing demonstrations of this truth, and continue to serve as the paradigm for our own transfigurations. The story of his agony in facing the cross, his acceptance of the cross, his crucifixion and resurrection, further reveal the paradoxical nature of suffering: the genuinely negative effects of evil as the necessary condition of our destined transfiguration.

Transfiguration: New But Old

Although the story of the transfiguration of Jesus in Mark 9:2-5, describes a physical transformation of Jesus, it is clear that the meaning of this physical appearance is spiritual: his physical change is an outward manifestation of his spiritual union with God. It is interesting to note that as Jesus, Peter, James and John descended the mountain after the transfiguration the disciples ask Jesus, "Yet why does Scripture say of the Son of Man that he must suffer much and be despised?" (9:12). The connection between transfiguration and suffering is immediate and inextricable. Though Jesus has undoubtedly attained *zoe* in the transfiguration he will not be released from his suffering. On the contrary, the two are essentially linked. The hedonistic objection that happiness, as a greater balance of pleasure over pain, is the state that creatures should expect from an omnipotent, omniscient, and omnibenevolent divine being is obscene in the face of the cross. The greatest value, the *summum bonum*, is the happiness which transcends the hedonistic calculus, namely the transfiguration of human persons from *bios* to *zoe*.

The process of transformation does not alter the sinful or simply human nature of persons. (An early heresy did claim that believers were no longer capable of sin.) We retain our human nature which is the condition for the possibility of sin. Faith transfigures because it explains the purpose of human existence, and because it empowers human persons to attain *zoe*, the likeness of God.

The transformation from *bios* to *zoe* is a process which takes a lifetime to accomplish. This is not to say that there is a determinate space of time in which the process is complete or that every one will accomplish the transformation in his or her lifetime. One's entire life is the opportunity for transformation. It is possible to interpret every event or decision in one's life in the context of this transformation. It is true that some events lend themselves better than others to this hermeneutic. For example, cutting the grass may not inspire this interpretation as much as a family wedding. But cutting the grass may indeed be an opportunity for reflection upon one's relationship with nature, place in the universe, and social responsibilities. If human existence is intended for transfiguration, then every human experience is a potential opportunity for interpretation in the context of that truth. There are certain life experiences, however, which affect us profoundly and irrevocably. These are the moments that shape our lives and most demand, and paradoxically may seem to resist, the transfiguration hermeneutic. The person who is reborn remains a human being in the material world, thereby affirming the fundamental existential paradox, that is, we are called to live as moral and spiritual persons in a material and resistant environment.

Transfiguration is a process whereby suffering may be endured and valued even though it is not eliminated. The transfiguration process reveals our individual relationship with God as dependent creatures and the social nature of the self. Failure to take cognizance of either aspect leads to the frustration which discourages faith. For instance, if a community believes that it can accomplish the transformation from *bios* to *zoe* through its own efforts, it relinquishes the aspects of grace and intervention.[12] On the other hand, ignorance of the social aspect of personhood can encourage individuals to rely upon miraculous interventions while neglecting to accept real material aid that is readily available through human agency. Perhaps the failure to give one or the other of these aspects their due explains why some persons do not experience suffering as a transforming experience.

If we neglect the social revelation of suffering—that we are dependent upon others and obligated by love to sustain one another (materially and spiritually)—then it is easy for some to experience only the negative characteristics of suffering. Or if we rigorously meet the material aspects of a crisis and respond as a community with great effort to remove a suffering that persists but forget that divine wisdom prevails, then it is easy for some to experience only the negative characteristics of suffering. In either case, the absence of the transfiguration hermeneutic leads to individual or collective despair. Our most serious mistake is to expect that suffering should be removed in all cases. The cup was not taken from Christ's lips, and thus the transfiguration was completed.

The communal nature of the cross is witnessed in the many exhortations of Jesus that we care for one another. Solidarity with one another in suffering is an essential aspect of the hope to be found in the face of evil. The hope of prayer is more often answered in the acts of fellow persons rather than in extraordinary interventions. Persons who fail to encounter the hopeful power of God in the midst of evil are often isolated from other persons or abandoned by insensitive structures or institutions. The Christian call is to shoulder the burden of the cross for others, as did Simon the Cyrenean for Jesus. In fact, for some who are suffering the negative effects of evil, the solidarity shown by others itself may be the revelation of God's power.

Conclusion

As moral and spiritual beings we are called to improve ourselves and our material condition. We are called to alleviate the suffering of others. This effort stems from an internal state of grace, namely, compassion and love for and solidarity with others in the vale of soul-making. Our continuous effort to right what is wrong exists only by virtue of our faith in the community of persons and the responsibilities which emerge from that reality.

Transfiguration theodicy provides the psychological benefit of optimism, for when our efforts at righting what is wrong do fail we can acknowledge the positive interior transforming effect of our efforts. Though this may be weak solace for those who labor against egregious evils, it is solace none the less. Transfiguration theodicy informs our efforts with the positive knowledge that even if we fail at the material level, our efforts are fruitful at the level of *zoe*.[13]

The suffering of Christ on the cross, the laying down of his life for us, is the paradigm of solidarity among persons. This divine and universal act did not transform the material world at the level of *bios*. It did not eliminate disease, poverty, injustice, or human nature. But it did forever transform material reality by its revelation of God's presence in the midst of suffering.

Theodicy cannot hope to explain why Jesus suffered on the cross. It can only accept the fact that God sent a son, an only son, and that his suffering was not eliminated. Moreover, Jesus' suffering was essential to his transfiguration and to ours. A theodicy of any promise must begin with this fact, for no matter how evil came to be, God has pronounced loudly that it remains in the earthly lives of the people of faith. A transfiguration theodicy establishes its positive value, and thus provides a rational basis for the claim that evil is consistent with an omniscient, omnipotent, and omnibenevolent God. The metaphor for a transfiguration theodicy is not the fall, but the cross. My account of a transfiguration theodicy does not explain the existence of evil, but attempts to derive meaning from its reality, and relies ultimately upon a point of revealed theology rather than natural theology.

NOTES

1. John Hick, *Evil and the God of Love* (San Francisco: Harper and Row, 1977).

2. The theory of positive value is developed in my book, *The Co-Existence of God and Evil* (Peter Lang, 1991). Briefly, an event, object, or action may retain its bad-making characteristics but have extrinsic value as a means towards some greater good. The overall value of a thing, i.e., the judgment that it is better that it obtain than that it not obtain, or worse that it obtain than that it not obtain, is the weighing of its intrinsic and extrinsic good-making and bad-making characteristics. If the vale has bad characteristics but is necessary for soul-making, and soul-making is a good sufficient to justify the vale, then the vale has positive, rather than negative value, even though it retains all its bad-making characteristics.

3. By non-rational agents I mean events such as earthquakes, hurricanes, floods, etc.; or non-human beings such as members of the animal community. These remarks are intended to address the moral nature of actions taken by irrational human persons, by angels, or by other non-human persons whose capacity for intentionality is subject to discussion.

4. John Stuart Mill, *Three Essays on Religion* (London: Longmans, Green and Co., 1875), pp. 176-90, 194.

5. *The New American Bible* (Nashville, Camden, New York: Thomas Nelson Publishers, 1970), pp. 1228-1229.

6. *Ibid*, p. 1094.

7. In addition to the stipulative definition I have given of suffering, it may be helpful here to add these clarifications: suffering is the experiencing of actions or events whose bad-making characteristics outweigh their good-making characteristics. These actions or events may be intended or unintended, and intentionality may be either a good- or bad-making characteristic of the action or event. The suffering may appear to be unmerited or merited, and this, too, may be a good- or a bad-making characteristic of the action or event.

8. Mill, *op. cit.*

9. C.S. Lewis, *The Problem of Pain* (London: Geoffrey Bles, 1940), pp. 14-24.

10. "Fallacies in the Argument from Gratuitous Suffering," *The New Scholasticism*, Autumn 1986, Volume LX, No. 4, pp. 485-89.

11. I do not mean that Christ is no more than exemplary cause, but that his transfiguration functions as exemplary cause as well as revelatory and redemptive act.

12. This is not to say that grace or divine intervention can be thwarted by the human failure to seek them, but that over-reliance on human efforts can lead to frustration because it ignores the action of the divine in historical events. Cognizance of this fact is necessary for a peaceful acceptance of the actual outcomes of one's efforts.

13. I am grateful to Philip Quinn, University of Notre Dame, for his comment on this point. Although his concern was that transfiguration theodicy might lead to a pessimistic approach toward the alleviation of evil on the material plane, I believe its result is quite the opposite.

5

The Ambiguity of the Symbol of the Cross:
Legitimating and Overcoming Evil

By Mary Ann Stenger

T he central Christian symbol of the cross has been given a variety of meanings through the centuries. Some of these meanings focus directly on the issue of evil, but the interpretations can vary from overcoming evil to legitimating the endurance of evil. This ambiguity in the symbol of the cross has been exploited at times by dominant groups against the less powerful. I will explore here the symbol of the cross in relationship to evil, with special reference to violence against women and other oppressed peoples. First, the structure of the symbol of the cross will be analyzed to show how the diverse interpretations developed. Secondly, the use of the cross to justify or allow violence will be explored. Finally, the possibilities of using the symbol of the cross to help resist evil and violence will be analyzed.

The Structure of the Symbol of the Cross

The cross was a Roman means of execution, and even before Jesus' death on a cross, it was used as a metaphor of suffering and agony.[1] The reference to "taking up one's cross" (Matt. 10:38) in the sayings of Jesus invokes images of self-sacrifice. In the Gospels, taking up one's cross signifies the ultimate demands of being a disciple of Jesus. "And he who does not take his cross and follow me is not worthy of me. He who finds his life will lose it, and he who loses his life for my sake will find it" (Matthew 10:38-39).

Jesus' death on the cross reinforces those meanings and adds theological significance. Jesus' self-sacrifice is connected with restoring a right relationship between God and humans. Jesus is understood as dying for human sins (not his own), as the ultimate sacrifice and atonement before God. Jaroslav Pelikan argues: "The followers of Jesus came very early to the conclusion that he had lived in order to die, that his death was not the interruption of his life at all but its ultimate purpose."[2] It is not surprising that the cross develops as the central Christian symbol, used even by denominations that prohibit any other symbols.

The apostle Paul develops a theology of the cross in his letters, making the event the central event and tying its meanings to the key ritual events in the life of a Christian—baptism and communion.[3]

Meaning in baptism:

Do you not know that all of us who have been baptized into Christ Jesus were baptized into his death? Therefore we have been buried with him by baptism into death, so that, just as Christ was raised from the dead by the glory of the Father, so we too might walk in newness of life (Romans 6:3-4).

Meaning in communion:

The cup of blessing that we bless, is it not a sharing in the blood of Christ? The bread that we break, is it not a sharing in the body of Christ?" (I Corinthians 10:16).

For as often as you eat this bread and drink the cup, you proclaim the Lord's death until he comes" (I Corinthians 11:26).

In both baptism and communion, the Christian is sharing in the death of Jesus: being baptized into his death, sharing in the body and blood of Christ, and proclaiming the Lord's death.

The death of Jesus on the cross could have brought an end to Jesus' religious movement. But instead it becomes the focus of Christian faith. Of course, the interpretation of the cross cannot be separated from faith in the resurrection of Jesus. But for the individual Christian, following Jesus is connected with taking up one's cross as a necessary prerequisite to participating in the resurrection. From Christians' earliest theological reflections, the cross carries the meaning of self-sacrifice. Discipleship entails sacrifice and suffering.

Another key interpretation given to the cross focuses on the love of God for humans shown in God's sacrifice of the only Son. "No one has greater love than this, to lay down one's life for one's friends" (John 15:13). Theologians argued that "nowhere else but in Jesus and in his cross was the true nature of love visible. . . True love was self-sacrificing love, and God had demonstrated it uniquely by giving up his own Son to the death of the cross."[4]

Already with Paul, a lifestyle of self-sacrifice is encouraged for disciples. For example, he argues for not marrying as a way of devoting oneself to religious affairs rather than family obligations (I Corinthians 7). The Gospel of Mark shows Jesus issuing a clarion call for disciples to sacrifice themselves: "If any want to become my followers, let them deny themselves and take up their cross and follow me" (8:34). The following verse suggests a connection with martyrdom: "For those who want to save their life will lose it, and those who lose their life for my sake, and for the sake of the gospel, will save it" (Mark 8:35). For several centuries of the church, martyrdom was the primary model for taking up one's cross, to the extent that some people deeply desired the opportunity to become martyrs. This desire for suffering was connected with the expectation of the Kingdom of God; it was assumed that suffering was a sign and a necessary precursor to the coming of the Kingdom.[5] Just as the cross had to precede the resurrection, so also suffering for the sake of the gospel, taking up one's cross, had to precede the fulfillment of the Kingdom.

At the same time that martyrdom was honored, others chose the ascetic life as a way of self-denial. Eventually asceticism was structured into the monastic life, continuing specific practices of self-denial and associating them with taking up one's cross. St. Francis of Assisi is the preeminent example, not only focussing his devotions on Jesus Christ crucified but also receiving the stigmata, the marks of the cross, upon his own body.

Twentieth-century theologian Paul Tillich interprets the symbol of the cross as Jesus sacrificing himself as Jesus to be the Christ, to be transparent to God.

> Jesus of Nazareth is the medium of the final revelation because he sacrifices himself completely to Jesus as the Christ. He not only sacrifices his life, as many martyrs and many ordinary people have done, but he also sacrifices everything in him and of him which could bring people to him as an "overwhelming personality" instead of bringing them to that in him which is greater than he and they.[6]

Jesus dies to himself, sacrificing his finite human characteristics (gender, religion, historical period, etc.). Jesus is not to be treated as a divine hero or as an idol. Jesus' sacrifice on the cross is the basis of a central theme for Tillich, the Protestant principle which guards against idolatry. This principle allows for ultimate truth to be expressed in finite forms and symbols but also states that no truth of faith is ultimate except the truth which says that no human possesses that truth.[7] In other words, truth is expressed through forms and symbols which sacrifice their own ultimacy in order to show ultimacy, with the primary example as the cross of the Christ.

The theme of sacrifice as a central meaning of the cross pervades Christian theology from its earliest days to the present. Its practical implications call for self-sacrifice for disciples of Jesus as the Christ. The two main sacraments of baptism and communion remind people of Jesus' sacrifice on the cross and invite people to share in that sacrifice. Sacrifice is central in many religious traditions because it is associated with effecting a better religious relationship. Whether presenting specific offerings or altering one's lifestyle to be more ascetic (even for a period of time), sacrifice serves the purpose of improving the connection between humans and the ultimate, divine power. Within Christianity, the cross carries the meaning of liberation and salvation along with the theme of sacrifice.

Paul's theology of the cross emphasizes the liberation brought about through Jesus' death, focussing on freedom from sin and freedom from death.

Freedom from sin:

> While we were still weak, at the right time Christ died for the ungodly. . . But God proves his love for us in that while we still were sinners Christ died for us. Much more surely then, now that we have

been justified by his blood, will we be saved through him from the wrath of God. For if while we were enemies, we were reconciled to God by the death of his Son, much more surely, having been reconciled, will we be saved by his life (Romans 5:6, 8-10).

Freedom from death:

. . .One man's act of righteousness leads to justification and life for all. . . Just as sin exercised dominion in death, so grace might also exercise dominion through justification leading to eternal life through Jesus Christ our Lord (Romans 5:18b, 20b-21).

The cross, then, is not only a symbol of sacrifice but also a symbol of salvation. It is seen as the event which restores a right relationship between humans and God, thereby freeing humans from the debt of sin and from the punishment for sin which is death.

The liberation from sin and death wrought by Jesus on the cross provided freedom from the detailed requirements of Jewish law. Paul uses the imagery of the cross to defend his authority when he argues that observance of Jewish law is not necessary, arguing that he has died to himself and that Christ lives in him (Galatians 2:20). For Paul, the sacrifice on the cross brings liberation.

The connection of the cross with freedom from evil and death can be seen in the early church practice of marking oneself, other people, or objects with the sign of the cross. Although making the sign of the cross is not mentioned in the New Testament, it is spoken of early in Christian history as being used to ward off evil powers.[8] For early Christians, the cross showed God's power, connecting it with the understanding that the power of evil had been broken through the death of Jesus, the Son of God.[9]

In *Cur Deus Homo?* (1097 C.E.) Anselm of Canterbury attempts to prove rationally what Paul had stated in I Corinthians, that what would appear in human wisdom as folly is the wisdom of God.[10] Anselm concentrated on the interpretation of the crucifixion as satisfying the debt that human sinners owed to God. Sinners could not pay the debt, but the innocent, divine one, Jesus the Son of God, could offer himself as payment for others. Anselm tries to show that there is an underlying rationality to the incarnation and the cross.

Paul Tillich's use of the cross also carries with it the underlying theme of liberation. The paradox and sacrifice of the cross is seen as a guard against idolatry and injustice. Tillich recognizes that when something or someone is absolutized, treated as an idol, the result is injustice for others. One person or one group claims ultimate power, implying the inferiority of those under that power. Tillich speaks of justice as a "criterion which judges idolatrous holiness."[11] The sacrifice on the cross avoids such idolatrous holiness. As its structure becomes a criterion against idolatry, the cross can be seen also as a criterion against injustice. Critiques of unjust laws or systems can be seen as efforts to liberate them from idolatrous identification with the divine or ultimate. Tillich's Protestant principle is rooted in the cross, working against absolutization of the finite and against the injustice which results from such absolutization.

The cross, then, symbolizes the liberation from sin and death made possible through Jesus' sacrifice. Jesus' death on the cross made it possible for people to be brought into a right relationship with God, a reconciliation no longer broken by sin. Tillich expands this meaning in arguing that Jesus's death on the cross symbolizes freedom from idolatry and its resulting injustice.

Just as there is paradox in Jesus as the divine incarnation, so also there is paradox in the symbolic meanings of the cross. The cross carries two meanings: self-sacrifice and overcoming of sin and death. Discipleship may entail sacrifice and suffering, but being a disciple of Jesus Christ will free one from the powers of sin and death. Extending that to the social world, the cross can be a symbol of liberation from injustice.

Use of the Cross to Legitimate Violence

The cross as a symbol of self-sacrifice and sharing in the suffering of Jesus can be a positive symbol for those who choose to undertake a more disciplined or ascetic lifestyle. Countless numbers of Christians through the centuries have made that choice and have found meaning in their self-sacrifice through the cross of Jesus. But a key word here is choice. If people freely choose to inflict suffering on themselves because of the higher meanings that it brings, most would accept such practice (as long as the inflictions are not too severe, a standard which changes through cultures and time periods).

However, there are those whose sufferings and self-sacrifice is not chosen and where the infliction is done by others: abuse of women and violence against African-Americans. The cross has sometimes been used to encourage victims to accept and endure their pain and suffering. The practical effect of such legitimation is to keep the victims as victims and to turn the cross into a symbol of oppression.

Within Christianity, women have been connected with evil through the role of Eve in the story of the fall and for most of Christian history have been considered inferior and subordinate to men. But Christianity also posited a spiritual equality of men and women (Galatians 3:28) and called on Christian men to love their wives and never treat them harshly (Colossians 3:19). Yet feminist critiques of Christianity have pointed out numerous examples of Christian legitimation of violence against women, ranging from the witch hunts of the past to present day spouse abuse.

The cross is a symbol in the church's persecution of witches, not as a symbol of self-sacrifice but as a symbol of the power of the church over against the feared power of witches. One of the methods that can be used to protect places, people or animals against the power of witches is to write in four places in the form of a cross the words that were posted on top of Jesus' cross: "*Iesus Nazarenus Rex Iudaeorum.*"[12] The meaning of the cross underlying such actions is that of freedom from sin, extended here to freedom from the power of devils and witches. But since the majority of prosecuted witches were women, the cross also served as a legitimation of the violence of those prosecutions.

Feminist philosopher Mary Daly outlined the relationship between the image of Jesus as a sacrificial victim on the cross and the sacrifice imposed on women and other minority groups. She names this relationship the scapegoat syndrome.[13] She argues that people are unable to imitate Jesus as the sacrificial victim and end up transferring their own guilt to another. In Paul's theology that other to whom the guilt is transferred is Jesus. But Daly argues that in fact people transfer their guilt to others, that is, others are forced to be the sacrificial victims.[14] Others are blamed, and punishment for one's own guilt is inflicted on others. Instead of Jesus as the only sacrificial victim who takes away all guilt through the cross, others become the scapegoats and the new victims.

In *Gyn/Ecology* Daly extends this connection between Jesus' sacrifice on the cross and the abuse of women, arguing that the glorification of suffering on the cross has been extended into a secular sadomasochistic claim that female suffering is joy.[15] Daly's examples include Hannah Tillich's description of her theologian husband Paul watching a pornographic film depicting females hanging on crosses and covers of rock albums with "pictures of women chained, women hanged, women gang-raped."[16] Daly is not arguing that Christianity is responsible for sadomasochism but rather that "Christianity, with its torture cross symbolism, has been one expression of this basic pattern."[17]

Psychologist of religion, William Beers, explores the connection between the cross of Christ, sacrifice and women, noting that Tertullian blamed women for bringing death into the world, including the death of the Son of God. Beers argues, "The execution of Jesus of Nazareth was rationalized into a myth in which women were to blame."[18] Beers analyzes religious rituals of sacrifice, including the Christian Eucharist rather than the abusive sacrifices imposed on women which Daly describes. But he does argue for psychological interpretation of the Eucharist in which the body and blood of Christ replaces the nurturing body of the mother, part of a more extensive process of diminishing the theological significance of women.[19] The sacrifice of Jesus on the cross symbolized in the breaking of the bread and pouring of the wine is connected subtly to the sacrifice of women, their loss of central religious meanings and roles.

Harder to document but relevant to the discussion here is a related use of the cross to legitimate women's sacrifice as victims of abuse or even rape. How many priests and ministers told female victims that the violence was their cross to bear, invoking the bearing of the cross as the necessary means to true Christian discipleship? Although such advice may have been intended as consolation and support for victims, it carried the not so subtle legitimation of violence against women. Over against Jesus' agony on the cross, how could a woman complain? How could a woman ask that her cross be removed since that cross might be her very means of showing her true discipleship for Jesus? Enduring her plight passively and quietly, as Jesus endured the cross, was her lot and destiny. Sometimes the overlay of the sacrality of marriage and the submissiveness of wife to husband added to this legitimation. But the cross, added to the other legitimations, turned its meaning into domination by other powers rather than liberation from those powers.

Although most Christian groups today would abhor racial violence directed toward African-Americans, they cannot ignore the
past history of slavery and white supremacist groups in the United
States. Christian theology was used (and still is by some groups) to
support racist attitudes and actions. We will look briefly at the
treatment of slavery within the New Testament and then consider
the role of the cross in legitimations of racism.

Slavery was an accepted institution within the Roman Empire at
the time when Christianity began as an organized religion. Sociological studies of early Christianity show that slaves were among the
large numbers of dispossessed who joined the Christian movement.[20]
Several early Christian texts do not attack the social institution of
slavery but rather exhort the slaveholders to treat their slaves justly
and fairly (Colossians 4:1). Paul's letter to Philemon hopes for
positive treatment when Philemon's slave Onesimus is returned, but
it does not call for freeing him. Yet Paul's letters also contain this
famous verse, thought to have been a baptismal formula: "There is
neither Jew nor Greek, there is neither slave nor free, there is
neither male nor female; for you are all one in Christ Jesus"
(Galatians 3:28). Paul goes on to use slavery as a metaphor for
bondage to the law, contrasted with freedom through faith in Christ.
Within the faith community, the social status of slave was rejected,
but that did not carry over to rejection of slavery as a social
institution within the Roman Empire.

The American form of slavery, rooted in racism, is particularly
repugnant to our modern sensibilities. But in exploring the evil of
slavery, one cannot ignore the fact that the slaveholders saw themselves as Christian and even legitimated their position as a means to
bring slaves to Christianity. Many slaves responded and were
allowed their own separate churches. Separate denominations or
separate churches for African-Americans developed rather than the
churches living out the baptismal formula of oneness in Christ Jesus.

The end of slavery as a legal institution in the United States did
not end segregation within Christianity or among Christians who
believed their racism against African-Americans was supported by
God. Nor did the civil rights movement and civil rights laws in the
1960's and 1970's end it. A personally memorable and chilling
moment from a national meeting of Christian youth in 1964 is relevant here. The meeting was racially integrated, but some white

southern participants raised the Confederate flag, spoke out for white supremacy, and then announced that if they were wrong, through Christ God would forgive them in the end anyway. The doctrine of atonement, rooted in the cross, took a diabolical turn here.

This climate of assumed Christian support for racism was countered by the active involvement of many white Christians in the marches against segregation and in efforts to integrate Christian denominations and churches. Equality in Christ became the ideal under which denominations once separated over race now unified. For many, their Christian faith was the basis of their struggle for civil rights throughout their communities.

But others continued to believe in the superiority of whites and the inferiority of blacks and saw their beliefs as fitting with Christianity. The Ku Klux Klan, a white supremacist organization still active today, makes references to Christianity in its literature and uses a burning cross as a sign of their responsibility for specific acts of violence against African-Americans. A burning cross represents hatred and a rejection of the humanity and rights of African-Americans. The Klan's choice of the cross as their symbol shows their connection of Christianity with racism and violence.

Womanist theologian Delores Williams analyzes the situation of black women who were used as surrogate mothers, expected to love other people's children more than themselves and to bear pain and hardship. She asks whether the atonement model that treats Jesus as the surrogate for the sins of humanity can serve as a liberating model to black women.[21] "If black women accept this image of redemption, can they not also passively accept the exploitation surrogacy brings? . . .Can there be salvific power in Christian images of oppression (for example, Jesus on the cross) meant to teach something about redemption?"[22] These questions point to the negative side of the symbol of the cross. As a central symbol which elevates suffering and sacrifice as divine, it can and has been used to legitimate others' self-sacrifice. But the cross also carries the meaning of liberation.

Use of the Cross to Resist Violence
and to Liberate from Violence

The above discussions of the cross in connection with violence against women and violence against African-Americans show that some have used the cross to legitimate their domination over others and the accompanying evil acts against those others. But it is intriguing to recognize that this has not resulted in a full-scale rejection of the cross as a symbol to victims. Rather, Jesus' suffering on the cross often resonates with the oppressed who feel that Jesus understands and knows their suffering. And the cross often works as a symbol of liberation from oppression and violence.

Theologian Susan Thistlethwaite gives several examples of abused women or minority women who have experienced the symbol of the cross as Jesus empathizing with their suffering. As a woman who had been raped "lay on the heap of trash, injured and bleeding and wondering whether she was about to be killed, she had a vision of Jesus as a crucified woman who said to her from the cross, 'You don't have to be ashamed, I know what you are suffering.'"[23] Thistlethwaite describes women who find healing in statues of Christa, female figures in the form of a crucifix. "Christa is not experienced by many women as legitimating violence against them but as identifying with their pain and freeing them from the guilt that somehow, because of the original sin of being female, they deserved what they got."[24] Although these cases show the figure on the cross as a female rather than Jesus, the image of the suffering on the cross as redemptive has carried over to the Christa figures.

Themes from African-American spirituals also suggest that the cross provided a liberating image to the oppressed. "Nobody knows the trouble I've seen; nobody knows but Jesus" suggests that only the suffering Jesus could identify with the pain and suffering of the oppressed black, whether during or after slavery. Most of the verses of "Were you there when they crucified my Lord?" focus on the agony and suffering of Jesus rather than the resurrection. A glorified image would offer little basis for identification with the oppressed, but the cross symbolizes that identification and shared experience of suffering.

Theologian Deotis Roberts notes that the privileged are more apt to identify with a regal or otherworldly model of Christ while the oppressed and persecuted see Christ as a liberator. He argues that that is why the cross is central in Minjung (Korean liberation) and black theologies. "But the cross is not a symbol of escape; rather it is a symbol of engagement with evil and suffering. Christ's victorious resurrection is seen in relation to the cross as its sequel and ultimate vindication."[25] The cross does not stand alone but as the precursor to the resurrection; but perhaps, it is more significant that the resurrection does not stand alone but receives its full meaning as victory over the evil and suffering shown in Jesus' death on the cross.

Delores Williams emphasizes Jesus' life of right relationships with the oppressed and his resurrection as the symbols of redemption more than the cross. But she recognizes that the cross is important as a reminder of collective destruction of people and movements working for equality and transformations of the status quo.[26] She argues that Jesus came for life, but she knows that black women cannot forget the cross. The cross show God's identification with the oppressed, but it should not be glorified.

The cross of Christ as a liberating image, then, comes not in a narrow focus on the cross alone but in its connection with the resurrection. On the one hand, resurrection without the cross is not a liberating image for the oppressed. The power of the resurrection is in its vindication of the powerless, the symbol of life, not just over death, but of life for the victim, the one who has suffered violence at the hands of others. Thus, in spite of the use of the cross to legitimate that very violence, the power of the symbol of the cross in conjunction with the resurrection remains strong as an image of liberation from violence.

Conclusion

The ambiguity of the cross shows how the same religious symbol can be used as part of religious legitimations of violence and evil and as an image of liberation from violence and evil. We humans find meaning in religious symbols, but we are capable of manipulating our interpretations to fit our own needs and purposes. Evil and violence are not inherent in religion, but the power of religion as a legitimator of evil and violence throughout history cannot be ignored. People have recognized that religious legitimation connects ordinary human action and ideas to the unchanging, transcendent power of the sacred or God. That connection of the infinite to the finite is inherent in religion, but the abuse of that connection is not. The process of making religious legitimations can involve turning the finite human event, person, ideas, or movement into an idol, an absolutization of the finite. Such idolatry generally entails domination of one group over another, acted out in the injustice of evil and violence against the other.

Paul Tillich's use of the cross as a criterion against such idolatry builds upon the ambiguity in the symbol or more accurately, the paradox in the symbol of the cross. Idolatry and its accompanying injustice can be guarded against by working to maintain the underlying paradox in religion, that religious symbols and actions can express ultimacy but are not themselves ultimate. We always need to be on guard against absolutizing our finite actions and ideas. The sacrifice on the cross can symbolize the rejection of such absolutization. Religious leaders and theologians need to make people aware of the danger in religious legitimations and to encourage them to challenge such abuses of religion.

NOTES

1. Benedict T. Viviano, O.P., "The Gospel According to Matthew," *The New Jerome Biblical Commentary* (Englewood Cliffs, NJ: Prentice Hall, 1990), p. 660.
2. Jaroslav Pelikan, *Jesus Through the Centuries: His Place in the History of Culture* (New York: Harper and Row, 1985), p. 95.
3. All biblical reference are from *The Holy Bible*, New Revised Standard Version (New York: Oxford University Press, 1989).
4. Pelikan, *op. cit.*, p. 106.
5. See Howard Clark Kee, *Jesus in History: An Approach to the Study of the Gospels* (New York: Harcourt, Brace, and World, Inc., 1970), p. 92 for a discussion of this point in the gospels.
6. Paul Tillich, *Systematic Theology*, Vol. 1 (Chicago: University of Chicago, 1951), p. 136.
7. Paul Tillich, *Dynamics of Faith* (New York: Harper and Row, 1957), p. 98.
8. Pelikan, *op. cit.*, p. 96.
9. *Ibid.*, p. 98. "The cross was believed to possess all of this victorious power because it had been the instrument for the greatest victory of them all, the cosmic victory of the power of God over the power of the devil in the death and resurrection of Jesus" (pp. 99-100).
10. I Corinthians 1:22-24: "For Jews demand signs and Greeks seek wisdom,

but we preach Christ crucified, a stumbling block to Jews and folly to Gentiles, but to those who are called, both Jews and Greeks, Christ the power of God and the wisdom of God." Also see Pelikan, pp. 106ff.

11. Paul Tillich, *Systematic Theology*, Vol. I, p. 216.

12. Heinrich Kramer and James Sprenger, *The Malleus Maleficarum*, trans. by Montague Summers (New York: Dover Publications, 1971), p. 92.

13. Mary Daly, *Beyond God the Father: Toward a Philosophy of Women's Liberation* (Boston: Beacon Press, 1973), p. 75.

14. *Ibid.*, p. 76.

15. Mary Daly, *Gyn/Ecology: The Metaethics of Radical Feminism* (Boston: Beacon Press, 1978), pp. 93-94.

16. *Ibid.*, p. 94.

17. *Ibid.*, p. 96.

18. William Beers, *Women and Sacrifice: Male Narcissism and the Psychology of Religion* (Detroit: Wayne State University Press, 1992), p. 172.

19. *Ibid.*, pp. 172, 176, 178-179.

20. See John Gager, *Kingdom and Community: The Social World of Early Christianity* (Englewood Cliffs, New Jersey: Prentice-Hall, Inc., 1975), chapter 4.

21. Delores Williams, "Black Women's Surrogacy Experience and the Christian Notion of Redemption," in *After Patriarchy: Feminist Transformations of the World Religions*, ed. Paula Cooey, William Eakin, and Jay McDaniel (Maryknoll, NY: Orbis Books, 1991), pp. 8-9.

22. *Ibid.*, p. 9.

23. Susan Thistlethwaite, *Sex, Race, and God: Christian Feminism in Black and White* (New York: Crossroad, 1991), p. 93.

24. *Ibid.*

25. Deotis Roberts, *Black Theology in Dialogue* (Philadelphia, PA: Westminster, 1987), p. 109.

26. Delores Williams, *op. cit.*, p. 12.

6

The Problem of Evil:
An Islamic Approach

By Muhammad Al-Ghazali

I slam, which literally means submission, may be defined as voluntary subordination of human discretion to the will of God. The divine will is embodied in the decrees of God articulated in his revelation (*Qur'an*) and interpreted by his last Prophet, Muhammad, (peace be upon him) through oral explanation and practical example (*Sunnah*). Approval or disapproval of Islam is accorded by the criteria of the *Qur'an* and the *Sunnah*. Since the scope of explicit verdicts provided in these twin sources of guidance is limited, there remains a wide area for human reason to pronounce its judgment concerning such matters on which these sources are silent. Such judgment must not violate the doctrinal framework laid down in the *Qur'an* and the *Sunnah*.

Islam, according to the injunctions of God and instructions of his Prophet (peace be upon him), is a commitment of the mind and heart that is compatible with human nature.[1] Islam, therefore, takes a realistic and friendly attitude to human nature. It does not oblige its adherents to follow a course of action decidedly incongruent with the innate urges of human nature. These natural urges are identifiable in their universal manifestation in spite of all diversities of creed and culture, genealogy and geography, socio-economics or history.

The *Qur'an* points to an innate duality within the human person. This duality invests an individual with a simultaneous capacity for good and evil. Where the *Qur'an* mentions the divine act of creation in which God inaugurated human life in history, it also speaks of God breathing into a human being the divine spirit together with the earthliness of humanity.[2] This duality represents unlimited opportunities to relate to matter, mind and spirit, all granted by God to humanity. One is not, therefore, expected to dedicate himself/herself exclusively to spiritual endeavors at the detriment of an individual's instinctive needs and aesthetic aspirations. Such a person is not only authorized, but asked to satisfy legitimate physical desires provided one does not lose balance in this process. Thus in the very creation of human beings, God intended to combine the possibility of evil with the prospects of good.

God created humanity in the best fashion.[3] God placed the human person at the center of this cosmic order as his *Khalifah*, vicegerent.[4] This lofty locus of vicegerency implies that a person is entitled to enjoy the treasures of this earth subject to the observance of the terms and conditions of the office of vicegerency. It further requires that one is granted freedom to accept or reject the terms of this august office. Such freedom demands that evil opportunities should always remain available along with the promise of good. Hence, Islam does not contemplate a human condition in which evil tendencies might be totally eliminated. For this would mean utter disregard of human nature and distortion of its temperament. That was why the angels who had been created with an exclusive capacity for good, expressed bewilderment over the possibilities of evil being placed at the disposal of humanity and rightly predicted that human beings would fill the earth with mischief and bloodshed.[5]

The significant point to note here is that when a creature with both options pursues the path of good and shuns the avenues of evil by one's own choice, such a person surpasses all angelic levels of spirituality. The entire potential of human personality in all its diversity is thus realizable through this essential duality. For example, if there is no instinct for self-preservation or the fear of death, there can be no bravery. If there is no greed, there is no meaning of generosity. If there is no hunger, there is no use to fast. If there is no lust, there would be no concept of chastity. Therefore, in the Islamic view of things, duality is naturally ingrained in the very constitution of human beings and should be preserved at all times. The *Qur'an* or the *Sunnah* do not envisage any human existential condition free from all elements of evil. For the very realization of good is contingent upon the possibility of its opposite. The definition of good involves positing the self-conscious human subject at the center of this bipolarity.

At the same time the human person has been granted the higher faculty of judgment whereby one is able to discriminate between good and evil. This ability to distinguish good from evil is innate in a person's natural constitution. Their understanding of good and evil and their mutual distinction is primarily derived from intuition. It is further reinforced and elaborated by divine guidance communicated to an individual through the Prophet (peace be upon him) and concretized in his ideal example. That is why the essential values of good, for example, truth, mercy, generosity, justice and gratefulness and their opposite evils, namely falsehood, cruelty, miserliness, ungratefulness and oppression are universally recognized for what they are by all. Thus a person enjoys immense prospects of spiritual and moral elevation by realizing one's vast potential for good. At the same time, one has the option to gravitate entirely to a baser level of behavior if one chooses to pursue the path of evil. The challenge, which is quite formidable but at the same time highly rewarding in terms of unlimited spiritual ascension and perfect bliss, is that humanity is required to maintain an equilibrium between the two urges. These urges are apparently opposite but essentially compatible. They are harmonious in the state of inner balance but incongruent in a condition of disequilibrium. The human person is required to be neither exclusively devoted to spirituality nor wholly dedicated to animality. One is asked to embrace both and to shun neither. Therein lies the greatness of humanity. It is a divine mercy that the realization of human greatness was made possible through prescribing a course of action fully compatible with human nature.

It is to be noted that unlike all other animals, a human being remains dissatisfied despite the fullest satisfaction of one's beastly desires. One aspires toward constant improvement and refinement in the quality of life. A person may undertake unlimited intellectual endeavors to inquire, explain and innovate, and a large number of people may benefit from the fruits of such intellectual and artistic achievements. If human beings were selfish in a total sense, there would have been no progress possible in human culture and civilization. All developments of the past in the spheres of culture and civilization afford ample evidence of this innate altruism of humankind.

Islam did not leave the task of forging this formidable balance between the higher and lower planes of personality to the whims and vagaries of individuals. On the contrary, the prophets who have been commissioned by God to preach Islam to humanity from the genesis of humankind to the advent of the Prophet Muhammad (peace be upon him) have exemplified in their own patterns of living, the manners and modes of effecting this balance. These distinguished figures of wisdom, knowledge and piety also initiated vigorous collective campaigns for promoting good and suppressing evil at the level of society. They presented in their examples, a pattern for balanced behavior in the individual and collective dimensions of life. It is this balance effected in the inner self under the guidance of prophetic example which alone is capable of providing total fulfillment to human beings. One develops a natural love for good and a personal abhorrence for evil. One is filled with happiness by performing virtue and with remorse and repentance when evil is committed. This identification of one's will with God's will constitutes the essence of piety. But the criteria for distinguishing between good and evil deeds is not their outer objective manifestation but their inner subjective motivation which is fully known to God. Thus God judges humans by their intentions and not by the results of their efforts. This realistic aspect of Islam demonstrates the mercy and compassion of God to creatures in that God has charged them with obligations commensurate with their capacity.[6]

Thus the great task for humankind under the Islamic agenda of life is to constantly engage in reforming intentions and purifying them of malice, avarice, and all vicious wishes. For this is surely within the capacity of each human being. The rest is forgivable because God is all merciful and compassion overtakes God's wrath and envelops all things in existence.[7]

In the worldview of Islam, the human person is the goal of this world and not vice versa. The material world is placed at the service of humanity. Each person has been urged to serve God so as to attain lasting bliss in the life of the hereafter.[8] For the immediate world of matter, despite its charms and pleasures, is not worth one's while. In this worldview, life presents itself as a great challenge. Either one should enthrone one's higher self within the inner kingdom of the body, mind, heart and spirit or establish in it the supreme rule of the lower self. If a person sincerely pursues the former path, such a one will be rewarded with inner peace and tranquility here and with lasting bliss hereafter. If one willfully follows the latter way, such a person might attain some timely pleasure by an exhaustive satisfaction of baser desires but will surely be deprived of inner peace and felicity here as well as of salvation and success hereafter.

The main emphasis of the teachings of Islam is, therefore, a constant concern and endless effort to purify the intentions of the inner self. This, according to the *Qur'an*, constitutes one of the cardinal functions of the Prophet (peace be upon him). Such inner purification of the self is a fundamental objective because in Islam, the root of all evil is the inner human intention.[9] Without continuous vigilance over the evil tendencies of the self and an earnest endeavor to reform and rectify its immoral ambitions, the problem of evil cannot be redressed. Unless serious effort is made at various levels and from different directions to check evil at its birth place, namely, the human psyche, no external influence can be of much avail. Use of coercion might yield some results in the form of superficial drills of morality, but mere force can neither reform the inner self nor motivate it to good instead of evil intentions.

Evil rampant in the world is begotten from a perversion of human emotion, intuition and intellection leading to a corruption of intentions. This perversion also diminishes one's ability to perceive truth because persistent pursuit of evil weakens the human psyche. A sick psyche cannot distinguish truth from falsehood. As the tongue tastes sweet as bitter in certain feverish conditions, so the sick soul often fails to discern right from wrong. This inner perversion gradually develops into an apotheosis of the ego. This apotheosis is not made by any oral testimony or overt proclamation. It is perpetrated by the inner attitude of an unbalanced and exclusive pursuit of a selfish purpose in disregard of all norms and canons of higher morality.

The ultimate purpose to which Islam aims is not, however, confined to the personal well-being and inner peace of individuals through effecting a balance between their bodies and souls. This focus on individual purity and personal piety is no doubt a basic concern of Islam. But its ultimate objective lies in the realization of *adl*, justice at all levels of human endeavor and social concourse.[10]

Justice as Islam views it, is not something apart or independent from the balance and harmony that we have thus far elaborated. For the very quintessence of justice is harmony and balance. If harmony is achieved in the psychic interiors and mindsets of individuals, it should ipso facto lead to an outer balance between our attitude to a variety of entities. From the Islamic point of view, justice effects an equilibrium between a diversity of obligations. The general definition of *adl* (Islamic term for justice literally meaning balance) is: placing something in its proper stead, and its opposite *zulm* would be defined as placing something in an improper or wrong place where it does not belong. Thus individuals who are charged with a definite set of obligations are required by the dictates of the supreme value of justice to perform their duties toward all entities without disturbing the necessary balance. This provides us with a universal meaning of justice: balance within and balance without. By the same token the antithesis of justice also becomes easily definable with universal significance.

If a human being invested with tremendous inner potential for intellectual ingenuity and moral excellence, animal gratification and spiritual upliftment, emotional contentment and chaos, peace of heart and anarchy of mind, succeeds in striking a balance and harmony between these internal forces, then that individual is bound to make substantive contributions to the outward and popular ascendancy of justice. Thus the inner duality between animality and spirituality within the human person manifests itself at all levels of the human situation. It has been the primordial challenge to actualize one's natural inner harmony in order to realize justice at all subsequent levels of relationships with fellow beings as well as with other creatures of God.

Moreover, the above definition of justice affords a comprehensive and total approach to the problem of good and evil in all conditions of human existence. With this definition in view we may contend that maintaining a balanced position vis-à-vis all the gravitational pulls that characterize human reality constitutes good. And losing this balance is evil. This conception of good and evil is valid in all space-time conditions. Furthermore, the idea of balance as the mainstay of all forms of justice and disequilibrium as the crux of all mischief and miscarriages of justice extends beyond the human sphere to the realm of the natural environment as well.

The whole pathogenesis of humankind is ultimately traceable to a loss of balance between various demands of the body and soul. Any slight or serious disorder in human physiology or psychic normalcy is to be explained in terms of some excesses or omissions either in nutrition, habit or exposure to nature or interaction with fellow beings. In other words, all ailments of the body or maladies of the soul result from some misappropriation of their properties.

More significantly, such a comprehensive concept of justice as an all-pervading value can give proper orientation to one's relationships with nature. Any excess or omission in a person's exploitation of the treasures of nature results in the loss of balance and harmony in their mutual relationship. This brings home the point that any infringement or offense against the legitimate rights of others whether humans, animals, members of the vegetable kingdom or other entities of the natural world, is bound to bring evil consequences for the imminent or ultimate well-being and survival of the perpetrators themselves. Is this not also fully testified by the incontrovertible empirical evidence of science?

To maintain harmony and balance in order to afford to all what is legitimately their due assumes a greater significance to the human social enterprise. This is so precisely because all evil known in human history has arisen from humankind's malice and ill will against and among each other. This cardinal sin is a result of a person's willful loss of the necessary balance between animality and spirituality. One becomes egocentric when animal desires dominate the entire self and thus overpower the personality. When a human being earnestly undertakes the effort to maintain the required balance within one's personal inner kingdom, such an individual is able to overcome greed, grudge, malice and jealousy by a systematic training of the self. Such a person no longer regards oneself to be the sole master of one's destiny and the molder of one's inner and outer world. This individual accepts the role as a trustee of life and nature. In accepting one's obligations to others, an individual engages in an endless sincere effort to pursue the benefit, happiness and welfare of others. This altruism need not be pursued at the cost of one's own vital interests; for throughout balance should not be lost. A human being should neither be totally slanted towards selfishness nor entirely tilted to selflessness.

This requires that a person acknowledges the rights of all those humans with whom interaction might take place in existential life. One is urged in the first place to faithfully observe obligations to parents.[11] The obligation to one's parents is so fundamental in Islam that it comes only next to monotheism in the *Qur'anic* description of the priorities of human moral conduct. This stress on the obligation to parents implies that one is not authorized to cultivate the same amount and intensity of love for others. This would be at the expense of the natural balance in human relations. Similarly the love and affection due to one's real brothers and sisters should not be showered upon others at the cost of one's brothers and sisters. So also the status of mother supersedes all other human relations. A person is required to accord one's kindest treatment to one's mother. Also the intimate love, sincerity and close companionship due to one's spouse is not due to anyone else. Otherwise one would lose the essential balance of human relations and life would be deprived of harmony and peace. Moreover, the society at large would run the risk of facing such horrible consequences as it has so far suffered in the form of rising divorce, broken hearts and homes, matrimonial infidelity, incest and desecration of all human bonds. The latest example of this desecration is the judgment of American courts under which children have been allowed to divorce, so to speak, their parents. With this judgment, the sanctity of the parental bond has been reduced to mere contractual reciprocity. Similarly the love of one's children, so strongly rooted in humanity's natural disposition, should not be withheld from or offered to others rather than to one's own offspring. Disturbance of this balance results in irreparable psychic abnormalities, damaging the inner health and harmony of life. Such deviations from the natural course of life invariably threatens human peace and tranquility in serious proportions.

Any disturbance in the natural balance of human relations tarnishes the temperament of humanity and as a result deprives it of its inherent harmony and health. Eventually this disequilibrium sows the early seeds of *zulm* (improper balance), the antithesis of *adl* (proper balance), by dislodging the near and dear ones from their rightful place in the human heart. This brings a rupture to the composure and serenity in the interior of the human personality. Moreover, misappropriation of one's love and affection at the level of the individual disturbs the overall integrity and solidarity of the social situation. It engenders self-interest rather than the selfless building of sincerity and altruism.

If the whole spiritual texture and moral fiber of society rests ultimately on the primacy of justice as a norm of human conduct, then the task of defining the meaning of justice cannot be left to the whims of individuals. The centrality of justice as the main anchor of human integrity, on the contrary, calls for a permanent set of norms that must be universally acknowledged. These norms must be based on immutable connotations of right and wrong. Hence, good and evil cannot be defined by the arbitration of human desire nor allowed to be defied by the selfish utilitarian caprice of individuals. Rather, right and wrong, good and evil, virtue and vice ought to be permanently settled by express divine decrees articulated through the mediation of prophets and concretized in history by their exemplary models.

Moreover, from the Islamic point of view, moral duties are classified into two broad categories: obligations to God and obligations to humanity. Obligations to humanity precede one's obligations to God according to the consensus of Muslim scholars. This order of precedence is justified by the fact that God is all merciful and compassionate. But humankind by nature is tempered with reciprocity. A human being is authorized to retaliate if wronged by others, but at the same time strongly urged to forgive. When one finds both options open but adopts the way of clemency and compassion, such a person indeed achieves a great moral victory. If you have no option but to forgive, there is no virtue in forgiveness.

In the sphere of human obligations to God, such as worship, the individual is the gainer or loser. If one worships God with sincerity and dedication, such a person is the gainer; if one omits anything in that respect, that person alone is the loser. But in the case of human rights, the adversity resulting from one's evil act is incurred by others. This individual thus becomes guilty of disseminating evil which is a greater crime than that committed in the narrow personal sphere.

Evil in its various categories cannot always be eliminated or suppressed by an individual's own limited efforts. There is an essential evil, namely, the imbalance of the inner self which is the individual's own responsibility to curb and control. There is a kind of evil which needs to be resisted at the level of the family. If this primary social unit is strong enough, as it should be, then it would check and possibly eliminate many forms of evil by the strength of the matrimonial bond before they assume social proportions. There are manifestations of evil at the social level. It is the collective duty of the society to check and obstruct its expansion by a strong mechanism of social censure. There is yet a higher evil perpetrated at the political plane. Since this category of evil is often backed by naked physical force, it must be checked by equivalent force. Because when evil is spread in the land through the instrument of promethean political power, mere passive preaching can hardly be of any avail.

It needs to be emphasized that in order to devise a viable strategy to fight evil in all its forms, we must address ourselves to reform the thought and behavior of humankind in order to restore balance and harmony in human life at all levels. We should adopt all means to impress upon individuals, societies and state, the dire need to revise and rectify current attitudes, conventions and policies that may drift more and more toward selfish pursuit of interests. While we do not deny the natural right of a person to improve living by all legitimate means, we need to underline the message that material progress should not be myopically pursued at the cost of moral scruples and spiritual norms. Is this not also the conclusion of the scientific enterprise?

NOTES

1. *Qur'an*:30:30.
2. *Ibid*:15:29.
3. *Ibid*:95:3.
4. *Ibid*:2:30.
5. *Ibid*.
6. *Ibid*:2:286.
7. *Ibid*:7:156.
8. *Ibid*:2:25.
9. *Ibid*:12:53.
10. *Ibid*:57:25.
11. *Ibid*:17:23-24.

7

Feminist Theology as a Means of Combatting Injustice Toward Women in Muslim Communities and Culture

By Riffat Hassan

Women such as Khadijah and 'A'ishah (wives of the Prophet Muhammad) and Rabi'a al-Basri (the outstanding woman Sufi) figure significantly in early Islam. Nonetheless, the Islamic tradition has, by and large, remained strongly patriarchal till today. This means, among other things, that the sources of the Islamic tradition, mainly, the *Qur'an* (which Muslims believe to be God's Word transmitted through the Angel Gabriel to the Prophet Muhammad), *Sunnah* (the practice of the Prophet Muhammad), *Hadith* (the oral traditions attributed to the Prophet Muhammad), and *Fiqh* (jurisprudence) have been interpreted only by Muslim men who have arrogated to themselves the task of defining the ontological, theological, sociological and eschatological status of Muslim women. It is hardly surprising that until now the majority of Muslim women who have been kept for centuries in physical, mental and emotional bondage, have accepted this situation passively. Here it

needs to be mentioned that while the rate of literacy is low in many
Muslim countries, the rate of literacy of Muslim women, especially
those who live in rural areas where most of the population lives, is
amongst the lowest in the world.

In recent years, largely due to the pressure of anti-women laws
which have been promulgated under the cover of "islamization" in
some parts of the Muslim world, women with some degree of
education and awareness are beginning to realize that religion is
being used as an instrument of oppression rather than as a means
of liberation. To understand the powerful impetus to "islamize"
Muslim societies, especially with regard to women-related norms
and values, it is necessary to know that of all the challenges con-
fronting the Muslim world perhaps the greatest is that of modernity.
Muslims, in general, tend to think of modernity in two ways: as
modernization which is associated with science, technology and
material progress; and as Westernization which is associated with
promiscuity and all kinds of social problems ranging from latch-key
children to drug and alcohol abuse. While modernization is
considered highly desirable, Westernization is considered equally
undesirable. An emancipated Muslim woman is seen by many
Muslims as a symbol not of modernization but of Westernization.
She appears to be in violation of what traditional societies consider
to be a necessary barrier between private space where women
belong and public space which belongs to men. The presence of
women in men's space is considered to be highly dangerous for, as
a popular *hadith* states, whenever a man and a woman are alone, *ash-
Shaitan* (the Satan) is bound to be there. In today's Muslim world,
due to the pressure of political and socio-economic realities, a significant number of women may be seen in public space. Caretakers of
Muslim traditionalism feel gravely threatened by this phenomenon
which they consider to be an onslaught of Westernization under the
guise of modernization. They believe that it is necessary to put
women back in private space (which also designates their place) if
the integrity of the Islamic way of life is to be preserved.

Although I had begun my study of theological issues pertaining
to women in the Islamic tradition in 1974, it was not until 1983-84
when I spent almost two years in Pakistan that my career as an activist began. The enactment of the Hadud Ordinance (1979) according
to which women's testimony was declared to be inadmissible in

Hadd crimes, including the crime of rape, was accompanied by a wave of violence toward women and a deluge of anti-women literature which swept across the country. Many women in Pakistan were jolted out of their slumber by the "islamization" of the legal system which through the promulgation of laws such as the Hadud Ordinance and the Law of Evidence (1984), as well as the threat of other discriminatory legislation (such as the law of Qisas and Diyat or blood-money), reduced their status systematically to less than that of men. It soon became apparent that forces of religious conservatism were determined to cut women down to one-half or less of men, and that this attitude stemmed from a desire to keep women in their place, which means secondary, subordinate and inferior to men.

Reflecting upon the scene, I asked myself how it was possible for manifestly unjust laws to be implemented in a country which professed a passionate commitment to both Islam and modernity. The answer to my question was so obvious that I was startled that it had not struck me before. Pakistani society (or other Muslim societies) could enact or accept laws which specified that women were less than men in fundamental ways because Muslims, in general, consider it a self-evident truth that women are not equal to men. Among the arguments used to overwhelm any proponent of gender equality, the following are perhaps the most popular: that according to the *Qur'an*, men are *qawwamun* (generally translated as rulers or managers) in relation to women[1]; that according to the *Qur'an*, a man's share in inheritance is twice that of a woman[2]; that according to the *Qur'an*, the witness of one man is equal to that of two women[3]; that according to the Prophet, women are deficient both in prayer (due to menstruation) and in intellect (due to their witness counting for less than a man's).[4] (Elsewhere in my work I have shown how the first three amongst the statements referred to above, are not warranted by an unbiased, accurate reading of the *Qur'anic* texts on which they are based.)

Since, in all probability, I was the only Muslim woman in the country who had been engaged in a study of women's issues from a nonpatriarchal, theological perspective, I was approached numerous times by women leaders (including members of the Pakistan Commission on the Status of Women, before whom I gave my testimony in May 1984) to state what my findings were and if they could be used to improve the situation of Pakistani women. I was urged by women activists who were mobilizing and leading women's protests in a country under martial law, to help them refute the arguments that were being used against them. Though I felt eager to help, I was not sure if the best strategy was simply to respond to each argument that was being used to deprive women of their human (as well as Islamic) rights. What had to be done, first and foremost, in my opinion, was to examine the theological ground in which all the antiwomen arguments were rooted to see if, indeed, a case could be made for asserting that from the point of view of normative Islam, men and women were essentially equal, despite biological and other differences.

As a result of further study and reflection I came to perceive that in the Islamic tradition, as well as in the Jewish and the Christian, there are three theological assumptions on which the superstructure of men's alleged superiority to women has been erected. These three assumptions are: that God's primary creation is man, not woman, since woman is believed to have been created from man's rib, hence derivative and secondary ontologically; that woman, not man, was the primary agent of what is generally referred to as man's fall or man's expulsion from the garden of Eden, hence all daughters of Eve are to be regarded with hatred, suspicion and contempt; and that woman was created not only from man but also for man, which makes her existence merely instrumental and not fundamental. The three theological questions to which the above assumptions may appropriately be regarded as answers are: How was woman created? Was woman responsible for the fall of man? Why was woman created?

It is not possible, within the scope of this discussion, to deal exhaustively with any of the above questions. However, in what follows, an effort has been made to highlight the way in which sources of normative Islam have been interpreted to show that women are inferior to men.

How Was Woman Created?

The ordinary Muslim believes, as seriously as the ordinary Jew or Christian, that Adam was God's primary creation and that Eve was made from Adam's rib. While this myth is obviously rooted in the Yahwist's account of creation in Genesis 2:18-24, it has no basis whatever in the *Qur'an* which describes the creation of humanity in completely egalitarian terms. In the thirty or so passages pertaining to the subject of human creation, the *Qur'an* uses generic terms for humanity (*an-nas, al-insan, bashar*) and there is no mention in it of *Hawwa'* or Eve. The word Adam occurs twenty-five times in the *Qur'an,* but it is used in twenty-one cases as a symbol for self-conscious humanity. Here, it is pertinent to point out that the word Adam is a Hebrew word (from *adamah,* meaning the soil) and it functions generally as a collective noun referring to the human rather than to a male person. In the *Qur'an,* the word Adam (which Arabic borrowed from Hebrew) mostly does not refer to a particular human being. Rather, it refers to human beings in a particular way. As pointed out by Muhammad Iqbal:

> Indeed, in the verses which deal with the origin of man as a living being, the *Qur'an* uses the words *Bashar* or *Insan,* not Adam which it reserves for man in his capacity of God's vicegerent on earth. The purpose of the *Qur'an* is further secured by the omission of proper names mentioned in the biblical narration—Adam and Eve. The term Adam is retained and used more as a concept than as a name of a concrete human individual. The word is not without authority in the *Qur'an* itself.[5]

An analysis of the *Qur'anic* descriptions of human creation shows how the *Qur'an* evenhandedly uses both feminine and masculine terms and imagery to describe the creation of humanity from a single source. That God's original creation was undifferentiated humanity and not either man or woman (who appeared simultaneously at a subsequent time) is implicit in a number of *Qur'anic* passages. If the *Qur'an* makes no distinction between the creation of man and woman—as it clearly does not—why do Muslims believe that *Hawwa'* was created from Adam's rib? It is difficult to imagine that Muslims got this idea directly from Genesis 2 since very few Muslims read the Bible. It is much more likely that the rib story entered the Islamic tradition through being incorporated in the *Hadith* literature during the early centuries of Islam. In this context the following six *ahadith* are particularly important since they are cited in *Sahih al-Bukhari* and *Sahih Muslim* which Sunni Muslims regard as the two most authoritative *Hadith* collections whose authority is exceeded only by the *Qur'an:*

1. Treat women nicely, for a woman is created from a rib, and the most curved portion of the rib is its upper portion, so if you would try to straighten it, it will break, but if you leave it as it is, it will remain crooked. So treat women nicely.[6]

2. The woman is like a rib, if you try to straighten her, she will break. So if you want to benefit from her, do so while she still has some crookedness.[7]

3. Whoever believes in Allah and the last day should not hurt (trouble) his neighbor. And I advise you to take care of the women, for they are created from a rib and the most crooked part of the rib is its upper part; if you try to straighten it, it will break, and if you leave it, it will remain crooked, so I urge you to take care of women.[8]

4. Woman is like a rib. When you attempt to straighten it, you would break it. And if you leave her alone you would benefit by her, and crookedness will remain in her.[9]

5. Woman has been created from a rib and will in no way be straightened for you; so if you wish to benefit by her, benefit by her while crookedness remains in her. And if you attempt to straighten her, you will break her, and breaking her is divorcing her.[10]

6. He who believes in Allah and the hereafter, if he witnesses any matter he should talk in good terms about it or keep quiet. Act kindly towards women, for woman is created from a rib, and the most crooked part of the rib is its top. If you attempt to straighten it, you will break it, and if you leave it, its crookedness will remain there, so act kindly towards women.[11]

Elsewhere I have examined the above *ahadith* and shown them to be weak with regard to their formal aspect (i.e., with reference to their *isnad* or list of transmitters). As far as their content (*matn*) is concerned, it is obviously in opposition to the *Qur'anic* accounts about human creation. Since all Muslim scholars agree on the principle that any *Hadith* which is in contradiction to the *Qur'an* cannot be accepted as authentic, the above-mentioned *ahadith* ought to be rejected on material grounds. However, they still continue to be a part of the Islamic tradition. This is due certainly, in significant measure, to the fact that they are included in the *Hadith* collections by Muhammad ibn Isma'il al-Bukhari (810-70 C.E.) and Muslim bin al-Hallaj (817-75 C.E.), collectively known as the *Sahihan* (from *sahih* meaning sound or authentic) which "form an almost unassailable authority, subject indeed to criticism in details, yet deriving an indestructible influence from the *ijma* or general consent of the community in custom and belief, which it is their function to authenticate."[12] The continuing popularity of these *ahadith* among Muslims in general also indicates that they articulate something deeply embedded in Muslim culture, namely, the belief that women are derivative and secondary in the context of human creation.

Theologically, the history of women's inferior status in the Islamic (as well as the Jewish and Christian) tradition began with the story of *Hawwa's* creation from a (crooked) rib. Changing her status requires returning to the point of creation and setting the record straight. Given the way the rib story has been used, it is impossible to over-emphasize its importance. The issue of woman's creation is more fundamental theologically than any other. This is so because if man and woman had been created equal by God who is the ultimate giver of value, then they cannot become unequal, essentially, at a subsequent time. On the other hand, if man and woman had been created unequal by God, then they cannot become equal, essentially, at a subsequent time. If one upholds the view that man and woman were created equal by God which is the teaching of the *Qur'an*, then the existing inequality between men and women cannot be seen as having been mandated by God but must be seen as a subversion of God's original plan for humanity.

Was Woman Responsible for the Fall of Man?

Muslims, like Jews and Christians, generally answer the above question affirmatively though such an answer is not warranted by the *Qur'an*. Here, it needs to be pointed out that the *Qur'anic* account of the fall episode differs significantly from the biblical account. In Genesis 3 no explanation is given as to why the serpent tempts either Eve alone or both Adam and Eve; in the *Qur'an* the reason why *ash-Shaitan* (or Iblis) sets out to beguile the human pair in the garden is stated clearly in a number of passages.[13] The refusal of *ash-Shaitan* to obey God's command to bow in submission to Adam follows from his belief that being a creature of fire, he is elementally superior to Adam who is an earth-creature. When condemned for his arrogance by God and ordered to depart in a state of abject disgrace, *ash-Shaitan* throws a challenge to God: he will prove to God that Adam and Adam's progeny are ungrateful, weak and easily lured by temptations and, thus, unworthy of the honor conferred on them by God. Not attempting to hide his intentions to come upon human beings from all sides, *ash-Shaitan* asks for and is granted, a reprieve until the day of the appointed time. Not only is the reprieve granted, but God also tells *ash-Shaitan* to use all his wiles and forces to assault human beings and see if they would follow him. A cosmic drama now begins involving the eternal opposition between the principles of good and evil which is lived out as human beings, exercising their moral autonomy, choose between the straight path and the crooked path.

In terms of the *Qur'anic* narrative what happens to the human pair in the garden is a sequel to the interchange between God and *ash-Shaitan*. In the sequel we learn that the human pair have been commanded not to go near the tree lest they become *zalimin* (improper actors). Seduced by *ash-Shaitan*, they disobey God. However, in Surah 7: *Al-A'raf*:23 they acknowledge before God that they have done *zulm* (improper actions) to themselves and earnestly seek God's forgiveness and mercy. They are told to go forth and descend from the garden, but in addressing them the *Qur'an* uses the dual form of address only once (in Surah 18: *Ta-Ha*:123); for the rest the plural form is used which necessarily refers to more than two persons and is generally understood as referring to humanity as a whole.

In the framework of *Qur'anic* theology, the order to go forth from the garden given to Adam or children of Adam cannot be considered a punishment because Adam was always meant to be God's vicegerent on earth (Surah 2: *Al-Baqarah*:30). The earth is not a place of banishment but is declared by the *Qur'an* to he humanity's dwelling place and a source of profit to it.[14]

There is, strictly speaking, no fall in the *Qur'an*. What the *Qur'anic* narration focuses upon is the moral choice that humanity is required to make when confronted by the alternatives presented by God and *ash-Shaitan*. This becomes clear if one reflects on Surah 2: *Al-Baqarah*: 35 and Surah 7: *Al-A'raf*:19, in which it is stated, "You (dual) go not near this Tree, lest you (dual) become the '*zalimin*.'" In other words, the human pair is being told that if they go near the tree, then they will be counted among those who perpetrate *zulm* (improper actions). Commenting on the root *zlm*, Toshihiko Izutsu says:

> The primary meaning of ZLM is, in the opinion of many author-itative lexicologists, that of "putting in a wrong place." In the moral sphere it seems to mean primarily "to act in such a way as to trans-gress the proper limit and encroach upon the right of some other person." Briefly and generally speaking "zulm" is to do injustice in the sense of going beyond one's bounds and doing what one has no right to.[15]

By transgressing the limits set by God, the human pair become guilty of *zulm* toward themselves. This *zulm* consists in their taking on the responsibility for choosing between good and evil.

As pointed out by Iqbal:

> *Qur'anic* legend of the fall has nothing to do with the first appearance of man on this planet. Its purpose is rather to indicate man's rise from a primitive state of instinctive appetite to the conscious possession of a free self, capable of doubt and disobedience. The fall does not mean any moral depravity; it is man's transition from simple consciousness to the first flash of self-consciousness. . .Nor does the *Qur'an* regard the earth as a torture-hall where an elementally wicked humanity is imprisoned for an original act of sin. Man's first act of disobedience was also his first act of free choice; and that is why, according to the *Qur'anic* narration, Adam's first transgression was forgiven. . .A being whose movements are wholly determined like a machine cannot produce goodness. Freedom is thus a condition of goodness. But to permit the emergence of a finite ego who has the power to choose. . .is really to take a great risk; for the freedom to choose good involves also the freedom to choose what is the opposite of good. That God has taken this risk shows His immense faith in man; it is now for man to justify this faith.[16]

Even though there is no fall or original sin in the *Qur'an*, the association of the episode described in Genesis 3 with fallen humanity and illicit sexuality which has played such a massive role in perpetuating the myth of feminine evil in the Christian tradition, also exists in the minds of many Muslims and has had extremely negative impact on the lives of millions of Muslim women. The following comment of A. A. Maududi, one of contemporary Islam's most influential scholars is representative of the thinking of many, if not most, Muslims:

> The sex instinct is the greatest weakness of the human race. That is why Satan selected this weak spot for his attack on the adversary and devised the scheme to strike at their modesty. Therefore the first step he took in this direction was to expose their nakedness to them so as to open the door to indecency before them and beguile them into sexuality. Even to this day, Satan and his disciples are adopting the same scheme of depriving the woman of the feelings of modesty and shyness, and they cannot think of any scheme of "progress" unless they expose and exhibit the woman to all and sundry.[17]

Though the branding of women as the devil's gateway[18] is not at all the intent of the *Qur'anic* narration of the fall story, Muslims, no less than Jews and Christians, have used the story to vent their misogynistic feelings. This is clear from the continuing popularity of *ahadith* such as the following:

> The Prophet said, "After me, I have not left any affliction more harmful to men than women."[19]
>
> Ibn Abbas reported that Allah's Messenger said: "I had a chance to look into paradise and I found that the majority of the people were poor and I looked into the fire and there I found the majority constituted women."[20]

Abu Sa'id Khudri reported that Allah's Messenger said: "The world is sweet and green (alluring) and verily Allah is going to install you as viceregent in it in order to see how you act. So avoid the allurement of women: verily, the first trial for the people of Isra'il was caused by women."[21]

Why Was Woman Created?

The *Qur'an*, which does not discriminate against women in the context of creation or the fall episode, does not support the view held by many Muslims, Christians and Jews that women were created not only from man but also for man. That God's creation as a whole is for just ends (Surah 15: *Al-Hijr*:85) and not for idle sport (Surah 21: *Al-Anbiya*:16) are major themes of the *Qur'an*. Humanity, consisting of both men and women, is fashioned in the best of molds

(Surah 95: *At-Tin*:4) and is called to righteousness which requires the honoring of *haquq Allah* (rights of God) as well as *haquq al-'ibad* (rights of creatures). Not only does the *Qur'an* make it clear that man and woman stand absolutely equal in the sight of God, but also that they are members and protectors of each other. In other words, the *Qur'an* does not create a hierarchy in which men are placed above women nor does it pit men against women in an adversary relationship. They are created as equal creatures of a universal, just and merciful God whose pleasure it is that they live together in harmony and righteousness.

In spite of the *Qur'anic* affirmation of gender equality, Muslim societies, in general, have never regarded men and women as equal, particularly in the context of marriage. Fatima Mernissi has aptly observed:

> One of the distinctive characteristics of Muslim sexuality is its territoriality, which reflects a specific division of labor and a specific conception of society and of power. The territoriality of Muslim sexuality sets ranks, tasks, and authority patterns. Spatially confined the woman was taken care of materially by the man who possessed her, in return for her total obedience and her sexual and repro- ductive services. The whole system was organized so that the Muslim "ummah" was actually a society of male citizens who possessed among other things the female half of the population. . . Muslim men have always had more rights and privileges than Muslim women, including even the right to kill their women. . .The man imposes on the woman, an artificially narrow existence, both physically and spiritually.[22]

Underlying the rejection in Muslim societies of the idea of gender equality is the deeply rooted belief that women—who are inferior in creation (having been made from a crooked rib) and in righteous- ness (having helped *ash-Shaitan* in defeating God's plan for Adam)— have been created mainly to be of use to men who are superior to them. The alleged superiority of men to women which permeates the Islamic (as well as the Jewish and Christian) tradition is grounded not only in *Hadith* literature but also in popular interpretations of some *Qur'anic* passages. Two *Qur'anic* passages (Surah 4: *An-Nisa'*:34 and Surah 2: *Al-Baqarah:288*) in particular are generally cited to support the contention that men have a degree of advantage over women. Of these, the first reads as follows in A. A. Maududi's translation of the Arabic text:

> Men are the managers of the affairs of women because Allah has made the one superior to the other and because men spend of their wealth on women. Virtuous women are, therefore, obedient; they guard their rights carefully in their absence under the care and watch of Allah. As for those women whose defiance you have cause to fear, admonish them and keep them apart from your beds and beat them. Then, if they submit to you, do not look for excuses to punish them: note it well that there is Allah above you, who is Supreme and Great.[23]

It is difficult to overstate the negative impact which the popular Muslim understanding of the above verse has had on the lives of Muslim women. Elsewhere I have done detailed analysis of this verse to show how it has been misinterpreted. For instance, the key word in the first sentence is *qawwamun*. This word is most often translated as *hakim* or rulers. By making men rulers over women, a hierarchy akin to the one created by St. Paul and his followers in the Christian tradition is set up in the Islamic *ummah*. Linguistically, the word *qawwamun* refers to those who provide a means of support or livelihood. In my exegesis of this verse I have argued that the function of supporting women economically has been assigned to men in the context of child-bearing, a function which can only be performed by women. The intent of this verse is not to give men power over women but, rather, to ensure that while women are performing the important tasks of child-bearing and child-raising they do not have the additional responsibility of being breadwinners as well. The root word *daraba*, which has been generally translated as beating, is one of the commonest root words in the Arabic language with a large number of possible meanings. That the vast majority of translators (who happen to be all men) have chosen to translate this word as beating clearly indicates a bias in favor of a male-controlled, male-oriented society.

The second *Qur'anic* passage, which is cited to support the idea that men are superior to women, is in the specific context of *iddat*, a three-month waiting period prescribed for women between the pronouncement of divorce and remarriage. The advantage men have in this regard is that they do not have to observe this waiting period due to the face that, unlike women, they do not become pregnant (the three-month waiting period is to make certain that the woman is not pregnant). That the intent of this verse is to ensure justice is made clear by its emphasis that "women shall have rights similar to the rights against them, according to what is equitable."

The reading of the *Qur'an* through the lens of the *Hadith* is, in my opinion, a major reason for the misreading and misinterpretation of many passages which have been used to deny women equality and justice. The following *Hadith* is often cited to elevate man to the status of *majazi khuda* (god in earthly form):

> A man came. . .with his daughter and said, "This my daughter refuses to get married." The Prophet said, "Obey your father." She said, "by the name of Him who sent you in truth, I will not marry until you inform me what is the right of the husband over his wife." He said, . . ."If it were permitted for one human being to bow down (*sajada*) to another I would have ordered the woman to bow down to her husband when he enters into her, because of God's grace on her." The daughter answered, "By the name of Him who sent you, with truth I would never marry!"[24]

A faith as rigidly monotheistic as Islam which makes *shirk* or association of anyone with God the one unforgivable sin, cannot conceivably permit any human being to worship anyone but God. However, this *Hadith* makes it appear that if not God's, it was the Prophet's wish to make the wife prostrate herself before her husband. Since each word, act or exhortation of the Prophet is held to be sacred by Muslims in general, this *Hadith* has had much impact on Muslim women. How such a *Hadith* could be attributed to the Prophet who regarded the principle *Tauhid* (Oneness of God) as the basis of Islam, is, of course, utterly shocking.

Conclusion

Reference has been made in the foregoing account to the fundamental theological assumptions that have colored the way in which Muslim culture, in general, has viewed women. These assumptions have had serious negative consequences and implications, both theoretical and practical, for Muslim women throughout Muslim history until the present day. At the same time, the *Qur'an* does not discriminate against women despite the sad and bitter fact of history in that the cumulative (Jewish, Christian, Hellenistic, Bedouin, and other) biases existed in the Arab-Islamic culture of the early centuries of Islam. Such biases infiltrated the Islamic tradition, largely through the *Hadith* literature, and undermined the intent of the *Qur'an* to liberate women from the status of chattel or inferior creatures, making them free and equal to men. Not only does the *Qur'an* emphasize that righteousness is identical in the case of man or woman, but it affirms, clearly and consistently, women's equality with men and their fundamental right to actualize the human potential that they share equally with men. In fact, when seen through a non-patriarchal lens, the *Qur'an* goes beyond egalitarianism. It exhibits particular solicitude toward women as also toward other classes of disadvantaged persons. Further, it provides particular safeguards for protecting women's special sexual/biological functions such as carrying, delivering, suckling, and rearing offspring.

God, who speaks through the *Qur'an*, is characterized by justice, and it is stated clearly in the *Qur'an* that God can never be guilty of *zulm* (unfairness, tyranny, oppression, or wrong-doing). Hence, the *Qur'an*, as God's Word, cannot be made the source of human injustice, and the injustice to which Muslim women have been subjected cannot be regarded as God-derived. The goal of *Qur'anic* Islam is to establish peace which can only exist within a just environment. Here it is of importance to note that there is more *Qur'anic* legislation pertaining to the establishment of justice in the context of family relationships than on any other subject. This points to the assumption implicit in much *Qur'anic* legislation, namely, that if human beings can learn to order their homes justly so that the rights of all within it—children, women, men—are safeguarded, then they can also order justly their society and the world at large. In other words, the *Qur'an* regards the home as a microcosm of the *ummah* and world community, and emphasizes the importance of making it the abode of peace through just living.

The importance of developing what the West calls feminist theology in the context of the Islamic tradition is paramount today in order to liberate not only Muslim women, but also Muslim men, from unjust structures and systems of thought which make a peer relationship between men and women impossible. It is good to know that in the last hundred years there have been at least two significant

Muslim male scholars and activists: Qasim Amin from Egypt and Mumraz Ali from India. Both have been staunch advocates of women's rights. It is profoundly discouraging, however, to contemplate how few Muslim women there are in the world today who possess the competence, even if they have the courage and commitment, to engage in a scholarly study of Islam's primary sources in order to participate in the theological discussions on women-related issues which are taking place in most contemporary Muslim societies. Such participation is imperative if *Qur'anic* Islam is to emerge in Muslim societies and communities.

NOTES

1. Reference is made, here, to Surah 4: *An-Nisa'*: 34.
2. Reference is made, here, to Surah 4: *An-Nisa'*:11.
3. Reference is made, here, to Surah 2: *Al-Baqarah*:282.
4. Reference is made, here, to *ahadith* (plural of *hadith* meaning an oral tradition) cited in *Sahih al-Bukhari* and *Sahih Muslim*; see footnote 6 and 9 for translations.
5. Muhammad Iqbal, *The Reconstruction of Religious Thought in Islam* (Lahore: Shaikh Muhammad Ashraf, 1962), p. 83.
6. M.M. Khan, translation of *Sahih Al-Bukhari* (Lahore: Kazi Publications 1971), p. 346.
7. *Ibid.*, p. 80.
8. *Ibid.*, p. 81.
9. A.H. Siddiqui, (translation of *Sahih Muslim*, Volume 2 (Lahore: Shaikh Muhammad Ashraf, 1972), p. 752.
10. *Ibid.*
11. *Ibid.*, pp. 752-753.
12. Alfred Guillaume, *The Traditions of Islam* (Beirut: Khayats, 1966), p. 31.
13. For instance, Surah 15: *Al-Hijr*:26-43; Surah 17: *Bani Isra'l*:61-64; Surah 18: *Al-Kahf*:50; and Surah 38: *Sad*:71-85.
14. Muhammad Iqbal, p. 84.
15. Toshihiko Izutsu, *The Structure of Ethical Terms in the Koran* (Mita, Siba, Minatoku, Tokyo: Keio Institute of Philosophical Studies, 1959), pp. 152-153.
16. Muhammad Iqbal, p. 85.
17. A.A. Maududi, *The Meaning of the Qur'an*, Volume 2 (Lahore: Islamic Publications Ltd., 1976), p. 16, n. 13.
18. This well known expression comes from Tertullian, a North African Church Father.
19. M.M. Khan, *op. cit.*, p. 22.

20. A.H. Siddiqui, *op. cit.*, p. 1431.

21. *Ibid.*

22. Mernissi, Fatima, *Beyond the Veil* (Cambridge: Schenkman Publishing Company, 1975), p. 103.

23. A.A. Maududi, *The Meaning of the Qur'an*, Volume 2 (Lahore: Islamic Publications Ltd., 1971), p. 321.

24. Sadiq Hasan Khan, *Husn al-Uswa* (Publication details unavailable), p. 281.

PART TWO

Responses from Asian Traditions

8

A Theoretical Explanation of Evil in Theravada Buddhism

By Medagama Vajiragnana

E vil in Buddhism means that which is opposed to the attainment of enlightenment or *nibbana*. *Nibbana* is ultimate reality, the highest state which lies beyond both good and evil. It is the cessation of craving and attachment. Whatever leads to that aim is good; whatever keeps one away from it is evil. Evil disturbs the mind of the individual and prevents the knowledge of enlightenment from being communicated to others.

"The root of all evil is ignorance (especially of the four noble truths) and false views."[1] In the parable of the deer,[2] ignorance is the decoy by which the enemy, Mara, leads the deer (humankind) astray into dangerous ground. The Buddha himself said, "I do not perceive any single hindrance other than the hindrance of ignorance by which humankind is so obstructed."[3]

According to Buddhism, basic ignorance is one's failure to see that the world is unsatisfactory. *Samsara* is the word used to describe the sum total of conditioned existence, the round of cyclic existence or rebirth. "Ignorance is the deep delusion wherein we here so long are circling round."[4] The very nature of *samsara* is non-satisfaction, and the realization of this is regarded as the first noble truth, which must be understood if one hopes to realize *nibbana*.

The state of ignorance is universal. Only an enlightened being has eliminated ignorance completely. Evil is a matter of degree. Nothing is absolutely good or absolutely bad. In the world both good and evil exist as relative to each other. Buddhism maintains that evil is ultimately in the mind. Therefore, Buddhism is essentially a mind-culture. Any improvement must occur initially in the mind of the person. The importance of being aware of, and controlling, one's thoughts is continually stressed.

"Good is that which is the outcome of unselfishness, or absence of craving, while evil is that which is produced by craving and is rooted in self."[5] A person is, by nature, good. At birth the mind is pure and self-luminous in its nature, but it is stained by defilements which come through the sense doors. Therefore, a person does evil things not because of an inherent propensity for wickedness but because of ignorance. Thus the ideal way to combat evil is through correct knowledge.

The Buddha gave neither an explanation of the ultimate source of the world nor of good and evil. He saw no beginning to the process of *samsara*. He was more interested in teaching the way to obtain release from suffering than in giving philosophical explanations of the beginning of the universe. "Just as the mighty ocean is of one flavor, the flavor of salt, even this *dhamma* [my teaching] is of one flavor, the flavor of deliverance."[6]

The Buddha taught that goodness has the power to overcome and defeat evil, because goodness is an aspect of the nature of ultimate reality. Therefore, evil should be treated as educative. Without the existence of evil, the realization of the ultimate goal is not possible. It is attributed to Nagarjuna that without contacting or associating with *samsara*, one cannot realize *nibbana*. Evil is a necessary ingredient on the path to *nibbana*; without it there would be no need to strive for spiritual progress.

The Concept of Mara

In order to understand the pervasive nature of evil, Buddhists employ the concept of Mara. Mara is a symbol for evil, death, and the whole of cyclic existence. Mara is everything that binds one to realms of birth and death, capturing and ensnaring the mind, and keeping it from enlightenment. Mara's voice appears entirely reasonable.

There are five manifestations of Mara: deity Mara, defilements, kammic activities, aggregates, and death.

The defilements or passions are greed, hatred and delusion. All unwholesome actions of body, speech and mind are rooted in at least one of these three. "There is no fire like lust, no grip like hate, no net like delusion, no river like craving."[7]

Khanda is a word used by the Buddha to define the five grasping groups or aggregates which constitute an individual. These are combinations of ever-changing physical and mental forces or energies. The five are form, feeling, perception, mental formations and consciousness. According to Buddhism there is no such thing as an individual apart from these five aggregates. If we say that Mara is these five aggregates, we are saying that the individual is Mara. Mara symbolizes the entire existence of unenlightened humanity.

Death is the supreme form of Mara. It is a fundamental tenet of Buddhist doctrine that life is *duhkha*. This is a Pali word which is difficult to translate into English, but which has the sense of unsatisfactoriness or imperfection. The Buddha said, "Birth is *duhkha*, decay is *duhkha*, sickness is *duhkha*, death is *duhkha*. . . association with the unpleasant is *duhkha*, dissociation from the pleasant is *duhkha*; not to get what one wants is *duhkha*—in brief, the five aggregates of attachment are *duhkha*."[8] Death may be regarded as an example of *duhkha* in its most extreme form. Mara is, therefore, not simply a kind of force which operates outside and upon oneself, but it is part of one's very existence. Mara is the whole of life apart from *nibbana*, that is, the whole of *samsaric* existence. Mara's realm is equated with birth and death and the fear that is associated with them.

Evil Actions

There is no one word in Pali which is the exact equivalent of the English word evil. The word which is frequently used in Pali is *papa*, which means that which defiles the mind. It is associated with the three immoral roots: greed, hatred, and delusion. All evil actions are rooted in one or more of these three qualities. Greed and hatred are not found together, but they both occur together with delusion.

Delusion can also be found by itself. The opposite of *papa* is *punna*, which is associated with the three moral roots: generosity, love and wisdom. The other terms which are used mean skillful and unskillful, or wholesome and unwholesome.

There are ten kinds of evil action. Three of these are deeds of body (killing, stealing and sexual misconduct); four are deeds of speech (lying, slandering, harsh speech and frivolous talk); three are deeds of mind (covetousness, ill-will and false views). There are three kinds of false view: denying the result of *kamma*, denying the cause and the result, and denying action and the result.

This brings us to a discussion of the word *kamma* as it is used in Buddhism. It is simply the law of cause and effect. Wholesome actions produce wholesome effects, unwholesome actions produce unwholesome effects. Above all it is volition that precedes the action that determines whether it is wholesome or unwholesome. The Buddha's teaching on volition and *kamma* has been beautifully expressed in the opening stanzas of the *Dhammapada*:

> All (mental) states have mind as their forerunner, mind is their chief, and they are mind-made. If one speaks or acts with a defiled mind, then suffering follows one even as the wheel follows the hoof of the draught-ox.

> All (mental) states have mind as their forerunner, mind is their chief, and they are mind-made. If one speaks or acts with a pure mind, happiness follows one as one's shadow that does not leave one.[9]

Elsewhere in the *Dhammapada* it is also said, "By oneself is evil done, and by oneself one becomes pure. The pure and the impure come from oneself; no man can purify another."[10] This position has also been likened to one building a wall or digging a ditch: one goes up or down strictly in accordance with one's own effort. Just as a seed that has been sown in soil produces plants according to its intrinsic nature, so too each action will produce its appropriate effects. "All beings have *kamma* as their own, their inheritance, their congenital cause, their kinsman, their refuge. It is *kamma* that differentiates beings into low and high states."[11]

Kamma operates without the intervention of an external, independent or ruling agency. It is a natural law of justice. It has nothing to do with the idea of punishment or reward meted out by an omniscient and omnipotent law-giver, or even an all-compassionate Buddha. The cause produces the effect; the effect explains the cause. Action causes reaction. "So, when a fool does wrong deeds, he does not realize (their evil nature); by his own deeds the stupid man is tormented, like one burnt by fire."[12]

Ultimately, one's aim is to become enlightened, that is, an *arahant*, which may be translated as a saint. The deeds of a saint are said to have gone beyond both good and evil; such actions are pure and do not produce kammic effects. The Buddha said, "Righteous things you have to give up: how much more the unrighteous things."[13]

Response to Evil

In general, the way to overcome Mara is the same way that leads to liberation in the Buddhist sense. When he was being tempted by Mara, immediately prior to his enlightenment, the Buddha said he possessed the following qualities which made him victorious: confidence, self-control, perseverance, and wisdom. The Buddha's enlightenment has been portrayed as a triumph over Mara by dispelling the darkness of ignorance. The way to defeat Mara is by following what we call the Noble Eightfold Path.

This path has been divided into three parts: morality, mental discipline and wisdom. In terms of the Noble Eightfold Path, morality refers to right speech, right action and right livelihood. It is often thought that Buddhists are concerned solely with matters such as concentration or meditation, but it is impossible to train the mind unless one has first purified one's actions by carefully observing a moral code. "What is the basis of higher states? Morality of perfect purity."[14] Moral precepts are, therefore, the preliminaries and accompaniments to attaining the highest state.

The Buddhist must conduct life on an ethical basis, which means controlling all actions of thought, word and deed. For the lay Buddhist, this means observing five precepts: to refrain from taking life; to refrain from taking that which is not freely given; to refrain from sexual misconduct; to refrain from harsh or false speech; and to refrain from taking intoxicating drinks or drugs. On certain days, the number of precepts may be increased to eight or ten.

The precepts are not commandments issued on the authority of the Buddha, and the Buddha does not assign either punishment for breaking them or reward for keeping them. The Buddha counseled his followers to act properly by pointing out to them the consequences of their actions and encouraged them to live their lives in a skillful fashion if they wished to avoid experiencing the undesirable effects of unskillful actions.

It should not be thought that the Buddha concerned himself solely with humanity's spiritual well-being and disregarded the layperson's concern with the more mundane affairs of everyday life. The Buddha stated that vice breeds in society owing to poverty, and that poverty is due to the maldistribution of economic goods. The Buddha did not condemn the creation of material wealth by legitimate means, but he did say that it should be spent liberally and wisely on one's relatives and friends. He condemned the miserly hoarding of wealth as well as squandering it carelessly.

In the Noble Eightfold Path, right effort, right mindfulness and right concentration constitute mental discipline. Right effort is the energetic will (i) to prevent evil and unwholesome states of mind from arising, (ii) to eliminate such evil and unwholesome states that have arisen, (iii) to cause good and wholesome states of mind to arise, and (iv) to develop and bring to perfection the good and wholesome states of mind already arisen. One element of this effort is said to be the development of the factors of enlightenment as a method of overcoming Mara's forces. These factors are: mindfulness, investigation of the doctrine, energy, joy, relaxation of body and mind, concentration, and equanimity. Of these seven factors of enlightenment, two are especially important: mindfulness and concentration.

It is principally by mindfulness that Mara can be defeated. This awareness leads to the recognition of Mara. The Buddha said that this method of vanquishing Mara can be verified experientially. For example, a bad or disturbing thought will not be able to have any sway over you once you become aware of it. Such awareness leads to the recognition of Mara. The Buddha is unassailable by Mara because the Buddha recognizes Mara as soon as the latter appears, and to recognize Mara is to deflate Mara. In his encounters with the Buddha, Mara repeats constantly the refrain, "The Lord knows me! The Righteous One knows me!"[15] The Buddha emphasized the importance of mindfulness as the way to resist Mara. He said, "Keep to your own pastures, brethren, walk on your native haunts. If you thus walk in them, then Mara will find no landing place, no basis of attack."[16] One's proper range is explained as the practice of the four foundations of mindfulness, that is mindfulness of body, mindfulness of feeling, mindfulness of mind, and mindfulness of mental objects.

Mara gains access to the monk who has not developed mindfulness of body, just as a heavy stone thrown into a mound of moist clay would have easy entrance or as a dry stick easily ignites and burns.[17] Where, however, a monk has developed mindfulness of body, then Mara is repelled. By constant mindfulness one should be aware of one's actions and so strive to eliminate those rooted in the three negative roots of greed, hatred and delusion, and to develop those rooted in the three wholesome roots of generosity, love and wisdom.

The Buddha gave the following instructions to his own son, Rahula, "Rahula, for what purpose is a mirror?" "For the purpose of reflecting, Lord." "Similarly, Rahula, after reflecting should bodily action be done; after reflecting should verbal action be done; after reflecting should mental action be done."[18] The Buddha goes on to say that such reflecting must be done before, during and after performing any bodily action. He then gives the same admonitions with regard to verbal and mental actions. One has to reflect on how the results of any action will affect not only other people but also oneself. Buddhism does not counsel us to act in a way that might cause harm to ourselves even though the consequences for other people might be beneficial. Acts of so-called self-sacrifice are not necessarily skillful.

Right concentration has three stages: preparatory concentration, approach concentration and attainment concentration. The third stage is marked by the attainment of *jhana*, absorption. This is a high degree of concentration which is achieved through meditation practice on one of forty subjects of tranquility meditation. It is a unified state of the normally scattered mind; it centers upon a single object by the inhibition of certain unwholesome mental states. There are eight *jhanas* that are emphasized as important for the defeat of Mara.

The remaining two factors of the Noble Eightfold Path are right understanding and right thought. Right understanding refers to understanding of the Four Noble Truths. These are: the truth of *duhkha*; the truth of the cause or the origin of *duhkha*; the truth of the end of *duhkha*; and the truth of the way to the end of *duhkha*. This understanding leads to seeing things as they really are, that is, ultimate reality, which is the end of ignorance and the attainment of true wisdom.

We have already observed that it is one's thoughts that either defile or purify a person. Evil thoughts tend to debase one, just as good thoughts tend to elevate one. Right thought eliminates evil thoughts and develops pure thoughts.

There are four modes of living which are essential to Buddhist practice. The first of these is called loving-kindness. "There, O monks, the monk with a mind full of loving-kindness pervading first one direction, then a second one, then a third one, then a fourth one, just so above, below, and all around; and everywhere identifying himself with all, he is pervading the whole world with his mind full of loving-kindness, with the mind wide, developed, unbounded, free from hate and ill-will."[19] The Buddha continued in the same vein to describe compassion, altruistic joy, and equanimity.

Thus the correct response to evil is to strive to remove ignorance from one's own mind. One's primary responsibility is to purify one's own actions. This process will naturally lead to an improvement in the ills which pollute society. As long as people leave unresolved actual or potential sources of evil within themselves, social activity will be either futile or incomplete. Preoccupation with social activities must not be made the excuse to neglect one's first duty to tidy up one's own house.

In formulating a response to evil there are two moral qualities which should be mentioned. They are so highly regarded that they were described by the Buddha as world protectors. These are moral shame and moral dread. The proximate cause of moral shame is said to be self-respect, and the cause of moral dread is respect for others conscience and accountability. One who has moral shame recoils from evil just as a cock's feather shrinks in front of fire. However, a person without moral dread is like a moth that is singed by fire. A moth, unaware of the consequences, is attracted by fire and will get burnt. In the same way a person without moral dread will commit evil actions. Moral shame comes from within, moral dread from the outside.

There are three criteria for distinguishing between good and evil. First, in deciding if the result will be good one must reflect on it personally, weighing matters for oneself and making oneself the judge. This is equivalent to respect for self. Second, public opinion is taken as the judge. This is equivalent to respect for others. Finally, the *dhamma*, the teaching, is taken as the means of reaching a decision. Of these three criteria, the first is regarded as the most suitable.

On the level of day-to-day living, the Buddhist counters evil by "going for refuge." Refuge is used here in the sense of that which protects, defends or preserves. This procedure consists of simply repeating three times the statement: I go to the Buddha for refuge; I go to the *dhamma* for refuge; I go to the *sangha* for refuge. This is the fundamental act of a Buddhist, committing him/herself, with body, speech and mind, to follow the Buddha, his teachings (the *dhamma*) and the noble disciples (the *sangha*), collectively called the triple gem. "I go to the Buddha for refuge" means that I take the Buddha as an ideal, and I commit myself with resolution to follow him to gain supreme wisdom (enlightenment), that will enable me to overcome evil.

The *dhamma* is the teaching of the Buddha embodied in the Noble Eightfold Path, consisting of ethical conduct, mental discipline and wisdom. This is the path leading to enlightenment. "I go to the *dhamma* for refuge" means that I commit myself with resolution to follow the *dhamma* to gain supreme wisdom (enlightenment), which will enable me to overcome evil.

The *sangha* is the spiritual community of disciples. The *sangha* which is referred to in this context is the spiritual *sangha*, rather than the institutional *sangha* of monks and nuns. The term spiritual *sangha* applies to those who have attained the spiritual height of the path of sainthood and its fruition, whether they are ordained or not. "I go to the *sangha* for refuge" means that I commit fully with resolution to develop myself with my own effort to attain the spiritual heights attained by the spiritual community of disciples, and thus gain supreme wisdom that will enable me to overcome evil.

NOTES

1. W. Rahula, *What the Buddha Taught* (London: Gordon Fraser, 1985), p. 3.
2. Mahasaccaka Sutta, *Majjhima Nikaya* I, 240. Page and volume numbers refer to the Pali Text Society editions.
3. *Itivuttaka* 14.
4. *Sutta Nipata* v. 730.
5. Francis Story, *The Buddhist Outlook* (Sri Lanka, 1973), p. 79.
6. *Udana*, 5, 5, 12 p. 56.
7. *Dhammapada* v.251.
8. Dhammacakkappavattana-sutta, *Samyutta Nikaya*, LVI, 11.
9. *Dhammapada* v.1-2.
10. *Dhammapada* v.165.
11. *Majjhima Nikaya*, III, 135.
12. *Dhammapada* v.136.
13. *Majjhima Nikaya* I, 22, p. 135.
14. *Samyutta Nikaya* v.143.
15. Mara Samyutta, *Samyutta Nikaya*.
16. Cakkavatti-sihanada Sutta, *Digha Nikaya*, III.58.
17. *Majjhima Nikaya* III.88.
18. *Majjhima Nikaya* II.88.
19. Tevijja Sutta, *Digha Nikaya* 13.

9

Mara as Evil in Buddhism

By Chandra Wikramagamage

The Buddhist canon and post-canonical literature use the term Mara, which in English could be rendered as evil.[1] This terminology seemed to have been borrowed by the Buddhist from the Brahmana texts where the word much used is *Papma Mrtyh*.[2] Again the term *Papima Mara*[3] seen in the Buddhist canon could be an adaptation from the above word. This evidence shows that the belief in Mara was prevalent in India even before the birth of the Buddha. Thus the belief in Mara is by no means folklore but a traditional religious belief. *Mrtyh* which means Maccu in the Pali texts refers to death, and death is interpreted as the messenger of Yama, the lord of death, according to the Vedic literature. In Buddhist literature Maccu is used for death as well as Mara.[4] The word Namuci in Hindu literature cannot and does not refer to the same Mara but to something else, since we know that Namuci is the demon responsible for drought and was put to death by Indra, the king of gods.[5] The Buddhists and the Buddhist literature use the word Namuci as a synonym for Mara which has a different root and nomenclature and which in English could mean evil. The above words were well established in the pre-Buddhist era in India, and all these words stress the meaning and explanation of death and the forces of death.

The Buddha propagated his philosophy with Magadha as its center and no doubt he would have used the language prevalent then for this purpose. Buddhists in Sri Lanka believe the language used by the Buddha is Magadhi which is a close dialect of Pali. It was imperative that this new philosophy was projected to the people in a language much older for it to be more effective and forceful and to be held in reverence. In this attempt to popularize, the Buddha used familiar words, examples, similes, and folk tales to bring out new meaning and emphasis to the *dhamma* (the teaching). Popular words then could be given new meanings and different inter-pretations. In this attempt certain beliefs and ideas of the people entered into the new religion or the new philosophy. Hence even the Buddha in his preaching the *dhamma* could have used then relevant terms or words such as, Mara, Maccu, Namuci, and Kanha in his sermons to give meaning to evil. This usage was due to an acceptance of old beliefs and traditions. However, the Buddha, in keeping with the existing beliefs of the people, had adapted them into more effective means to explain his own philosophy.

According to Buddhism, evil is not an extraordinary force or per-son, but something that any intelligent being could understand or something that one could perceive through one's own intelligence. The Buddha interpreted the six faculties, namely, the eye, ear, nose, tongue, body, and mind as Mara and that which arises as a con-sequence of this contact also as Mara.[6] According to the theory of causality, craving, hatred, and ignorance lead to grasping external objects such as matter, sound, etc., resulting in becoming which leads to new birth. Hence this series would continue until the last stage of decay, death, sorrow, lamentation, grief and despair are reached. Thus all conditional things could be regarded as Mara.

The deeds (*kamma*) as referred to in Buddhist teachings could also be taken as Mara, especially the merits and sins or good and bad deeds which contribute to the continuation of life in this universe. Accordingly, they are the world of desire, world of form, and the plane devoid of any material body. During their lifetime, beings are subjected to becoming, birth, decay, and death. Hence life is referred to as *samsara* or existence which in turn is the subject of Mara. Good or meritorious deeds in this world help us to achieve worldly happiness, and bad deeds or worldly sins lead us to the underworld; both are subjected to suffering because even worldly happiness leads to suffering.[7] The good and bad deeds are the results of craving, hatred and ignorance. The Buddha, one who had renounced the good as well as the bad, was distanced from these worldly things, desire, form and the material body. All beings during their lifetime accumulate merit and demerit. Their lives are enriched by their own deeds and acts, and they continue their existence in this universe. Sins are ten-fold. Taking away the life of a being, killing, theft, adultery, lying and sneaking, acts of sin caused by a word or verbal commitments, stinginess or being miserly, and the thoughts of hatred are the sins caused by the mind. These acts could be referred to as Mara or the binding forces of Mara.

In the deeper context of life there is no individuality, though traditionally reference is made to a person as an individual. Buddhism is a philosophy devoid of individualism, but in common usage the individual means the five aggregates or the five *skanda*, and all these in turn could be referred to as Mara,[8] the root cause of death and suffering. We are not able to go beyond this force of death.

Mara is no extraordinary force or individual but nature itself. This fact will help one to realize that the individual who makes such a statement, and the one who responds to this statement are both Mara. Can I avoid death? Or can you? Neither of us could. This is the bitter truth that all know for certain. This is the truth and the natural end of all living beings or things, the common and the inevitable result of all causes and their effects. At this very moment one may have many odd ailments such as physical aches and pains. Old age is the common legacy of humanity, a natural force, an inevitable thing, the tragedy of truth that none can avoid. That again is the force of nature, birth and death, the formation and destruction of what is happening all around us. Being or non-being, everything ends and hence everything is Mara.

This raises an enigmatic question. What happens to us after death? Do we escape from Mara after death? Different religions at different times, in different ways have put forward various explanations. Does death terminate or relieve us from the path of Mara? There is no known universal answer to this. None can say for certain what happens after death. This is our ignorance.

Ignorance is also Mara. Ignorance is sin. The good or the bad deeds stimulate consciousness and consciousness in turn creates names and forms or living matter; this in turn creates the six aggregates of senses and mind, the psycho-physical phenomena of living beings, the formation and the reaction of the sense organs and the senses. These contacts create feelings and the feelings lead to craving and grasping, resulting in new birth. Birth leads to disease, decay and to death. Hence where one encounters decay and death there dwells Mara. Where there is suffering there dwells Mara. Thus the only liberation from Mara is one's own conquering of birth, decay, disease, and Mara or death, through one's own understanding of the root causes and conquering of ignorance, that is, ignorance of the aforesaid causes and their effects.

Thus far I have interpreted Mara according to early Buddhist scriptures. It is necessary, however, to indicate what has been added through popular beliefs and folklore. This will help one to understand and differentiate the Buddhist concept of evil from other concepts that have entered Buddhism throughout history.

Vasavatti Mara

The existence of a heaven under the rule of a cruel god called Vasavatti Mara is common in the folklore of the Southeast Asian Buddhist community. This god cherishes sins and sinners and harms the good and acts against those who seek or work towards liberation from this world.

In the Buddhist scripture legends were included in compiling the life of the Buddha. One story relates that on the day that Prince Siddhartha renounced worldly life and left the palace, Vasavatti Mara beseeched him to abandon the quest. And as the story goes, we know that Prince Siddhartha renounced the world and donned robes on the bank of the river and with deep devotion and determination, meditated and achieved his ambition. It is said that Vasavatti Mara, knowing that Prince Siddhartha would attain Buddhahood in seven days had come again to dissuade him and pleaded, knowing that he was weak in body but not in mind said:

> Death hath come so close upon you and why not attempt to live, for by living one could achieve more in life. By living and living as a layman only, you could gain the bliss of life. The path and attainment of nirvana is very arduous. Sage Siddhartha thus hearing these sentiments of Mara replied "Have you come to weaken my

attempts and desires Papima Mara. I am not swayed by those
morsels of happiness and contentment, your promises of the bliss of
life. Do you know that I have forsaken a kingdom and a throne,
therefore it would be more worthy if you could encourage someone
who desires to attain the ultimate bliss through one's own
meritorious acts; this would certainly be more fruitful. What ask
thou of me, who has sacrificed and renounced all the worldly
happiness to attain Buddhahood? It is frivolous to entice me with
your morsels. I do not desire worldly happiness anymore, I have
renounced this worldly happiness and the cravings. I have
conquered all your forces, such as desire, aversion, hunger and
thirst, craving, sloth and torpor, fear, doubt, self-will and cant, gains,
flattery, ill gained honors, exciting oneself and despising others.
This Namuci is your army; this is Kanha's fighting forces. . ."[9]

It is further said that sage Siddhartha was meditating at Bodh
Gaya under the tranquility of the Bo-tree, when Vasavatti Mara was
supposed to have come on an elephant with his retinue of followers
and attempted to entice and dissuade him from attaining Buddhahood. The three daughters of Mara, Tanha, Rati and Raga, symbolizing desire, avarice and lust respectively, seeing the father so
disappointed, dejected and grieved, came to entice sage Siddhartha
back to mundane things in life. Their attempts bore no fruit, as he
was above all desires. Thus the conquering of Mara gave rise to very
meaningful and intensely popular folklore called the defeat of Mara.

One can easily differentiate or extract the truth about the
Vasavatti Mara from traditional folklore. Clearly the tenfold forces
of Mara are the sins of mortals, and the allusion to the daughters of
Mara refers but to these sins. *Tanha* or the craving is one of the
three main sins; *rati* represents aversion and *raga* represents lust. If
the existence of Vasavatti Mara according to folklore could be
believed, then undoubtedly he could have had a more forceful army
and weaponry of war and not mental forces alone. The forces of
Mara could be alluded to as the weaponry of attack. The Pali text
clearly states that what Prince Siddhartha overpowered under the
Bo-tree were the sensual forces of sins. Therefore, Vasavatti Mara
is a mythical figure; his army, his daughters are creations of the
imagination. The higher doctrine of Buddhist philosophy does not
give emphasis to Vasavatti Mara.

Classification of Mara

The single word *dhamma* in Pali could be said to contain eighty-four thousand parts or all of the Buddhist philosophy. Likewise, the single word Mara has a plurality of meanings. This single word could mean the stimulation of the sensual organs like the eye, ear, nose, tongue, and skin to matter, sound, smell, taste, touch and their responses. Hence we could differentiate twelve Maras. The higher doctrine classifies them as *skanda*, (aggregates) *dhatu* (elements), and *ayatana* (spheres), which could be treated as the threefold division of Mara. This is the oldest classification and the addition of Vasavatti Mara must have come at a later era from a legend then popular in society.

In the beginning, the new Buddhist philosophy was grasped and understood only by the intelligentsia. When it was later accepted as a world religion, thriving among other believers, it also absorbed many new elements, new interpretations even to the concept of Mara. Mara and the forces of Mara became more popular and acceptable among the common people. The Buddha often said that there is no force greater to overcome than the force of Mara. The Buddha explicitly indicated that the path to avoid Mara is most strenuous and arduous, and to destroy it completely without recurrence is to destroy *skanda* (aggregates), *dhatu* (elements), and *ayatana* (spheres).

Mara as depicted and interpreted in Buddhism is not only a feature of human life, but also embraces the cause and the effect of all the living and the non-living. If desired one could be relieved from this force of nature, and such relief would be the status of a supramundane state, the only absolute reality. What is the real need for this relief? It is to avoid the circle of suffering, birth, decay, disease, and death, the natural process. The only escape or relief from this cycle is to understand the cause and effect and to relinquish attachment.

The legends of Mara presented in the pre-Buddhist era were adapted according to Buddhist concepts. The exclusive Buddhist concept of Mara refers only to nature itself and is developed in accordance with the theory of natural evolution. Hence it is Mara, evil. Yet pre-Buddhist Mara legends with Buddhist interpretations have been more popular among the people.

NOTES

1. Morally bad; wicked, harmful or tending to harm, esp. intentionally or characteristically; disagreeable or unpleasant; unlucky; causing misfortune. *The Concise Oxford Dictionary*; new edition (Delhi, 1990), p. 405. Sinhalese Buddhists interpret the term Mara as something which makes people unwholesome.

2. E. Windish, *Mara and Buddha* (Leipzig, 1859), p. 185.

3. *Majjhima Nikaya*, I, ed. by Trenckner (London: Pali Text Society, 1888), pp. 327; 332-333; *Digha Nikaya*, ed. by T.W. Rhys Davids and J.E. Carpenter (London: Pali Text Society, 1890-1911), vol. II, p. 112. Papima Mara is synonym of Vasawatti Mara.

4. T.O. Ling, *Buddhism and the Mythology of Evil* (London, 1962), p. 57.

5. T.O. Ling, *op. cit.*, p. 55. *Namuci* in one Buddhist canon is also a synonym of Vasawatti Mara. *Kanha, Antaka, pamattabandhu* are other synonyms of the same.

6. *Samyutta Nikaya* (Buddhajayanti, ed.) (Colombo, 1960), p. 218.

7. *Itivuttaka Pali* (London: Pali Text Society, 1948), pp. 56, 92.

8. *Samyutta Nikaya*, *op. cit.*, Radha Sutta.

9. *Sutta Nipata* (London: Pali Text Society, 1965), pp. 74-78.

10

Three Levels of Evil in Advaita Vedanta and a Holographic Analogy

By Stephen Kaplan

A dvaita Vedanta, one of the leading schools of Hindu thought, presents a complex of ideas directed toward the subject of evil. On the one hand, the evil an individual endures is consequent upon the evil an individual has done in the past. On another hand, Advaita Vedanta attributes suffering, evil, and the problems of the world not to actions but to ignorance (*avidya*). This tactic reduces human problems to an epistemological mistake that is to be understood within the context of *maya* (illusion). For Advaitins such as Gaudapada, the epistemological treatment of evil is concomitant with the metaphysical doctrine of non-origination which informs us that Brahman is eternal, unchanging, being; and therefore, all change is unreal (*maya*), produced by ignorance. Thus in this sense, evil as *maya* does not exist. Nonetheless, Advaitins also tell us that evil is phenomenological; it is experienced.

This cursory overview of the Advaita Vedanta notion of evil raises much that is unsettling. First, we must ask ourselves what does it mean? What does it mean to say that evil is not real; it is only experienced? How can one say that evil is the consequence of what one has done in the past and then proceed to say that there are no individuals nor any past?

We must also ask ourselves a second question which while distinct from the former is related to it. I would like to ask whether the Advaita notion of evil can address the senseless violence and suffering that we uncover in our world. Can any of the theories about evil that we discuss make the thousands of such cases throughout the world palatable, justifiable, explainable, acceptable?

While I can make no pretense to answer the second question, I would at least like not to forget that it is the reason that we seek an answer to the first series of questions about Advaita Vedanta. I intend here to highlight three different strands within Advaita thinking on the problem of evil. These strands are simultaneously existing proposals, not historically sequential proposals. Historically, these three levels of explanation can be traced to Gaudapada, the teacher of the illustrious Sankara. The thoughts of Gaudapada, alleged to be the first person after the Upanisads to present the notion of *advaita* (non-dualism), have been crucial in the formulation of this presentation. The thoughts of Sankara will also be invoked giving one some sense that from its inception Advaita Vedanta has tackled the problem of evil in this multifaceted manner.

I am also including a review of Krishnachandra Bhattacharyya's presentation of evil. Bhattacharyya, a modern philosopher, has pondered Advaita notions through centuries of Indian and Western philosophy to present to us a modern phenomenological understanding of evil that is rooted in the problem of ignorance and embodied in the experience of pain.

Finally, I will try to illuminate the diverse answers that Advaita gives by utilizing a holographic analogy. Holography is the technique by which one produces three dimensional optical images from a film that contains no images. These images will appear to be real, but they are only experiences created by a duality of subject and object. The holographic film, an analogous reality, lacks this diversity of images.

The Three Levels of Evil

The late Professor B.K. Matilal observed:

Theodicy is an old and worn out issue. Probably nothing new can be said about it. It is also believed that theodicy was not a problem for the Indians, specially for the Hindus, because evil was, according to them, an illusion. Particularly, it is urged, in Sankara's Advaita Vedanta, the whole world is an illusion along with its evils, and hence the problem of evil is resolved. This belief is partly based upon a misconception. . .Besides, the rather pervasive, but uncritical and unexamined assumption that in Sankara's philosophy the world along with its evils is simply an illusion, leads to the misconception and false ideas about Indian philosophy in general and Sankara's philosophy in particular.[1]

The Advaita discussion of evil, like its discussion of other subjects, is multileveled. Advaita approaches numerous topics from creation to evil to *maya* from a number of different levels of truth and with a number of different types of philosophical discourse. The Advaita approach to a given topic is often the intermingling of these factors. One can see a subject such as *maya* treated from the different levels of truth found in the Advaita schema, namely, the highest truth (*paramartha*) and relative truth (*samvrti*), and also from a number of different modes of philosophical discourse such as metaphysical, epistemological and phenomenological.[2] The Advaita analysis of evil takes similar twists and turns. One must be cognizant of the entirety of the discussion as well as the specific nature of the discourse if one wishes to avoid one sided presentations and the misconceptions that Professor Matilal referred to above.

Advaitins present three levels of explanation for evil. On the one hand, one may look at evil from the metaphysical perspective, from the perspective of the highest truth. Succinctly put, from this perspective all is Brahman; all is the one unchanging being (*sat*), consciousness (*cit*), and bliss (*ananda*). This being is without measure and without end to measure; it is without beginning or end; it is eternal, unborn and unchanging. Ultimate truth is that there is no change, no birth, no causation, no coming into being nor any passing out of being. There is no duality (*advaita*). From this perspective, presented by Gaudapada under the notion of the doctrine of non-origination, there can be no evil because there are no individuals, no *jivas*. If no individuals ever come into being or pass out of existence, then evil has no ground upon which to take root. To this point Gaudapada says: "There is no destruction, nor origination. There is no bondage, nor anyone who seeks liberation. There is no desire for liberation, nor anyone liberated. This is the highest truth."[3]

This highest perspective reduces the world to illusion that is absolutely nought. Here the world of experience with its pain and evil is not only not given, it is not even denied as having once been experienced as real. Krishnachandra Bhattacharyya depicts this as a third level of *maya*.[4] If there is no world, nor even *maya*, there certainly can be no evil. Thus, one may say that, from this perspective, calling evil an illusion is both true and not true. It is true because evil is not what we think it to be; it is therefore an illusion. It is not true because there is no illusion, no *maya*. Even the illusion is reduced to nought.

The second type of explanation offered by Advaita proceeds in a very different direction. This level of explanation invokes the notions of *karma* and rebirth. This type of explanation is found in almost all forms of Indian thought in various ways. The notions of *karma* and rebirth inform us that the fortunes and misfortunes that presently befall an individual are the consequence of previous actions that an individual undertook. These previous actions may have taken place in a previous birth and the fruits of one's present action may ripen in this or some future life.[5] This cycle is without beginning. The confluence of the notion of *karma* and the notion that there is no beginning to the cycle of birth is inextricably intertwined with the Advaitin understanding of God and the related issue of theodicy. Sankara in the *Brahma Sutra Bhasya* makes the following points:

> The Lord, it is said, cannot be the cause of the world, because, on that hypothesis, the reproach of inequality of dispensation and cruelty would attach to him. . .To a Lord bringing about such an unequal condition of things, passion and malice would have to be ascribed. . .The Lord, we reply, cannot be reproached with inequality of dispensation and cruelty, 'because he is bound by regards'. . .the fact is, that in creating he is bound by certain regards, i.e., he has to look to merit and demerit. Hence the circumstance of

the creation being unequal is due to the merit and demerit of the living creatures created, and is not a fault for which the Lord is to blame.[6]

In the commentary to the next verse, Sankara replies to the following objection to his position, namely, that the Lord had to create the world, at some beginning moment, without consideration to good and bad *karma* and therefore the Lord must be responsible. Sankara responds to this objection by saying:

> . . .the transmigratory world is without beginning. The objection would be valid if the world had a beginning; but as it is without beginning, merit and inequality are, like seed and sprout, caused as well as causes, and there is therefore no logical objection to their operation.[7]

In these passages we do not find evil reduced to nought. In fact, evil is the paradigmatic issue from which the notion of Isvara (Lord) and creation are to be discerned. In order to extricate the Lord from the tangles of evil, Sankara is willing to argue that Isvara is not the sole force or factor in creation. Since the Lord would not create a world with such inequities, there must be other factors, in addition to Isvara's power, at work in the creation of the world. These other factors must have existed before the creation of any given world. Thus the transmigratory world must be beginningless. The other factors that establish the course of creation are the previous deeds, both meritorious and demeritorious, that individuals have undertaken. God is not the cause of evil. The evil that one encounters has no beginning except to say that it is traced to individuality. As we will see, tracing it to individuality leads us back to *maya*. Gaudapada informs us that the problems of the individual are the results of beginningless *maya*.[8]

The third perspective on evil found in Advaita Vedanta focuses on the nature of individuality. The structure of individuality with its concomitant notion of duality—subject and object—is for the Advaitin problematic. Both Gaudapada and Sankara follow the Upanisadic declarations that inform us that:

> For where there is duality as it were, there one sees the other, one smells the other, one tastes the other, one speaks to the other. . .But where everything has become just one's own self, by what and whom should one see, by what and whom should one smell, by what and

> whom should one taste. . .He (Self) is indestructible for He cannot
> be destroyed. He is unattached for He does not attach himself. He
> is unfettered, He does not suffer.[9]

Duality obscures knowledge of the self (*atman*) and that is certainly
problematic for the Advaitin. Sankara in the opening to the *Brahma
Sutra Bhasya* also informs us that we impose the characteristics of the
self upon the not self and the not self upon the self. This beginningless superimposition is correlated with ignorance and this, Sankara
says, is ". . .the cause of all evil."[10]

Radhakrishnan presents a definition of evil that follows along the
same lines:

> Evil is the free act of an individual who uses his freedom for his own
> exaltation. It is fundamentally the choice which affirms the finite,
> independent self, its lordship and acquisitiveness against the univer-
> sal will. Evil is the result of our alienation from the Real. If we do
> not break with evil, we cannot attain freedom.[11]

This definition stresses the notion that evil is the responsibility of the
individual—the individual's free act. Here also, it is not the responsibility of Isvara, the Lord. The problem is a human problem, not a
problem of divinity. Evil is associated with the individual's failure to
know the Real, Brahman, and it is thus antithetical to liberation.
From this third perspective evil is not reduced to nought; nor is it
attributed to retribution for particular acts that one has undertaken;
but rather, it is associated with our ordinary way of knowing the
world—a mistaken way.

Pain as Evil

Krishnachandra Bhattacharyya illuminates this third notion of
evil by locating it within the context not only of *moksa* but also of
pain. He says: "*Mukti* (liberation), whatever else it implies, is understood as absolute freedom from pain."[12] Freedom from pain would
be freedom from evil.

Bhattacharyya's explanation builds upon the discussion of individuality and duality. Pain as a fundamental fact of suffering has a
duality about it. Pain is at once both self and other. While impinging
upon the consciousness of the subject as other, pain must always be
appropriated as part of the subject to be felt as pain. Pain not

impinging upon the subject as a foreign element would be indistinguishable from the self and therefore not conceived to be a threat to the self. If it were no threat to self, it could not be conceived of as painful nor as evil. Thus, Bhattacharyya states that ". . .pain is known to be as much myself as given to or foreign to myself."[13]

Bhattacharyya's explanation of evil focuses our attention upon two types of wishes. He distinguishes a "secular wish" for freedom from pain and a "spiritual wish" for freedom from the "secular wish" that wishes to be free from pain. The secular wish to be free from pain appears rather natural and healthy. One who does not wish to be free from pain we assume desires to endure pain. Thus the desire to be free from pain is the prescribed route that one expects to take.

Bhattacharyya's analysis leads us to reexamine this understanding of the wish to be free from pain, the secular wish. He points out that this wish to be free from pain has the concomitant effect of establishing the reality of the experienced pain. With regard to this wish for the release from pain, he states:

> The wish presupposes the belief in the facthood of pain and yet if the wish were absent there would be no feeling of pain, for what is not wished to be terminated is not felt pain. The wish for freedom is the reflective self or reason itself which thus has to be regarded as conditioning the facthood of pain and as, therefore, acting suicidally. Reflection on pain, though implying the possibility of freedom from it, is in this sense an evil, the potentiality of pain. Reflection thus develops into reflection on itself as evil, freedom from which too is necessarily wished. The wish for freedom from the reflective wish to be free from pain is spiritual wish, the latter wish being secular.[14]

Several points are made that need to be explicated. First, Bhattacharyya is informing us that pain would not be pain if one did not desire to terminate it. The desire to terminate pain confirms the reality of the experience as pain. However, he also informs us that there can be no freedom from pain without the wish to be free from pain. Without this wish one cannot extricate oneself from pain. The wish to terminate the pain while giving hope that the pain can be terminated in fact confirms the feeling as pain. Thus, Bhattacharyya says that the wish to remove the pain is suicidal since it simultaneously establishes the experience of the pain. This first level of reflection he says ". . .is in this sense an evil, the potentiality of pain."

If the first level of reflection, namely, the wish to be free from pain, establishes the feeling as pain and is thus associated with evil, then freedom from pain and evil can only come in a second level of reflection. This second level of reflection is the wish to be free from the first wish. This second wish is the spiritual wish. It is the wish that seeks freedom from all pain because it does not wish to be free from any particular pain. This wish only wishes to be free from the wish for freedom from pain. It does not confirm the reality of that which it seeks to remove in the hope of removing it. Rather, the spiritual wish seeks to remove the conditions that affirm the experience of pain, namely, the secular wish for freedom from pain.

Bhattacharyya's analysis of evil into two wishes allows us to re-examine the notion that evil is an illusion. From this perspective, evil, associated with the particular experience of pain of an individual subject, is not a transcendental illusion imposed by an external deity, nor is this account of evil to be passed off as a cosmic illusion. Rather, here we see that evil is an illusion because it can be removed by removing the wish to remove it. It is an illusion precisely because it is based upon a wish. But neither the wish nor the illusion are transcendental in this account. Bhattacharyya says: "The illusion is to all an evil in itself, not as transcending or superseding the natural evil of pain but as wholly immanent in it."[15]

Bhattacharyya's analysis discloses that which allows individuality and duality to be correlated with evil. Individuality and duality, the normal standard bearers of the Advaita explanation of evil/suffering, are unquestionably to be associated with a lack of understanding of being, Brahman. Certainly for the Advaitin, one cannot gain liberation while under the influence of these two intoxicants. However, Bhattacharyya leads us to see that by themselves they do not present the reality of evil. In a world of complete pleasure—in a paradise of delights—one may not have liberation, but neither would one encounter evil. Bhattacharyya points out that evil is experienced, even for the metaphysically minded Advaitin, when pain enters into the consciousness of the individual. To remove pain is to remove evil and to do that one must attain liberation (*moksa*). He concludes his discussion by saying:

Pain as evil, therefore, is correlative to absolute freedom which implies freedom from pleasure also as good. It is because evil is correlated in the last resort with freedom and not with the good that freedom from pain is understood as the spiritual goal.[16]

Thus, we can see that Bhattacharyya's notion of pain as evil is not descriptive of one characteristic of evil, but rather this notion is characteristic of evil itself.

Structural and Comparative Analysis

Certainly, it is possible to say that evil is an illusion in Advaita Vedanta. However, one can now see that this has different connotations and, as Professor Matilal implied, it would be problematic to conflate these three levels of explanation.

On the one hand, the Advaitin says evil is an illusion because it is nought—not even experienced. All is Brahman and there is no change, birth, individuality, or suffering. On another hand, evil is an illusion that is experienced because an individual in knowing itself as individual experiences an object that impinges on its well being. Here Advaitains do not deny the experience of pain/evil; they only deny that it is ultimate reality—that it can be identified with Brahman, with liberation. Evil is associated with the (mistaken) way we know the world. It is the structure of experience that is associated with evil. This second approach is a systematic approach to evil. Like the second approach, the third perspective does not deny the experience of evil; however, this approach focuses on particular actions and their consequences. Here the problem is not systematic; it is particularistic. From this perspective, meritorious actions are distinguished from demeritorious actions. It is the particular actions that may lead to evil and not the ways of knowing in general that lead to evil.

We may say that these three approaches to evil offer 1) a systematic approach that focuses upon the structure of knowing and does not distinguish the particular merits of an action; 2) an analysis that focuses on particular merits/demerits of specific actions; and 3) an analysis that denies that there is any individuals, any particular actions and any evil.

These three levels of explanation of evil share a common feature and one that may be distinguished from some of the approaches to evil taken in Western theology. In the three levels of the Advaita analysis, the discussion focuses upon the subject—the experiencer of evil—not the agent who inflicts evil upon an other. Even with regard to the Advaita explanation of *karma*, the disucssion focuses upon what the individual has done in the past to merit his or her present suffering/evil. While this discussion begins with the agent of the good or bad deeds, the Advaita presentation quickly moves to the future subject who experiences the fruits of his/her own deeds. This discussion of evil actions is self-referential. It does not entail one person acting upon another person, but rather it focuses upon the consequence of the individual's action on their own self.

The second level of the Advaita discussion also focuses upon the individual who is the sufferer of the evil deed. Here evil is understood in terms of the way that the self knows itself. A mistaken way of knowing oneself is the root of suffering and evil. There is no reference to an independent agent who inflicts evil upon the individual. The third level denies the reality of a self that can suffer or experience evil. In these explanations the primary emphasis is not upon an agent who imposes evil, but rather upon the experiencer/subject of evil.

The Advaita approach can be distinguished from those approaches found within Western theology that focus on the agent who causes evil to another or permits evil to occur to another. For example, the Advaita approach can be distinguished from those positions that maintain that evil is the handiwork of a demonic/satanic figure or the testing of an individual by God. In addition, the Western discussion of natural evil places emphasis on the agent causing evil, rather than the subject experiencing evil. Natural evil, understood to be the evil that is inflicted upon humans and/or living systems, is attributed to natural processes. A discussion of natural evil may include the adverse effects that a subject has incurred but the experiencer of evil is now placed in the passive voice. The active voice is reserved for the natural process—the agent of evil. There is a similar twist in the Western discussion of moral evil. Discussions of moral evil focus upon the evil/sinful acts that one individual does that effect another individual or effect the evildoer's relationship with God. For example, we speak of the evil act that a murderer commits—the evil of the murderer. Certainly, we speak about the victim and the evil that the victim experienced, but the victim is the recipient of the evil. In such situations, evil is not defined by the subject of the experience but by the agent who inflicts the experience.

The Western emphasis on the agent can be highlighted by contrasting Bhattacharyya's approach. From the latter's perspective, evil exists only if the subject wishes it into experience. In the words of the *Brhadaranyaka Upanisad*: "He who sees all in the *atman*, evil does not overcome him; he overcomes all of evil."[17] This text is the root of Bhattacharyya's thought and it falls far from those traditions that demand that the experiencer of evil must also always be the captive of evil—once a victim, always a victim. From the Western perspective, evil is imposed upon an other and there is no escape from this imposition. The thought of an inescapable imposition is the ultimate evil for the Advaitin.

Three Levels of Evil and a Holographic Analogy

At this point, I offer a holographic analogy to this multileveled approach.[18] Like all analogies it has its limitations and strengths. (Here I can do no more than highlight some aspects of this analogy.[19]) As indicated, holography is the technique by which one reproduces three dimensional optical images. Holography should be distinguished from both photography and sculpture. Unlike photography, the images that are produced are three dimensional—they have height, width, and depth. In this sense they have the three dimensional optical properties of sculptures. They are suspended in space like three dimensional objects. However, unlike sculptures, holographic images are not objects. They cannot be touched. They are not projected onto a wall or a piece of paper like a two-dimensional photographic image. They are optical appearances.

Holography is unique not only because of the unusual three dimensional life-like images that it produces, but also because the film from which these images are produced is rather distinct. Holographic film does not contain the images that it reproduces.

Photographic film—the negative—contains the images that it reproduces. One can see these images when one holds the film to the light. There are no images on the holographic film. Technically, the hologram contains interference patterns from two interfering beams of coherent light. One of these beams of light from a laser reflects off a mirror. At the film these two beams of light converge and the interference patterns spread across the entirety of the film. This procedure does not result in discrete images on the film. In fact, rather astonishingly, because the film contains only interference patterns, each piece of the film is able to reproduce the entirety of the image. Cut the film into ten pieces and you can reproduce ten complete images. Put the film back together and only one scene reappears.

One can utilize the holographic film and the images it produces as an analogy for the Advaita understanding of reality and their concomitant analysis of evil. The film, like Brahman, does not have subject-object dichotomies, nor does it have the normal spacial-temporal relations of the world that it reproduces.[20] On the film each piece contains the whole. The film does not have individuals in the way that we experience it. On the film, like Brahman, there is no subject encountering evil, nor producing evil, nor encountering good, nor producing good. Again, each piece of the film is like all other pieces of the film in that there are no individual images and each piece can reproduce the entirety. In this sense, on the film like in Brahman, there is no change from one part to another part. If we compare the film to Brahman, then individuality and duality with their concomitant notions of good and evil do not exist.

To complete this holographic analogy, I would like to return to one of the questions that I initially asked: How can Advaita tell us that 1) evil does not exist, but 2) it is nonetheless experienced? How can the Advaitins assert the validity of both statements simulta-neously? By analogy to holography, it can be stated that at the same time and in the same place as the film exists, the holographic images appears.[21] Likewise, the Advaitin says that at the same time and in the same place as the nondualism of being (Brahman) exists there is the experience of individuality and evil. While the Advaitin considers Brahman the only reality and the realization of Brahman is identified with liberation, phenomenologically one still encounters individuals and evil. For Advaita the nonduality of Brahman is simultaneous with the phenomenological experience of individuality and evil. Brahman and the world are not separate nor are they sequential. The holographic film with its lack of subject-object relations is simultaneous with the subject-object relations of the holographic images. Thus by analogy with holography, one can see how nonduality and duality can exist simultaneously. By analogy, if one defined for soteriological purposes the film as real, one can say that the holographic images are unreal. These images appear, but they have no substance. They cannot be touched but they are definitely experienced. They are in fact only experienced when an individual perceives these experiences. They have no existence apart from their being experienced. The images do not exist on the film and they do not exist where one imagines them; namely, they do not exist suspended in space in front of the individual. They do not exist but they are experienced. This is similar to what Advaita says about individuality and evil. It is not real, but it is experienced.

I cannot pretend that the holographic analogy solves the problem of evil. I cannot assert that it makes evil and suffering more palatable. The intention here is to illuminate the relationship between the different levels of evil in the Advaita analysis.

NOTES

1. Bimal K. Matilal, "A Note on Samkara's Theodicy," *Journal of Indian Philosophy* 20: (1992), 363. Arthur L. Herman in *The Problem of Evil and Indian Thought* (Delhi: Motilal Barnasidass, 1977), makes a similar point: "The contention that evil is unreal is bandied about primarily by Vedantins like Samkara, or at least the position has been attributed to him. . .I am not convinced that Indians, even, are prepared to say that suffering is unreal. Surely one can grant them that it is not metaphysically, ultimately, absolutely really, real. . .But from the 'other' point of view evil, suffering, waste, terror, and fear are real enough." (p. 246).

2. For a similar description of Advaita philosophizing, see Eliot Deutsch, *Advaita Vedanta: A Philosophical Reconstruction* (Honolulu: University of Hawaii Press, 1973), p. 29. For an example of such a multileveled analysis of *maya* in Advaita thought see, by this author, *Hermeneutics, Holography, and Indian Idealism* (Delhi: Motilalal Banarsidass, 1987), Chapter 4.

3. Gaudapada, *Mandukyopanisad, Gaudapadiya Karika and Samkarabhasya* (Gorakhapur: Gita Press, Samvat 2026), 2:32. (Hereafter listed as *MK*, and all translations the responsibility of this author.)

4. Krishnachandra Bhattacharyya, *Studies in Philosophy*, Vol. I (Calcutta: Progressive Publishers, 1956), p. 101.

5. For an excellent discussion of the development of the notion of *karma*, specifically as it relates to Advaita see: Karl H. Potter, "The Karma Theory and Its Interpretation in Some Indian Philosophical Systems," in *Karma and Rebirth in Classical Indian Traditions*, Wendy Doniger O'Flaherty, ed.

(Berkeley: University of California, 1980), pp. 241-267.

6. Sankara, *The Vedanta Sutras of Badarayana with the Commentary by Sankara*, translated by George Thibaut (New York: Dover Publications, Inc., 1962), 2-1-34, p. 358. (Hereafter listed as *BSB*.)

7. *Ibid.*, 2-1-35, p. 360.

8. See *MK*, 1:16. Gaudapada's point in this verse is that the individual sleeps—does not comprehend the reality—because of beginningless *maya*.

9. *Brhadaranyaka Upanisad* IV.5.15. quoted from *The Principal Upanisads*, edited with Introduction, text translation and notes by S. Radhakrishnan (London: George Allen and Unwin Ltd., 1969), p. 286.

10. *BSB*, p. 15, 1.1.1.

11. Krishnachandra Bhattacharyya, *Studies in Philosophy*, Volume I, p. 104.

12. *Ibid.*, p. 135.

13. *Ibid.*, p. 136.

14. *Ibid.*, p. 135.

15. *Ibid.*, p. 140.

16. *Ibid.*, p. 142.

17. *Brhadaranyaka Upanisad*, IV.4.23, Sanskrit quoted from S. Radhakrishnan, *The Principal Upanisads*.

18. It may be helpful to note that Advaitins, like Gaudapada, often invoke two analogies to convey these three levels of explanation. Gaudapada utilizes the analogy of a "barren woman's son" to convey the notion of illusion that is absolutely nought. There is no such experience as a barren woman's son like there is no individuality. He utilizes the rope-snake analogy to convey the idea of an experience based upon subjectivity that is not real. When passing a rope in the dark one may experience a snake and fear it, but there is no snake. (See: *MK*: 3:27-28.)

19. For a more detailed discussion of some of these issues, see, by this author: "A Holographic Analysis of Religious Diversity: A Case Study of Hinduism and Christianity," *Journal of Religious Pluralism*, 2, 1993, 29-59.

20. For further elaboration and more technical explanation of these issues see by this author "A Holographic Alternative to a Traditional Yogacara Simile," *Eastern Buddhist*, XXIII, 1990, pp. 72-78; and David Bohm, *Wholeness and the Implicate Order* (London: Routledge and Kegan Paul, 1980), chs. 6 & 7.

21. There are many types of holograms and the specifics vary from type to type. I have in mind a transmission hologram producing virtual images. For a discussion of holography see: Howard Smith, *Principles of Holography* (New York: Wiley-Interscience, 1969).

11

Hindu Understandings of Evil:
From Tradition to Modern Thought

By William Cenkner

P hilosophical reflection in ancient India arose neither from wonder nor curiosity as was so frequently the case in the West but as a response to moral and physical evil in human life and in the world at large. The philosophical problem and the religious problem were the same: How to remove evil from human life. Liberation (*moksa*) or human freedom meant the removal of evil experienced as such. This was true in the classical traditions of India—Hinduism, yoga, Buddhism—since the basic perception of reality was the suffering of all (*sarvam duhkham*). Deliverance from suffering became the project of each Indian religious tradition.

The earliest Vedas and much of classical mythology in Hinduism reflect the conflict and tension among the gods, between the gods and demons, and between the divine and human orders of reality. Suffering or evil was a result of an inherent conflict in creation wherein the cosmic process was one of continual change and battle between the gods and anti-gods. This was not an eternal conflict between two opposing principles; it was not a dualism as frequently perceived in classical traditions. The two principles were in fact within the same frame of reference or within the same entity. Yama, the Lord of death, may be fearful, frightening and abhorrent for one person, but for another Yama was a gracious and inviting guest: "His sacred string is of gold. His face is charming, smiling. He wears a crown, earrings, and a garland of wild flowers."[1] The same is true for other gods who personify both good and evil. In the cosmic battle between good and evil, evil consistently lost to the power and ingenuity of the forces of good.

The above indicates that suffering is an experience that needs to be seen in perspective. Achieving such perspective will differ in the Vedas and throughout the Hindu tradition. Asceticism is critical to Hindu development because it attempts to set evil and suffering into perspective. Asceticism seeks to place evil in relation to the whole, into the greater picture of reality. One of the earliest forms of asceticism was sacrificial ritual. Ritual was intended to restore the good order of reality. In the conflict, for example, between the gods and the anti-gods, the gods always conquered in battle but the battle was never definitive for in time evil would again emerge. The gods would sacrifice and the human world would also imitate such sacrificial rituals in order to restore the reign of goodness. The descent of a god into history (*avatara*), likewise, was to restore goodness to the human order.

Two major developments advanced the notion of asceticism. The Upanishads, the final section of the ancient Vedas, realized that ritual had only a limited value. The major perception of the Upanishads was the essential unity of all reality; reality is undifferentiated, one, nondual. This perception can be experienced through meditation, reflection, self-transcendence. Evil is not denied. It is experienced. However, it is not final but transitory, passing. The world of apparent opposites—good and evil, pleasure and pain, healing and suffering—is a problem only as long as it appears as final and permanent.[2] The new Upanishadic asceticism, reflection and meditation, offers means for detachment from those objects that cause suffering and detachment from an ego that binds one to a world of limited perspective.

A second significant development in advancing the Hindu notion of asceticism in overcoming evil, other than ritual and meditation, takes place in the popular *Bhagavad Gita* where a particular form of action, action with nonattachment, becomes the new response to evil and suffering. Here one must act without being bound to the action: "To action alone hast thou a right and never at all to its fruit; let not the fruits of action be thy motive; neither let there be in thee any attachment to inaction. Fixed in yoga, do thy work, O Arjuna, abandoning attachment, with an even mind in success and failure, for evenness of mind is called yoga."[3] One has the capacity to act in such a way if one follows completely the inner law of one's own being (*dharma*) by recognizing value in the action itself regardless of its success or failure. Or one has the capacity to act without attachment to the fruits of the action if one is given fully to God in love (*bhakti*) and devotion.

Consequently, the traditional responses to evil have been ritual, reflection and meditation, detachment from the fruits of action, and love of the divine. The problem in the history of Hinduism, however, was to allow detachment to fall unknowingly into a form of indifference. A major task in modern times is to explore ways to avoid such indifference.

Range of Modern Opinion

Modern opinion in 19th- and 20th-century Hinduism is looked upon as a renaissance of thought and life. Traditional notions that the world in not inherently evil but that good and evil are present hand in hand, nevertheless, persist. The popularity of selfless action advanced by the *Gita* may now express itself in terms of social service or dedicated action against injustice. Ramakrishna, a traditional mystic figure of the late 19th century, speaks of the world as part of God's play (*lila*), God's cosmic and sportive activity: "That is His will, His play. In His *maya* there exists ignorance and knowledge. Darkness is needed too. It reveals all the more the glory of light. There is no doubt that anger, lust and greed are evil. Why, then, has God created them? In order to create saints. . .There is need of everything."[4] For Ramakrishna evil exists from a relative perspective, an unenlightened perspective, but from an absolute perspective there is no evil. He takes a traditional position in saying that evil does not exist with God-realization or self-realization.

The erudite disciple of Ramakrishna, Vivekananda, was also to reiterate traditional notions. He writes: "We have no theory of evil. We call it ignorance."[5] He follows much of Upanishadic thought by placing good and evil in the mind, looking upon good and evil as different manifestations of the same thing, and by viewing both as God's play in order to bring change to the very subject of evil, the human person. It is only with the fully 20th-century figures of Mahatma Gandhi, Sri Aurobindo Ghose, Rabindranath Tagore, and Sarvepalli Radhakrishnan that significant growth in the tradition takes place. Even these, however, are preceded by the 19th-century socio-religious reformers, Ram Mohan Roy and Keshab Chander Sen, who responded to social evil by seeking a total renovation of the social order. A renewed social consciousness becomes a major response to evil in modern times. This is true even among highly traditional groups and figures. The Sankaracarya of Kanchi, for example, has called for social reconstruction as a priority over spiritual renewal in these present times.

Mahatma Gandhi (1869-1948), set the pace and goal in the restoration of a just and honest social and political order as a response to what he attributed so much of the suffering and evil of modern India. His most memorable contribution was nonviolence (*ahimsa*) in the face of evil. *Ahimsa* is present in Indian literature and tradition from earliest times but it receives a dominant role only in the Jain tradition which significantly influenced Gandhi in his youth. Nonviolence was meant not merely for saints and social leaders but for ordinary peoples reflecting their strength of spirit, following the ancient law of self-sacrifice. It is not resignation to evil or suffering but "the non-violence of my conception is a more active and more real fighting against wickedness than retaliation whose very nature is to increase wickedness. I contemplate a mental, and therefore a moral opposition to immoralities."[6] Thus Gandhi attempted to neutralize evil through nonviolence, not by coersion but through conversion and transformation of the human spirit. It became a call to suffer in the face of evil for the sake of truth.

One of the most creative thinkers of modern India was Sri Aurobindo Ghose (1872-1950), who built a whole vision around the context of the involution and evolution of the divine in the creative process. For him the world process is fundamentally good but frequently its goodness is in a state of latency with evil or suffering seemingly more evident. Evil is a moment in the evolutionary and transformative process in which the human person finds himself/herself. It is due to ego-attachment in a stage of what Aurobindo calls the "surface mind."[7] What is new and significant in Aurobindo's thought is the evolution and inevitable divinization of nature and humanity since there exists no opposition between matter and spirit.[8] In creation spirit is latent matter, the inconscient of supreme consciousness. The response to evil from process philosophy in the West would find Aurobindo's thought highly compatible. It is my intent here, however, to highlight the contribution of Rabindranath Tagore and Sarvepalli Radhakrishnan.

Tagore on Evil

Tagore (1861-1941) is probably the most universal and comprehensive figure of modern India. He saw himself primarily as a poet but he also wrote novels, short stories, dramas, and philosophical essays. He was an accomplished musician, writing both music and words, and painter with over 2500 pieces credited to him. Not only was he a world traveler and lecturer but also the founder of experimental education on both school and university levels. In a more practical vein he established reconstruction of village life through experimental farming, crafts, and other self-help programs.

Tagore's fullest treatment of evil can be found in a book of essays titled *Sadhana*, most of which were lectures at Harvard University.[9] For Tagore the problem of evil reveals the limited, incomplete, and imperfect nature of creation itself. The human person is especially incomplete and human life is to seek greater completeness, greater fullness. The creative process in both its cosmic and human phases is the shedding of its incompleteness, its limited and imperfect nature. Imperfection reveals itself in limited power, limited will, intellect, and creativity. Such imperfection must pass through stages of realization, stages of greater growth. Existence tries to prove it is not inherently evil. Tagore writes: "An imperfection which is not all imperfection, but which has perfection for its ideal, must go through a perpetual realization."[10]

In conformity with Indian thought, ancient or modern, Tagore calls for a greater awareness, a greater consciousness of the inner self, the real person. He writes:

> To the man [sic] who lives for an idea, for his country, for the good of humanity, life has an extensive meaning, and to that extent pain becomes less important to him [sic]. To live the life of goodness is to

live the life of all. Pleasure is for one's own self, but goodness is concerned with the happiness of all humanity and for all time. From the point of view of the good, pleasure and pain appear in a different meaning; so much so, that pleasure may be shunned, and pain be courted in its place, and death itself be made welcome as giving a higher value to life. From these higher standpoints of a man's [sic] life, the standpoints of the good, pleasure and pain lose their absolute value.[11]

Tagore's call to moral life is really a call to a more universal life.

At the heart of Tagore's thought is the traditional notion of the individual seeking universality. This is true for him in every aspect of creation and the creative process. This, in brief, is the meaning of the spiritual journey for Tagore. The lesson to learn is how to turn pain into love, how to transmute suffering into joy. None of this is original to Tagore. His originality lies in the discovery of the principle of relatedness. Relationship is the means to the greater self, real personhood, a more universal life and ultimately a more universal self. In studying the life of Tagore one has to ask why he moved from one literary experience to another. If he saw himself primarily as a poet, as he did, why did he continue throughout his life to write novels, short stories, dramas, and songs? He was trying with each new genre to relate to greater reality by relating through and in other forms of literary expression. If he saw himself primarily as poet, why did he become an educationist, a painter, an experimental villager, a world lecturer and essayist? He was trying with each new venture to relate to diverse humanity and problems of modern life both in India and the world. The principle of relationship is Tagore's contribution in responding to the problem of evil in our time. In his own words: "Thus we find that, just as throughout our bodily organization there is a principle of relation by virtue of which we call the entire body our own, and can use it as such, so all through the universe there is that principle of uninterrupted relation by virtue of which we can call the whole world our extended body and use it accordingly."[12] There is no negation of the world or humanity in Tagore's thinking. Evil exists to measure the good; pain is to measure the value of joy; suffering is to draw attention to one's destiny. Purification as an aid to spiritual progress, from suffering to wholeness, is the typical and traditional element in Tagore's thought.

From a philosophical perspective evil is alienation, isolation and unrelatedness for Tagore. He seeks the infinite and universal in the finite and the particular. His response to evil is not to transcend the finite and the particular but to respond to evil in greater relatedness to the finite and the particular. It is at this point that Tagore separates himself from the idealist traditions of India. However, literary critics look upon Tagore as a humanist, naturalist, and idealist. He views humanity and nature interdependent and interrelated. He is considered an idealist because he always responds to evil and suffering within the context of society and the world. In this he is untypical of the traditional Hindu world and very much a figure of modernity. Similarly different from traditional thinkers is Tagore's active life in experimental education, village reconstruction, and international relations both in Asia and the West.

Radhakrishnan on Evil

Sarvepalli Radakrishnan (1888-1976) was born in South India within an orthodox Brahmin family but educated in Christian missionary schools and even a Christian college. Although known as an interpreter of traditional Indian philosophy, he was to some degree a comparative philosopher at home both in Indian and Western philosophical traditions. He wrote a classic history of Indian philosophy and became for a generation the interpreter of Hindu thought to the West. He was the first Asian to give the Gifford Lectures in the United Kingdom. He was also active in the social and political life of India. Radhakrishnan would begin each day translating or writing commentaries on Hindu scriptures while serving as ambassador to Moscow in the post-war years, or chairman of UNESCO, or president of India during the Nehru years. We discover again a factor of significance among modern Indian thinkers: persons of profound reflection with highly active public lives.

More than most Indian thinkers, Radhakrishnan was fully knowledgeable in both traditional Christian explanations and Western philosophical understandings of evil. What he seems to take from these traditions is the role of human freedom in handling the problem of evil. He writes that "The world is moving to the manifestation of free spirits into whom the souls of men [sic] are evolving."[13] The alternative to a mechanistic world is a world of freedom in which error, ugliness, and evil are not excluded. Evil for him is an evolutionary by-product. The world and humanity move from imperfection to perfection through the spiritual ascent from matter. Such growth takes place through pain and suffering, through creativity. Creativity occurs in and through evil and pain.

Like most Indian thinkers, Radhakrishnan accepts evil as a fact of experience but not as an ultimate fact of existence. In typical Vedantic fashion, he draws upon the distinction between the world of appearance and the world of reality. Namely, in the world of appearance, the temporary and existential world of ordinary experience, evil surrounds human life; but in the world of reality, the permanent and transcendent world of self-realization, evil is transformed into bliss. Some would attribute Radhakrishnan's insight to the Western philosopher Bradley but the same insight, according to this writer, may be found in both contemporary and medieval interpretations of Vedantic philosophy.[14] Nevertheless, the purpose of evil is to serve as an incentive or signpost to progress and growth. In Radhakrishnan's language: "Pain and trouble purify the soul. The metal shines the brightest when it passes through the furnace. . ."[15] All seeking of the true, good and beautiful is in response to the false, evil and ugly. In this sense evil is the cause of a human dialectic from which creativity and growth emerge. Human ideals can only be attained through such a dialectic. Radhakrishnan writes: "The most poignant pain can be joyously accepted if it is recognized as contributory to the realization of one's ideals."[16] None of this is necessarily new or novel to traditional Indian understanding. What is new is the insertion of human freedom and its significance, an insight from the West, that he introduces into the discussion.

All the above could be argued by any theist, East or West. However, Radhakrishnan does depart from a fully theistic understanding on the issue of God's foreknowledge as a result of human freedom. If there is divine foreknowledge, human freedom is not fully free; if there is divine foreknowledge, God must be held responsible for not preventing such evil and suffering. Radhakrishnan believes that Isvara (the Lord) is responsible for evil in only an indirect way. Radhakrishnan remains very much an idealist in the Vedantic school of Hinduism, closer to Ramanuja than Sankara, but certainly influenced by Hegel and Western idealism.[17] His own philosophical understandings are best found in his book, *An Idealist View of Life*. Still very much a traditional thinker, he looks to the *Gita* and its dramatic struggle between the forces of good and evil as the drama of human life.

Contrast of Tagore and Radhakrishnan

Both Tagore and Radhakrishnan affirm the reality of evil as a fact of human experience because they affirm the reality of the world, an imperfect and limited world. They, likewise, maintain that such a fact has no ultimacy, namely, evil is overcome by the good as the classical myths demonstrated.[18] They also follow the Indian tradition by looking upon evil as a stage leading to the perfection of humanity. Tagore writes: "In fact, imperfection is not a negation of perfection; finitude is not contradictory to infinity: they are but completeness manifested in parts, infinity revealed within bounds."[19]

Tagore and Radhakrishnan articulate the problem of evil in similar but not exactly the same ways. India has consistently considered the problem of evil as an existential problem and not as an intellectual problem. These two modernists comprehend the problem from both perspectives. It is an existential problem because life is suffering; human life is bound to the cycles of rebirth. It is an intellectual problem because their theistic tendencies must reconcile evil with the goodness of God. In the final analysis they look upon evil as a spiritual problem, a problem of salvation/liberation, again a basic traditional response.

At first glance both seem to be in continuity with tradition when they point to the transcendence of ego or the overcoming of egotistic attitudes as the solution to the spiritual problem. However, since both place evil firmly in the created world, an imperfect and finite world, the solution of evil is sought concretely within the particularities of creation. Radhakrishnan speaks of the freedom one has in creation as does Tagore.[20] Tagore's contribution rests in the notion of relatedness and how this human dynamic advances growth and development and ultimately overcomes the evils of created life. What may be the most significant factor in their realization of placing evil firmly in the created world is not so much in their theoretical or intellectual response to evil but in their practical and social response to it.

Radhakrishnan's leadership in the political destiny of India and the world did not deter him from his consistent life of philosophical reflection. Political work was his practical response to the public evils of his day. Likewise, Tagore's forty year effort in experimental education, village restoration, and his life-long effort to bring the West and Asia into greater dialogue did not deter him from his prolific life as a man of letters. It was his public work that was his most concrete response to evil.

Conclusion

Several clarifications have emerged in discussion of modern Indian understandings of evil.[21] What frequently appears as good or evil depends on the perspective, stance, or mentality of the one receiving the perception. The consistent example of this is death. "What changes is not evil but what appears as evil."[22]

Throughout this discussion a classic distinction has been drawn between facts and ultimate facts. Evil is an experiential fact and as such is relative. Evil as nonexperiential is an abstraction and as such has little meaning in Indian thought. This is why the distinction between fact and ultimate fact is vital to the Indian perception.

Both Tagore and Radhakrishnan looked upon evil as error. This is also a typical Indian perception, namely, ignorance (*avidya*) and the progression toward the good is through the recognition of ignorance or errors. Consequently, progress in human growth and development, much like scientific progress, is through the recognition of error, ignorance, and evil.

It should be finally noted that neither thinker had a theoretical response to the modern holocausts. The wars in the West and in the Far East left Tagore depressed and without solution. The termination of the lives of European Jews and the atomic disasters in Japan began a new phase in the understandings of evil. No adequate theoretical response has come from India. What has emerged from these two modernists is their greater role in public affairs with advancing age and the increasing holocaust disasters.

NOTES

1. John Bowker, *Problems of Suffering in Religions of the World* (London: Cambridge University Press, 1970), p. 203. The most thorough study of this subject by a Western thinker is: Arthur L. Herman, *The Problem of Evil and Indian Thought* (Delhi: Motilal Banarsidass, 1976, 1993). In somewhat eccentric scholarship, Herman establishes that rebirth/transmigration resolves the theological problem of evil in Indian religion whether in Hinduism, Buddhism, Jainism, and the medieval philosophical schools. Under the rebirth solution and the principle of *karma*, there is a definite response to what happens by chance or accident and the emergence of universal/demonic evil and suffering. The rebirth/transmigration option should also please the theist for there is then no one chance or eternal damnation response to the spiritual journey. My concern in this article is not the nature of evil as much as the management of evil/suffering. This, I believe, is what traditional Hinduism was about in doing religion, that is, in ritual, meditation, selfless activity, and devotion. My intent is to show the experiential response to the fact of evil. This is what the Indian traditions, orthodox or heterodox, are working out in their spiritual journey.

2. *Ibid.*, p. 214.

3. *Ibid.*, p. 227. *Bhagavad Gita* 2. 47-48.

4. K.P.S. Choudhary, *Modern Indian Mysticism* (Delhi: Motilal Banarsidass, 1981), p. 108.

5. Swami Vivekananda, *Vedanta, Voice of Freedom* (New York: Philosophical Library, 1986), edit. Swami Chetanananda, p. 61; also confer pp. 137-38, 143, 163, 225, 246, 264.

6. Mahatma Gandhi, *Non-Violence in Peace and War* (Ahmedabad: Navajivan, 1942 & 1949), edit. Bharatan Kumarappa, 2 vol., Vol. 1, pp. 1-2.

7. Choudhary, *Modern Indian Mysticism*, pp. 238-241.

8. Rama Shanker Srivastava, *Contemporary Indian Philosophy* (Delhi: Munshi Ram Manohar Lal, 1965), p. 147.

9. Rabindranath Tagore, *Sadhana: The Realisation of Life* (London: Macmillan & Co., 1913), pp. 47-65.

10. *Ibid.*, p. 53.

11. *Ibid.*, pp. 56-57.

12. *Ibid.*, p. 62. Also refer to the chapters on Tagore in this author's *The Hindu Personality in Education: Tagore, Gandhi, Aurobindo* (Columbia, MO: South Asian Books, 1976).

13. S. Radhakrishnan, *Religion in a Changing World* (London: George Allen and Unwin Ltd., 1967), p. 92.

14. Harendra Prasad Sinhya, *Religious Philosophy of Tagore and Radhakrishnan* (Delhi: Motilal Banarsidass, 1993), p. 94.

15. *Ibid.*, p. 95.

16. *Ibid.*, p. 96.

17. Srivastava, *Contemporary Indian Philosophy*, pp. 257-336.

18. Sinha, *Religious Philosophy of Tagore and Radhakrishnan*, pp. 96ff.

19. *Ibid.*, quoted on p. 99, from *Sadhama*.

20. *Ibid.*, p. 103.

21. *Ibid.*, pp. 104ff.

22. *Ibid.*, p. 105.

12

A New Understanding of the Bhagavad Gita:
Trinitarian Evil

By Francis Xavier D'Sa

A theoretical reflection on any topic has its ultimate base in a person's world-view or universe of meaning (a horizon of understanding,[1] a *mythos,*[2] a language,[3] the world of being-and-understanding[4]). The world-view understood as the conscious, though not self-conscious, world-of-being-and-understanding is that space in which the human exists, that is, one stands among other entities but also stands apart from them. Outside this space no consciousness is possible for the human. When we speak of the human, the referent is not just the human but the human-in-the-world. Merely to speak of the human without the world is to speak of an abstraction.

This is a world of relationships. There is nothing in the world of the human which is not related and interrelated, dependent and interdependent. Hence world here refers not only to the physical world but also to the spiritual and moral world in which we are born, grow up and function in different capacities. The world of the human is a complex world which is animated by the universe of meaning. When we speak of reality it is this comprehensive world of which we speak. Our understanding of evil too will be of a piece with our understanding of reality itself.

This implies that each world-view has its own way of looking at evil. The understanding of one world-view needs to be qualified, corrected and complemented by the perception of evil from other world-views. From this flows the need of dialogue between the diverse world-views in order that a transcultural view of the reality of evil may emerge.

For an intercultural dialogue there is the prior need of a common space where the different world-views can meet. With this in mind, I am putting forward Raimundo Panikkar's theanthropocosmic view of reality as a possible place of encounter.[5] Panikkar is of the opinion that all cultures and religions have either explicity or implicitly at some time or other contained such a view of reality though they may have expressed it or hinted at it in their own way. In other words wherever there has been an integral experience of [ultimate] reality, it has taken place on a theanthropocosmic foundation. Because of the ethos of the age, more often than not each culture has had to express such an integral experience more in terms of its own (anthropocentric or cosmocentric) focus rather than in theanthropocosmic terms. In Panikkar's view it is the *kairos* of our age to gather together the fragments so that an integrated and integrating theanthropocosmic vision of reality may be born.

On such a backdrop I would like to sketch the *Bhagavad Gita*'s way of looking at the problem of reality. The intention is to prepare the *Gita*'s perspective on evil for a dialogue with other views of evil. I would like first to clarify my position.

Blindness to the Real means forgetfulness of the roots of one's being; this in turn refers to the forgetfulness of the unlimited in which all existence is grounded. In other words the ontological forgetfulness of the unlimited roots of existence reduces existence to limited, finite existence, and this is the source of evil. Finitude as such, that is, the finite without reference to the infinite, is the beginning of evil. The finite is merely the finite's way of looking at existence without reference to the infinite. But the finite grounded in the infinite is no more finite.

One might pursue the question further and ask, what is the ontological status of bondage in which evil is a reality? Methodologically the question arises from the fact of bondage, the fact of limitation. Standing within the realm of limitation, we cannot answer the question of the origin of limitation. Being unable to pose this question

from outside the realm of limitation, the question cannot be methodologically justified. Our starting-point and our understanding of
it are finite. But what we can do is to question our understanding of
finitude. Is the finite what we think it to be or is it another way of
expressing the fact of ontological blindness, the ontological forgetfulness of the infinite?

This view will not satisfy the naive realists who experience their
limitation and which they believe cannot be explained away. This
brings us back to the fact of ontological blindness. What does one say
to the blind who insist that there are no colors because they do not
see them? Our situation is similar to that of the blind. Are we not
blind to the infinite side of our being?

The origin of evil in the comprehensive sense is to be sought first
and foremost in the finitude of the human and one's world. The
finite is what is not finished, not perfect, not integrated until it
comes in contact with the infinite. Ultimately the finite as finite is
that which is reified; reification is possible when finite beings have
lost their moorings in and become alienated from the infinite. This,
I submit, is the source of evil.

If evil is inescapable for the finite, evil has a totally different
significance for the infinite. Or to put it differently, what we call evil
from our perspective need not be evil from the perspective of the
infinite. If we take the example of the holocaust does this imply then
that it is evil only from our perspective but not so from that of the
infinite? What is undeniable in the eyes of the finite and the infinite
is the fact of the extermination of millions of people. The point,
however, is about the aspect of evil that is predicated of this extermination. More specifically it refers to the evil intention which lies
at the root of such an enormity. Can the divine be blind to it? Here
we must remember that we can at the most speak of God in pictures.
God is not blind to it as a human is not blind to the fact of a fellow
human who has no eyes. Moreover, both the meaning and the significance of darkness in the case of a blind person cannot be
understood in terms of the blind person alone; the experience of the
non-blind is also essential.

There is more to it than mere privation. If the divine is really
divine it must know not only evil in the form of privation but also its
purpose, place and significance in the mosaic of history and salvation. Hence without equating the two examples, it could still be

asserted that the experience of evil in the case of human history cannot be understood in terms of human history alone. For if the significance of evil is not to be interpreted entirely negatively we need to postulate someone in whose hands the happenings of history rest and who alone can redeem evil on the canvas of history and salvation. Thus evil for a believer, far from being an argument against the divine, is an argument in favor of its existence.

What does this mean for us who do not have God's view and vision of things? It means that we cannot understand the significance of evil unitl we discover our real Self, the infinity of our being. Bede Griffiths, commenting on the *Bhagavad Gita*, writes:

> That means that we enter into the inner center of our being and at that center we realize that we are one with all people and with all things. This is the essential vision.[6]

Will such a line of thinking not lead to disastrous implications? If evil has ultimately a significance different from what we perceive, why should we not engage in evil provided that we can make sure that ultimately good will come out of it? What is the point of overcoming evil if ultimately all evil will be redeemed?

Without going into great detail we could briefly state the following. One, human consciousness has worked out some instances where evil is done so that good can come out of it. The history of surgery is one example; and the principle of a just war is another. Two, the point of the ultimate redemption of evil is to highlight the principle that human evil however colossal will never be able to overcome God's goodness. And the point in fighting evil is that we have to discover our real Self, the infinity of our being. This we cannot do unless we become free from all that blinds and misleads us. Hence fighting evil implies that we engage in working selflessly for the welfare of all (*Bhagavad Gita* 5.25; hereafter all references are to chapter and verse of this text).

But how can God, the good and the merciful, permit this? Evil can never become an argument against God's goodness and mercy for two reasons: one, we can never fathom God's goodness and mercy and two, our understanding of goodness and mercy is incapable of understanding God's goodness and mercy. The implication of this is that religious beliefs and metaphors (God as father, mother, etc.) have a different function, namely, to help us recognize our finitude and alienation and discover our roots in the infinite. Religious metaphors cannot be pressed too far; one metaphor cannot be made to answer all possible questions. In this regard the whole family of metaphors of a religious tradition should be of service in locating the specific function of a metaphor. It is here that the dialogue between religions and traditions as a corrective to the danger of anthropomorphism that is inherent in all religious language has its proper place.

Finally, a genuine religion must remind us constantly and continually that eternal life does not mean life without death! Eternal life is the integration between the temporal and the eternal, namely, the tempiternal.[7] From a tempiternal perspective evil, suffering and death have an altogether different significance.

Reality is Trinitarian

We have to revise our notions of reality. We have to begin with any everyday experience. If I say, for example, I see a tree from my window, there is something (the tree from my window) that I am drawing attention to. This is true of all discourse. Whatever may be the content of my discourse, there is something that I am asserting, denying, something that I am drawing attention to. Panikkar calls this the 'cosmic,' 'material,' 'objectifiable' dimension of reality. It is such an aspect of reality which lends itself to objectification. Everything has an objectifiable aspect. Even God has an objectifiable aspect.[8]

Coming back to our assertion, I see a tree from my window, I perceive that besides the cosmic dimension of reality, there is the objectifying dimension. Not only do I speak of the tree but there is also someone who is conscious of the tree. This is the dimension of consciousness that does the objectifying. Panikkar calls this the human dimension of reality. In as much as we speak of even the unknown, our very speaking of the unknown is its human dimension. For anything to *be*—phenomenologically—the dimension of human consciousness has to be connected with it.

Finally there is a depth-dimension to reality which connects the objectifiable aspect of reality with its objectifying aspect. This implies that both the objectifiable and the objectifying dimensions have a kind of unfinished, infinite character. The objectifiable can be objectified without any limit; water can be objectified from different angles. Similarly there is no limit to the human's objectifying capacity. The human's infinite capacity to objectify corresponds to the infinite objectifiablity of the cosmic. Panikkar calls this the depth-dimension, the spiritual or the divine dimension.[9]

Reality, that is, everything, is made up of these three dimensions. The cosmic, the human and the divine are not nouns but constitutive dimensions, aspects of reality. The cosmic dimension does not refer to the cosmos, nor the human dimensions to the human being nor the divine to God. The cosmos is made up of all three dimensions but stresses the cosmic dimension; the human being is made up of all three dimensions but stresses the human dimension and God is made up of all three dimensions but stresses the divine dimension. Each being is different because of the different ways in which it integrates the three dimensions. Accordingly the Real is the integration of all three dimensions.

The three dimensions of reality are in fact three communities interpenetrating each other and thus forming one trinitarian community of reality. This means the cosmic dimension in you, in me, in the tree, in everything is a community in which everything participates. The same is to be said with regard to the human and the divine dimensions. All three communities (cosmic, human and divine) together constitute the trinitarian community of reality. Reality is not a conglomeration of disconnected objects but one organic community in which the three communities participate. Each being is connected with every being. It is real in as much as it is connected with every being. Wholeness is what constitutes the measure of a being's reality. In as much as it lacks wholeness it is not real.

Trinitarian Evil

It is not surprising that our world is no longer a safe place to live in. The human is becoming less human, and the divine no longer holds primary significance, at least as far as our universe of meaning is concerned. Reality is becoming less real. Is it surprising then that meaning in life is in short supply? My aim is to point to the constant danger of the human being, the cosmos and the divine becoming less and less real because of blindness to each of the three dimensions of reality.

Clearly blindness to each of these aspects is different. Blindness to the cosmic turns the cosmos into a world of objects, a world of manipulation, a world with no significance. Blindness to the human makes the human being a living body with a dead spirit. One's so-called interpersonal relationships are in effect inter-living-object relationships. Blindness to the divine is manifested in the lack of depth in the relationships to the cosmic and the human. There is no depth in the world of objects nor in that of living objects. The fatal conclusion is that the human is becoming a mere human and the world is becoming mere matter; in neither of them can one find real meaning or mystery.

This is what I call trinitarian evil. It means that all evil has a trinitarian consequence: that is to say, neglect of the divine dimension is at the same time neglect in some way of the human and the cosmic; neglect of the human dimension is at the same time neglect of the divine and the cosmic dimension; and neglect of the cosmic dimension is at the same time neglect of the divine and the human. Trinitarian evil implies that whatever be the partiality we are involved in, it always affects the three dimensions of reality.

Accordingly we have evil wherever there is partiality. Evil is wherever one or the other dimension of reality is overlooked or denied. Where wholeness is rejected or neglected and partiality is the norm, there evil makes its appearance. What we usually call evil (crime, criminals, intention, motives, etc.) are all symptoms of the larger evil of blindness and partiality to one or the other dimension of reality. This is the base of all evil whether it is seen anthropocentrically (as sin, i.e., disobedience to God's will) or cosmocentrically (as evil [adharma, papam], i.e., lack of harmony with reality).

What is evil ontologically speaking? Evil is the movement against reality. Whereas the movement of being is towards fullness, evil is the attempt to empty reality of its meaning and significance. Meaning and significance emerge only from the direction of wholeness and fullness. Indeed where meaning and significance are missing or neglected, there is no fullness or wholeness possible. Reality is not to be understood statically. That which moves toward fullness and totality is the real. As something moves in the direction of fullness it is real, and as it moves away from it, it is evil. The question is not how evil is in the world but in what direction it is moving, in the direction of the real or its opposite, the non-real.

The ontological order is the order which comprehends wholeness; wholeness cannot be restricted to the moral order alone. The moral order is not independent of the ontological perspective; it has its foundation in the ontological order of harmony of the three constituents of reality. This implies two things: Not only is good and evil determined from an ontological perspective but also all notions of good and evil are of a piece with the ontological perspective. In the last analysis all notions of good and evil, if they are to have any basis, have to be intelligible in terms of their respective ontology.

Evil in the Bhagavad Gita

To understand the *Bhagavad Gita's* insight into evil we need briefly to study its view of reality. Reality has two aspects: the perishable and the imperishable. We begin with the imperishable (8.3), the immutable (9.14), the highest person (8.8; 15.17-19) and the Supreme Spirit (15.17b,31b) who embraces all that is. The Supreme Person, *purushottama*, is the beginning, middle and end of all things. Whatever is, is in and through the *purushottama*. *Purushottama* is the One-who-is-the-All because the All is sustained and held in being by the *purushottama* (11.40).

In the background of such a view is the metaphor of the cosmic person of the Rigvedic hymn X.90 (13.13-14). This is an analogy which the Indian tradition (especially Ramanuja of the Vaishnava tradition) has canonized: the universe as the body of the Supreme Spirit of the universe.[10] But unlike the everyday notion of spirit which is embodied in the body, the Indian analogy stresses the animation of the universe by the Supreme Spirit. The universe is in the Supreme Spirit (9.5) which is the *anima* animating the universe. The universe is animated by the Supreme Spirit.

However, we can speak of the Supreme Spirit only in terms of its body, the animated universe called *prakriti*. *Prakriti* is the cosmic process of change and becoming.[11] *Prakriti* is constituted by three constituents (*gunas*) called *sattva*, *rajas* and *tamas*.[12] *Sattva* accounts for what is light and bright, *rajas* for what is dynamic and *tamas* for what is dark and heavy. All three are to be understood primarily ontologically and only secondarily psychologically. Hence *sattva* has to do with what is light, namely, that which enlightens and is good; *rajas* has to do with what is dynamic, with the passionate, pleasing, and repelling; similarly *tamas* refers both to what is dark, dull and heavy, and to the stubborn and the stupid. The three basic movements of *prakriti* are the upward movement of *sattva*, the sideward movement of *rajas* and the downward movement of *tamas*. We could perhaps compare the threefold movement to the forces of an orbital movement wherein the centrifugal force is *sattva*, the centripetal is *tamas* and the orbital movement itself is *rajas*. All three go together, none can exist by itself and only when the three harmonize do we have the movement of an orbital process[13] (14.18).

This analogy which is primarily applied to the macrocosm (i.e., the universe) is also applicable to the microcosm, namely, the human being. The microcosm is neither separate nor different from the macrocosm.

The smooth and harmonious orbital movement that human existence is meant to be is neither smooth nor harmonious because each of the three forces pulls in its own direction without reference to the others. The result is that human existence is scattered and fragmented and so humans are unable to find their real identity in the Supreme Person. Bedeviled by a false sense of identity human beings cannot realize their true Self (3.27). This is bondage, the state where evil starts to raise its head as a matter of course.

With this background we are at the core of the problem of evil in the *Bhagavad Gita*. The state of evil in which humans find themselves is bondage. In the language of our analogy, bondage means the state in which we allow ourselves to be pushed and pulled by all the forces of the *prakriti*—a process which in effect alienates us from our real source and space, the *purushottama*. Bondage through attachment to each of these three constituents has a different effect. *Sattva* binds by attachment to happiness and knowledge; *rajas* to action and *tamas* to heedlessness, indolence and sleep (14.6-9).

What needs to be noted is the following: The movements towards happiness, knowledge, action, heedlessness, indolence and sleep are present wherever we have the three *gunas*; that means, as constituents of *prakriti* they are ubiquitous. This, however, is not the problem. Their movements are natural and one has to make use of them in order to discover the real roots of human existence, namely the Supreme Person.

Bondage enters the scene once we begin to give in to these movements; they then rule over us and our freedom disappears. We become the victims of these forces. We are ruled by the false sense of identity and are alienated from our true Self when these onto-logical (and not merely psychological) forces (of passion, greed, and delusion) lord it over us. Passion, greed and delusion are not so much psychological as ontological movements. To be in charge of them means to be led by the realm of the spirit (*purusha*); but to be led by them is to be blind to the realm of the spirit. Such blindness is existential blindness, the privation of existential openness.

Bondage is the movement that arises from the ego faculty (*ahamkara*) and liberation (*moksa*) is the movement that leads to the discovery of the true Self (*purusa*). In the language of the *Bhagavad Gita* bondage is the movement towards the non-real and liberation towards the Real. Consequently, if one follows the movement towards the non-real, the orbital movement of existence will turn out to be a vicious circle (*samsara*), a going in circles with no way out; and if one follows the movement towards the Real, one will be opened up to the infinite, to one's infinite capacity for fullfillment, which is another way of saying, one will be opened to the Real.

To quote the *Bhagavad Gita*:

> *SAT* - it means what is real and what is good, Arjuna; the word *SAT* is also used when an action merits praise. *SAT* is steadfastness in sacrifice, in penance, in charity; any action of this order is denoted by *SAT*. But oblation, charity, and penance offered without faith are called *ASAT*, for they have no reality here or in the world after death (17. 26-28).

One has to remember that in the *Gita*'s context sacrifice (*yajna*) is understood primarily ontologically, not ritualistically, much less psychologically (3. 4-19).[14] In the *Gita*, it must be remembered, faith, oblation, gift and austerity are primarily to be seen from the onto-logical and not from the moral viewpoint. The sequence is striking: reality, goodness and good work. And even good work is under-stood as action undertaken for the sake of the Supreme Person. Furthermore *sat* (being), the present participle of the verb 'to be' is contrasted with *asat* (non-being); the real vis-a-vis the non-real. Whatever is done without faith, oblation, is *asat*, it is nought, here or hereafter.[15] Indeed, the non-reality of such action is the precise point of the quotation.

Belief and unbelief are in the view of the *Gita* ontological categories.[16] The kind of being one is depends on the nature of one's faith.[17] Faith is ontological or existential openness. Without openness one stands on the moving sands of the non-real; accordingly, whatever one builds on will be built on the non-real. The openness of being means openness to the Real, to the infinitely Real. If the *Gita* speaks of three kinds of faith, *sattvic, rajasic* and *tamasic*, it is, in my interpretation, because the *sattvic* stresses the divine dimension, the *rajasic* the human and the *tamasic* the cosmic. An integral faith requires an integration of all three dimensions.

To put this more systematically: the real and the good are connected with faith, and the non-real and evil with the lack of faith. To believe is to see things as they really are; not to believe is to be unable to see reality as it is. Not to believe then is not to be in touch with reality. In the view of the *Gita*, this is the lowest form of evil since it is the same as having no reality here or in the world after death.

Overcoming Evil

Trying to overcome the triple evil is what the *Gita* tries to achieve through its triple yoga of knowledge, devotion and action.[18] *Jnana-yoga* (knowledge) challenges our notion of the divine; *bhakti-yoga* (devotion) purifies our understanding of the human and *karma-yoga* (action) questions the authenticity of our commitment to the cosmos. Genuine integral faith implies a notion of the divine that is neither rationalistic nor idealistic; an understanding of the human that is neither merely cosmic nor purely divine, and a commitment to the cosmos that is neither exclusively object-oriented nor exclusively other-worldly.

Overcoming evil is neither merely a subject of grace nor a totally human initiative. It is not a question of relying only on grace. There is need of human response. But neither is it a question of what we can do about this. The question we have to ask is this: Is wholeness a matter of doing or of discovering? Has not the paradigm of doing brought us to this impasse in the first place? It would be a fallacy to suggest that doing is part of our responsibility. Looking at doing in this way ignores that prior to doing there is need to listen and to discover something that is given. The *Bhagavad Gita's* view of doing is that all doing leads to bondage except selfless activity which is for the welfare of the whole (3.9). The *Gita* coordinates the centripetal force of selflessness with the centrifugal force of the welfare of all beings. What emerges from this is not so much action as participation in the natural orbital movement of reality where one is not different from reality. This is the experience of nonduality of the later Advaita schools.

The answer to evil, I submit, is to be sought in a fresh discovery, in a revision (*metanoia*) of reality. For this we need a mystagogy (in Indian terminology, a *sadhana*) like that of the *Gita* which will lead us from the unreal of instrumentalization to participation in the Real, from the darkness of fragmentation to the light of unity-in-diversity and from the death of limitation to the life of the unlimited.

NOTES

1. G. Oberhammer, *"Begegnung" als Kategorie der Religionshermeneutik* (Vienna: Publications of the De Nobili Research Library, 1989).
2. R. Panikkar, *Myth, Faith and Hermeneutics* (New York: Paulist Press, 1979), p. 3.
3. H-G. Gadamer, *Truth and Method* (London: Sheed and Ward, Reprint, 1985), pp. 269-274.
4. This is my own way of putting together these different aspects. I am in no way intending to equate world-view with the horizon of understanding or with *mythos* or language. These are to be understood not as equivalent but as homologous.
5. "Colligite Fragmenta. For an Integration of Reality," in: *Alienation to At-Oneness*, ed. by F.A. Eigo (Philadelphia: The Villanova University Press, 1977).
6. B. Griffiths, *River of Compassion. A Christian Commentary on the Bhagavad Gita* (New York: Amity House, 1987), p. 85. Comment on *Bhagavad Gita* 5.7 which speaks of one "whose soul is one with the soul of all."
7. See R. Panikkar, "Time and Sacrifice—The Sacrifice of Time and the Ritual of Modernity," in *The Study of Time*, ed. by J. T. Fraser, N. Lawrence and D. Park (Berlin: Springer Verlag, 1978), pp. 711ff.
8. See R. Panikkar, "The Cosmotheandric Intuition," *Jeevadhara*, 79 (January 1984), pp. 27-35.
9. *Ibid.*
10. See *Bhagavad Gita*, Ch. 12.
11. See *Bhagavad Gita*, Ch. 13.33; 14.3-4; 15.17-18.
12. See *Bhagavad Gita*, Ch. 14.5ff.

13. The weakness of the analogy is obvious: in an orbital movement the centripetal force has to be equal and opposite to the centrifugal movement which is not the case here. The point of the analogy is that just as all three forces in an orbital process are constitutive so too are all three *gunas* constitutive of the cosmic process.

14. R.C. Zaehner, *The Bhagavad-Gita: With a commentary based on the original sources* (London/Oxford/New York: Oxford University Press, 1969).

15. The *Aitareya Brahmana* 7, 10, 4 couples faith with truth which in the Upanishadic tradition is ontological truth. Truth (*satya*) is the abstract form of *sat* (being). In some philosophical traditions of India faith is said to be a positive attitude toward reality. See Paul Hacker, "Über den Glauben in der Religionsphilosophie des Hinduismus," *Zeitschrift für Missionswissenschaft und Reigionswissenschaft*, 38 (1954), pp. 51-66.

16. *Bhagavad Gita*, 17.3: "A person is made of faith: as a person's faith so the person."

17. R. Panikkar, "Faith as a Constitutive Human Dimension," in *Myth, Faith and Hermeneutics* (New York: Paulist Press, 1979), pp. 188-229.

18. See F. X. D'Sa, "The Yogi as a Contemplative in Action," in *Studies in Formative Spirituality*, Vol. XI:3 (1990), pp. 289-302.

PART THREE

Responses from
African Traditional Religion

13

Evil in Yoruba Religion and Culture

By E. O. Oyelade

T he Yoruba who occupy the western region of Nigeria are a homogeneous community. Although they speak varying dialects, they do understand one another. They are presently divided into five states: Lagos, Ogun, Oyo, Oshun and Ondo. This is a deeply religious community whose ways of life are essentially the products of religion. Religion and culture or religion and morality are inseparable. Separation attempts have been made and are still being made through foreign religions such as Islam and Christianity. But the cord of the extended family, described as the *Ebi* commonwealth,[1] is so strong that no individual, despite a new religion, can claim total separation from the traditional community. This community is a veritable platform where all kinds of evil forces disrupt the life of individuals. The Yoruba are ever aware of the presence of evil. Instead of running away, they simply live with it, seeking whatever solutions are possible and accepting with little or no complaints whatever cannot be overcome, as their lot in life.

In light of the above I have four objectives in this discussion. The first is to describe the beliefs of Yoruba traditional society to the problem of evil. The second is to examine four types of evil. The third objective is to examine critically how the Yoruba in their traditional settings seek to deal with the problem of evil. The fourth is to assess the value of evil and examine its future role in a society that is becoming quickly literate and mobile.

The Origin of Evil

Several words are used in Yoruba language to express the word evil. Among these are *ibi*—evil, *buburu*—wickedness, *aidara*—bad, *aito*—unrighteousness. It is the word *ibi* which corresponds most closely with the English word evil. There are several understandings about the origin of *ibi* in our world. For instance, one theory says that when a woman gives birth, the baby is *omo*; the placenta is *ibi-omo*, i.e., the evil of the baby. According to Chief Olumuyide Ogunyemi-Falua[2] both the placenta and the baby are *omo*; one is *omo* that can speak or make sounds, and the second is *omo* that is silent and cannot speak. The second is the caretaker of the human *omo* with whom all things are kept. But it is also the evil-Esu that followed *omo* from heaven. The Yoruba refer to it as a delicate thing that must not be broken. Because it is also a person; it has ears and can hear but it does not have a mouth to speak.

During labor the baby may decide to return to heaven. This is the time when the herbalist may speak to it through incantations.[3] They will plead with it to rethink and come out peacefully in order to complete its assignment. They will remind it that "the dog returns home with the person who takes it out." Then it will come out. After delivery, *ibi-omo*, the placenta or the silent child is put in a pot and buried in a cool place. It is generally believed that the spirit of *ibi-omo* is continuously revolting against the child and never departs until death separates them.

Bolaji Idowu identifies Esu as one of the sources of evil. According to him, the Yoruba believe that there is "an unmistakable element of evil in Esu. As a result all things evil are said to be the manifestation of his powers. Because of his wickedness he was feared by both humans and divinities. He is described as Esu, the enemy of the divinities. No wonder the Yoruba attributed every evil tendency in man to his agency."[4] For instance, when a man slapped his wife, it is the work of Esu; when a man got drunk and broke his leg, it is Esu; and when a man committed adultery with his brother's wife—surely it is Esu! So all wicked thoughts are given by Esu. A

wicked child is called the son of Esu. When a person is resolute
about initiating an action calculated to have evil effect, he is asked:
"Is Esu manipulating you?" Esu is described as Agbako who causes
accidents and misfortunes to travellers. A very cherished prayer is:
"You shall not meet with Agbako on your way."

But Esu is not totally characterized as the biblical Satan. Evil, for
Esu, is a hobby "just as any person corrupted by power which seems
uncontrolled may find sadistic relish in throwing his weight about in
unsympathetic, callous ways."[5] The worshippers of Esu are proud of
bearing names with Esu as prefix: Esubiyi, the scion of Esu;
Esugbayi, claimed by Esu; Esubunmi, Esu offers me a gift; Esudara,
Esu does wonders; Esudiya, Esu avenges me.

It appears that there are two sides to Esu in Yoruba religious
culture. Esu causes evil by giving misleading suggestions which end
in sadness or destruction. On the other hand Esu is a good divinity,
very close to Olodumare. Esu is able to obtain good things for its
worshippers. Esu may be made angry for the purpose of inflicting
injury on someone by using *adi*, (palm kernel oil) as a libation,
usually poured on the Esu rock. When the blessing of Esu is
required, *epo* (palm oil) is poured on the rock.

From Ifa records, the Yoruba believe in the existence of supernatural powers. According to Chief Olumuyide Ogunyemi-Falua
after the earth was created by Orunmila, Olodumare allowed the
earth to mature and expand. For more than a trillion years the
earth was inhabited by powerful beings, the divinities. There are two
types, the good and the evil. The good are also twofold, namely, the
gods and the ancestors. These good supernatural powers assist
humans in their daily activities if they are kind to their neighbors
and faithful to their god. On the other hand, the evil supernatural
powers are said to be two types: the belligerent enemies and the
witches. These supernatural powers work against human interests
by trying to disrupt human destiny. The most dreaded are death,
disease, infirmity or paralysis, and a loss that destroys or carries
away one's belongings. Another group are the witches or birds. The
witches are capable of assuming the form of birds whenever they
wish to attack or work against human interests.[6]

The wicked people who receive powers from the witches or the
divinities or other spirits are classified as part of the belligerent
powers. The main characteristic of these wicked beings is that they

always pretend to be helpers and admirers in order that they not be suspected for the evils they do.

These theories of the origin of evil are given realistic interpretations. Humankind lives in the midst of enemies seen and unseen. One must struggle to find safety in order to achieve goodness enshrined in one's destiny.

Types of Evil

The Yoruba divines have, however, tried to classify evil into four types: physical evil, moral evil, inflicted evil, and predestined evil.

The most disturbing manifestations of physical evil include the destruction of houses, property or persons by lightning or thunder. The Yoruba regard this as the function of Sango, historically, a powerful Oyo king who became a divinity after his death. He now resides in heaven and became in the apt words of Leo Frobenius "the Hurler of thunderbolts, the Lord of the storms, the God who burns down compounds and cities, the Render of trees and Slayer of men; cruel and savage. . . ."[7]

Another manifestation of evil is seen in the epidemic caused by Sopona, the god of smallpox. To illustrate how dreadful this disease is regarded, the late Obafemi Awolowo reported the outbreak of an epidemic of smallpox in 1920 in his hometown, Ikenne. The priests and their devotees had to observe a twenty-one-day purification ceremony to appease Sopona.[8] Among the titles assigned to Sopona are: Lord of the earth or world, hot earth, meaning that he is an earth divinity. During the outbreak, women must not sweep their houses and premises. Sopona is also referred to as the Lord of the open. For example, when one throws out water from inside the house one must say, excuse me or permit me, Lord, to throw out this water.

It is reported that Sopona can be employed against an enemy or as a source of income for priests. H. J. Elis (1892), a Wesleyan missionary, once had to plead with the Ogbonis (tribal elders) who arrested a person and charged him for murder because after he was healed of smallpox, his aunt became afflicted with it and died. The Ogbonis believed the healed person had transferred the disease to his aunt.[9] An unscrupulous priest may also exploit the situation by secretly spreading the infection in order to collect sacrificial objects and money from the relations of the victims.

Chief Olumuyide Ogunyemi-Falua claimed that one of the most devastating supernatural powers causing physical disasters is the god of the wind. He controls his messenger, whirlwind, and sends him to destroy all the obstacles that stand in his way as he journeys through forests and cities. The main task assigned to him by Olodumare is to transfer plant seeds from place to place, preserving the forestation of the earth. But the god of the wind is also a wise and powerful magician who often took people away, and having enslaved them, taught them magical powers. A popular Yoruba magician claimed that he spent seven years with the god of the wind [between heaven and earth].[10]

The general moral response of the Yoruba to physical evil is usually that of resignation and acceptance although efforts may later be made to prevent future occurrence. The usual greeting is: Greetings to you, the way things are around us, God will deliver us.

Bolaji Idowu asserts rightly that morality is the fruit of religion.[11] The Yoruba do not make any attempts to separate religion from morality, and it is impossible to do so without disastrous consequences. In the view of the Yoruba certain actions are morally approved and others are disapproved. Those that are forbidden are tabu. The expression "It is a tabu, it is not done" expresses the belief that if such a tabu is not observed, terrible consequences should be expected. The tabu is in consonance with the expressed injunctions of the deity or the divinities. Usually, these injunctions are made known through divination and the voice of the oracle. Therefore, the consequence of disobedience is believed to arrive some day when the avenger or other powers begin to act. It is a common saying:

The Avenger will avenge, he cannot but avenge.
He who queries will query, he cannot but query.
This oracle to Orunmila made him give strict
warnings to his male and female children.[12]

The Yoruba believe that *Orunmila* is the secret agent who discovers all the hidden behaviors of people and judges justly. He is referred to as the retributor who knows and judges the secrets of one's heart. It is expected that a family source of power given by the family divinity is secret and is not to be disclosed to an outsider. Any member of the extended family who is guilty of revealing the secret may be severely punished and ostracized. If two friends enter into an oath of agreement or a covenant, it is tabu to break the covenant. The defaulter is referred to as one who turns the earth upside down. If a person has sexual affairs with another man's wife, he is said to have eaten the tabu. All these unhealthy behaviors are disapproved of not only by the community, but they also stir up the anger of the divinities even Olodumare himself.

Inflicted evils are the result of the wicked activities of witches and medicine men. In this case the victim may not have committed any offense. One may be tempted to behave in a certain way in order to be punished for it. One may be punished simply as a demonstration of power. The powerful people of the earth are usually referred to as Aye.

> I have no pride before *aye*.
> I prostrate before young and old.
> I prostrate before you my fathers
> and mothers. I prostrate, let my
> humility be acceptable.

The Yoruba consider witches as the most dreaded group of Aye. Ifa poems describe the powers of the witches as more powerful than human beings, the divinities, or the ancestors. The creation divinities were humiliated by the witches.[13] Akin Omoyajowo has identified three methods of becoming a witch, namely, by inheritance, by swallowing witchcraft substances which are sold cheaply by women, or it may be imposed on people by demons.[14] According to Chief Olumuyide Ogunyemi-Falua, the witches are given power to do many things. They may make marks on a child's body or may cause a physical deformity while the baby is in its mother's womb; they may prevent delivery and cause the death of the child and its mother. Whatever one succeeds in doing is done by the witches and whatever fails is caused by their actions. The control of the earth is in the hands of the witches, so they can penetrate into any place they wish. Since they are to continue eternally, they must continue to initiate beloved ones into their cult.

It may be implied that the presence of the witches in the midst of human society is the proof of the reality of evil. Their presence also suggests the fact that the Yoruba believe that Olodumare is almighty and all-powerful, yet there is almost nothing society can do with the witches. Could this be regarded as self-limitation or does Olodumare allow the witches to operate in order to maintain God-consciousness in human societies? If the second suggestion is the case, then we may say that the end justifies the means.

Witches may have no guilty consciences. But the community has always been their judge. Witches, when discovered, are regarded as enemies who must be punished and sometimes destroyed. It is common belief that they cannot escape punishment since they must confess all their sins before death.

One of the strongest religio-cultural beliefs among the Yoruba is the doctrine of predestination. According to this general belief humans obtain their destiny in one of three ways: that to which one kneels and chooses; that to which one kneels and receives; and that which is imposed on one. In consequence of this the Yoruba believe that all events in this world whether good or bad are the outward manifestation of a person's destiny.[15]

The Yoruba, following the revelation in Ifa poetry, believe that "a man's destiny, that is to say his success or failure in life, depends to a large extent on the type of head (*ori*) he chose in heaven." In this context, everyone's *ori* is regarded as one's personal god who cares intimately about one's affairs. The *ori* is worshipped and propitiated.[16] Once a person arrives here on earth as destined, nothing can be changed. But unlike predestination in Islam which cannot be altered, the Yoruba allows room for modification for the better or for the worst.

Methods of Dealing with Evil

Evil is a reality in Yoruba society. Some of it cannot be controlled while most of the forces of evil may be prevented. The Yoruba are active in the search for preventive methods. Among the popular methods used are: sermonization, the medicine man, sacrifice, and the king. All traditional priests emphasize the results that follow evil deeds. The Ifa poems preached sanity and good will. The wicked should consider their sufferings in the afterlife. A popular Ifa lyric is as follows:

Perpetuate no evil in this world
for heaven's sake (repeated twice).

For when you get to the gate of heaven,
you will give account (of your stewardship).[17]

Preventive sermonization is especially popular during the various religious festivals. The drummers and the musicians emphasize the concept of retribution here on earth and yonder in heaven. The diviners are also preachers of divine retribution. When a medicine man is consulted, he assures the client that the penalty is sure to come as a result of wickedness.

According to R. J. Gehman, a medicine man functions similarly to a traditional doctor who seeks to help the sick and needy who are troubled by witches. In this regard a medicine man is not a herbalist in Gehman's view. This is not completely true among the Yoruba. The *babalawo*, the diviner connected with the cult of Orunmila very often is also *oloogun*, the medicine man; he is also *onisegun*, the herbalist. This is notwithstanding the fact that there are independent herbalists who specialize in curative medicine only. Even they sometimes consult diviners. The medicine man is the "doctor of traditional African culture endowed by his ancestral spirits with the power of counteracting witchcraft—hence called a witch doctor.[18]

The belief in the efficacy of traditional sacrifice can be confirmed by the fact that every morning in Ile-Ife, one of the well-known modern societies, you can find in many quarters remnants of sacrifices. According to the Yoruba sacrifice is a religious act which involves the rendering of something to a supernatural being or beings. The practice of sacrifice varies from religion to religion but essentially is similar. It has various intents and purposes.[19] Awolalu having observed various sacrificial rites affirms that it is not possible to speak of one purpose of sacrifice. It may be made to propitiate the angry spirit whose land or trees have been destroyed or to substitute for a sick human's life; or to seek the support of the divinity for one's community or farm or business; or to change an unfortunate situation into an auspicious one.[20] Offerings may be made to control and prevent the evil machinations of mysterious powers or to implore one's fate divinity to bring good things in life. Or sacrifice may invite the invisible spirits (the ancestors) to partake in the offered food and drink in order that they may be well-disposed to the living. This is a communication between the living and the living dead or to express gratitude to spiritual beings for the benefits received from them and in order to fulfil the vow made to their particular divinity who provided for their needs in a surprising way.[21]

Although Metuh agrees that sacrifices have varying purposes, he claims that no compulsion is put on the gods. "In the final analysis the believer knows that the gods will do as they like, no matter the cost of the sacrifice." Like Kristensen, Metuh sees sacrifice as a material corporal prayer, a form of communication with God. The gift or offering thus becomes a means of expressing the intensity of one's desire to communicate with God.[22]

This may be what sacrifice means in the Igbo community context. In the Yoruba view of life sacrifice must be dictated by the oracle. Once the oracle specifies, the result is assured. The oracle, especially Ifa divination, is the liaison between the enquirer and the divinity in charge. If it is a form of prayer, it is a realized prayer, a shout of victory.

When there is a physical disaster or the witches are becoming too outrageous, community representatives will visit the king and place before him their problems. The king in turn will, in consultation with his chiefs, send a special message to the head of all the *babalawo* or send a message to the mother of the town, the head of the witches. They will then make demands in order that the problems may be suppressed or removed completely. The king is usually all too pleased to provide the objects required to ward off the evils in society. Kingship rituals become the sacred canopy under which the entire society takes refuge.[23]

Conclusion

A final question to be asked is what are the advantages of evil in Yoruba religious culture? In the Yoruba view evil means suffering. To endure suffering is to be a real man or a real woman. This attitude toward evil has limited psychological effects. In the words of Fela Anikulapo, the great Nigerian musician, the African man is always suffering and smiling. A Yoruba proverb says, "He who prevents your good from reaching you, has taught you courage or strength." The presence of evil in society also teaches wisdom. It also teaches a person how to live and deal with the powerful people of this world. There is a proverb which says, "An adult who refuses to run away from a snake, awaits death." It is also said, "If you claim to be wise without suffering, who is your teacher?"[24]

Perhaps the greatest disadvantage of evil is the persistent fear planted in the hearts of Yoruba people. In most cases, one's homestead is the seat of evil. Many people have migrated to other towns and cities where their origins are unknown. It is believed that the wicked and the witches must know one's genealogy to do any harm.

From this study we have seen that evil is a practical phenomenon, not a theoretical or philosophical ideology. It is manifested in the daily life of the Yoruba community. The Yoruba people in a traditional society may have to live with evil for many more years. However, the advancement of Western education, philosophy and way of life are likely to reduce the fear associated with evil. For example, thunder does not really have any connection with Sango, a kingly divinity. It is a physical manifestation explained by scientists.

Looking more closely at the influence of Western education in traditional communities, one can see already a tendency to appropriate more and more scientific attitudes. Witchcraft is concentrated in the female community. Women's education is now very popular. Here we can expect two possibilities: first, there may emerge a new set of educated witches whose activities will be positive. There is a common belief in Africa that witches in Europe are recognized contributors toward scientific discoveries. If this is true, a similar advantage may be expected among the Yoruba. Second, the newly educated and elite women may reject witchcraft as a traditional folly which has caused underdevelopment. Presently, there is no positive contribution which witchcraft makes among the Yoruba.

In Yorubaland, we are also experiencing the establishment of new and elite urban communities, removed from traditional society. About ten kilometers away from Ibadan, an urban community called Ajoda New Town is developing. Most of the inhabitants are well-placed officials in government and private sectors. The children who grow up in this town may hear nothing about witches or evil spirits or wicked men of charms. Similar communities are growing up around the centers of higher learning especially, polytechnic institutes and universities. For example, Obafemi Awolowo University may be well described as a modern site where people are seldom exposed to the traditional ways of life, except for research purposes.

The growing number of medical centers is another hope of the future. The Yoruba communities have passed through an era called the Abiku plague where children in the womb are switched and replaced by witches or spirits. Such forces have the power to chase out the real natural children and occupy the wombs as *abiku* children. After birth they bring unrest to the family. The children are sickly, very expensive to nurse and frequently die. But they keep returning to the same mothers. With the advent of medical science, it was discovered that most of the children described as *abiku* were killed by diseases. Presently if there are any such children, they are very few in number. Medical science has also shown that so-called inflicted evils can be cured in the hospital. The preventive activities of hospitals and primary health care services are becoming more and more effective.

There is a new factor growing out of the established churches of the Western European missionary tradition. This is the new Pentecostal movement. Educated youths are very much involved in this movement. Apart from the emphasis on spiritual gifts, there is great opposition to what they describe as satanic forces. They are opposed to all forms of secret societies, moral laxity and the use of black magic. The emphasis is on the reality of Christ's miracles as a way to overcome such satanic forces. Coupled with these beliefs is a vigorous evangelistic movement, not only in the city communities but also in the village communities. They go about denouncing all forms of evil in traditional society.

For the last three decades there have been strong voices calling for the revival of African religions and cultures. For instance in February 1977 a Festival of Arts and Culture was held in Nigeria to highlight the contributions of the black race to world development. This was internalized in many African societies especially among the Yoruba people.[25] The Orisa traditional movement has become an international movement. The main objective is to revive the Yoruba traditional religions and cultures with a view to replanting them among blacks in the diaspora. Will these movements actively supporting traditional heritage result in a more sophisticated amalgam of the past and present? Whatever is done will not only determine the nature of survival from the evil forces surrounding the Yorubas, but it will also determine the rate of development in Yorubaland in particular and in Africa in general.

NOTES

1. I.A. Akinjogbin, *Dahomey and Its Neighbours*, 1708-1818 (London: Cambridge University Press, 1967), p. 9.
2. Chief Olumuyide Ogunyemi-Falua, is a traditional healer from Osi-Ekiti, the Apena of the Ogboni cult, and he is the Chairman, Research Network on traditional medicine based in the Faculty of Pharmacy at Obafemi Awolowo University, Ile-Ife, interviewed March 15, 1994.
3. Incantation is magical language making references to the origin of related things and ending with a command.
4. E. Bolaji Idowu, *Olodumare: God in Yoruba Belief* (London: Longman, 1962), pp. 83f.
5. *Ibid.*, p. 83.
6. Wande Abimbola, *Ifa: An Exposition of Ifa Literary Corpus* (Ibadan, Nigeria: Oxford University Press, 1976), pp. 151f.
7. *Op. cit.*, B. Idowu, p. 91.
8. Modupe Oduyoye, "The Spider, The Chameleon, and the Creation of the Earth," in *Traditional Religion in West Africa*, ed. E.A. Adegbola (Ibadan: Daystar Press, 1983), p. 381.
9. James Johnson, "Civil Leadership: Confrontations with the Ogboni, 1892," in *Traditional Religion in West Africa*, ed. E.A. Adegbola (Ibadan: Daystar Press, 1983), p. 104.
10. Unfortunately Aladokun, the magician, was slain by one of the mad men he was trying to heal.
11. *Op. cit.*, Bolaji Idowu, pp. 146f. Also see p. 198.
12. *Ibid.*, p. 198, in the original language.
13. Wande Abimbola, *Sixteen Great Poems of Ifa* (Zaria: UNESCO and Abimbola Pub., Gaskiya Corporation, 1975), pp. 292, 309.
14. J. Akin Omoyajowo, "What Is Witch-Craft," in *Traditional Religion in West Africa*, Ed. E.A. Adegbola (Ibadan: Daystar Press, 1983), pp. 317-318.
15. *Op. cit.*, Bolaji Idowu, p. 173.
16. *Op. cit.*, Wande Abimbola (*Corpus*), p. 113.
17. J.A. Ayorinde, in *Religion and Ethics in Nigeria*, Ed. S.O. Abogunrin (Ibadan: Daystar Press, 1986), p. 17.
18. R.J. Gehman, *African Traditional Religion in Biblical Perspective* (Kijabe, Kenya: Kesho Pubs., 1987), p. 75. For the activities of the Bamucapi of Malawi (1934) and the Atinga of West Africa (1957). *Op. cit.*, Omoyajowo, pp. 323-324.
19. J. Omosade Awolalu, *Yoruba Beliefs and Sacrificial Rites* (London: 1979), pp. 134f.

20. *Ibid.*
21. *Ibid.*, pp. 138-141.
22. Emefie Ikenga-Metuh, *African Religions in Western Conceptual Schemes: The Problem of Interpretation* (Bodija, Ibadan: Pastoral Institute Pub., 1985), p. 68.
23. J.K. Olupona, *Kingship, Religion, and Rituals in a Nigerian Community: A Phenomenological Study of Ondo Yoruba Festivals* (Stockholm, Sweden: Almqvist & Wiksel International, 1991), pp. 21, p. 4, 9, 43.
24. J.O. Ajibola, *Owe Yoruba* (Yoruba Proverbs) (Ibadan, Nigeria: Oxford University Press, 1976 ed.), pp. 1, 3.
25. Colin Legum (ed.), *African Contemporary Record, Annual Survey and Documents*, Vol. 9, 1976-1977 (London: Rex Collins, 1977), pp. B 676 - B 577.

14

Gods Versus Anti-Gods:
Conflict and Resolution in the Yoruba Cosmos

By Wande Abimbola

T he Yoruba are a West African people who live in Nigeria, where they are about 20 million people, Benin Republic and Togo, with some villages in Ghana. The Atlantic slave trade brought thousands of Yoruba-speaking people to Brazil, Cuba and other Caribbean islands from where a second wave of migration of Yoruba descendants went to the United States. Today millions of people are to be found in the Americas who are direct descendants of the original Yoruba slaves or who have embraced Yoruba religion in the form of Santeria, Candomble, Umbanda or Macumba. Haitian Vodum also has a very strong Yoruba literary, iconographic, ritual and philosophical base.

The aim here is to examine the Yoruba concept of evil and its inevitable conflict with the idea of good, and how the Yoruba have been able to maintain a balance or resolution through a symbolic system of codes of communication with their elaborate and elastic pantheon of supernatural powers. I will rely on the Ifa literary corpus which is by far the most important of the hundreds of sacred oral texts of the Yoruba, some of which have already gone into oblivion.[1] A study of the sacred texts of any religion, whether oral or written, is the primary way to understand the theology of a religion rather than the modern preoccupation of scholars of religion and anthropology with interviews of people. Interviews should come at a secondary level mainly to throw more light on the texts or to elucidate or explicate already collected data.

The Yoruba pantheon consists of six hundred and one supernatural powers, not four hundred as we often read in books. Ifa literature divides them into two categories: "Four hundred supernatural powers of the right; and two hundred original supernatural powers of the left."[2] The four hundred supernatural powers of the right are the *Orisa* who are sometimes said to be four hundred and one. The present writer is now of the view that the one on top of the four hundred does not refer to any particular divinity as such but rather to the principle of elasticity embedded in the pantheon.

According to the words of Ifa quoted above, the universe is divided into two halves, left and right. On the left of the universe is to be found the two hundred supernatural powers otherwise known as *Ajogun* (warriors), and on the right side are the four hundred supernatural powers known as *Orisa*. The *Ajogun* represent the principle of evil since they are completely malevolent without any redeeming features whatsoever. We employ a Portuguese term at this point and call them *deus de mal*. The four hundred and one supernatural powers are the *Orisa* or divinities. They are by nature benevolent even though they may fight a human being who sins against, prevents or corrupts the ethics, norms or taboos of society. They usually have no protection for any human being who does not offer sacrifice. We use the opposite Portuguese term *deus de ben* to describe these essentially benevolent supernatural powers.

There is, however, one particular supernatural power who straddles the right and the left of our universe. He is *Esu* who is an *Orisa* but who is also the lord and master of the *Ajogun*. A line from an Ifa verse puts the matter as follows: "Death, Disease, Loss, Paralysis, Big Trouble, Curse, Imprisonment, Affliction, They are all errand boys of *Esu*."

A simple sketch of this divided world of the Yoruba can be made, showing where each supernatural power functions. In this sketch is Olodumare, the Yoruba High God, who has no cult of his own among humans. He also has no temples or shrines. Sacrifices are never made to him. Consequently, he has no liturgy, iconography, or priesthood. He is the supreme example of an abstract divinity too

mighty to be captured by any artistic, literary, or idealistic simpli-
fication. Yet he is believed to be the creator of the universe. He
created the *Ajogun* and the *Orisa* with the possible exception of *Esu*
(the trickster) and *Ifa* who are believed to co-exist with him.

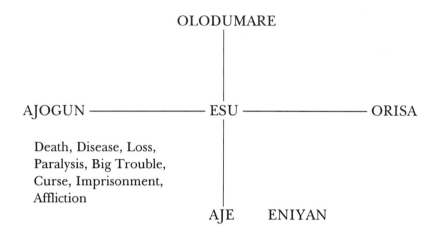

In the sketch above, the *Orisa* (*deus de ben*) are on the right side of
the universe. They are, as mentioned before, 400 plus one in number. They are benevolent to humans, and one can pray to them, and
what is more important, offer sacrifices to them in order to achieve
one's desires, such as money, a wife or husband, children, good
health, long life, employment, and protection from one's enemies.
When one offers a sacrifice to any *Orisa*, the sacrifice will be communicated by ones *Ori* (spiritual or inner head) to the *Orisa* in the
spiritual realm. The sacrifice will eventually be presented to *Esu* who
will in turn communicate one's wishes to *Olodumare* so that one's
prayers or desires may be accepted or come to pass.

In the case of a negative force generated by one of the evil supernatural powers, *Esu* will present the sacrifice to the *Ajogun* responsible for the affliction or evil concerned. As soon as the sacrifice is
accepted by the *Ajogun*, he (the *Ajogun* concerned) will leave the
victim alone or let the person off the hook. A balance or reparation
will then be restored in the life of the individual, family, or community concerned. The important point to remember is that the
individual must first of all perform sacrifice, otherwise *Esu* cannot
perform his mediating role. This is the import of the statement often

found in Ifa verse: "It is the person who performs sacrifice who receives the support of *Esu*."

The *Eniyan* indicated at the bottom of the right side of the diagram are the human beings of any social or economic class. They too harbor a germ of divinity in that each human being has a spiritual aspect known as *Ori* who is also regarded by the Yoruba as an *Orisa*. The communication process of a human being with the spiritual world starts with his own *Ori*. Anything which has not been accepted by a person's *Ori* cannot be approved by the *Orisa*. An Ifa verse puts this clearly as follows:

> *Ori* we salute you
> Who quickly remembers your own.
> You who blesses a person more quickly than the *Orisa*.
> There is no *Orisa* who by himself blesses a man
> Without the consent of his *Ori*.
> *Ori* we salute you.
> You who allow children to be born alive.
> A person whose sacrifice is accepted by *Ori*
> Should rejoice exceedingly.[3]

The *Aje,* who are sometimes known as *Eniyan* (negative people), play an important part in the Yoruba cosmos. Like witches in other cultures, they suck human blood, eat human flesh, and afflict human beings with diseases like impotence, stomach disorders, blood and liver diseases. They are therefore allies of the *Ajogun* in this respect. Their important messenger is a bird known as *ehuru*. They often take the form of this bird especially at night when they hold their nocturnal conferences and plan their attacks on human society. That is why they are known as *eleye* (owner of birds).

There are certain peculiarities about the *Aje* which we should briefly point out. In the first place, the *Aje* are believed to be women. In Yoruba thought only women can be *Aje*. A man, however negative or evil cannot be an *Aje*. Secondly, an evil force afflicting a human being and which is diagnosed as emanating from the *Aje* cannot be resolved by the offering of a normal sacrifice. Only a special type of sacrifice can partially affect the *Aje*. Moreover, only a human being's *Ori* can ultimately save that person from an attack emanating from the *Aje*. Hence, the following Ifa verse:

Travellers on the road to *Ipo*,
Travellers on the road to Ofa,
Only your *Ori* (spiritual heads)
Can save you from the *Eleye*.

Thirdly, the *Aje* are sometimes benevolent, and that is why they are regarded as humans in spite of their negative aspect. They can bless a human being by making the individual rich or successful in life. They therefore straddle both the left and the right side of the universe.

The left side of the universe is the abode of the *Ajogun*, the evil supernatural powers. As mentioned above, the *Ajogun* are negators of the *Orisa*. They are completely evil without any redeeming features. There are two hundred *Ajogun* and their eight principal war lords are those listed in the diagram above. They attack human beings and the *Orisa* without any reasonable cause, but sometimes the *Orisa* themselves are the aggressors.

A good number of Ifa verses deal with the idea of conflict and resolution in the Yoruba cosmos. Ifa *Elepe* (the King of *Epe*) was asked to perform sacrifice with an animal in order to ward off an impending attack of *Iku* (Death) and other evil supernatural powers. *Elepe* performed sacrifice and as a result he was able to exchange the animal for his own life. This verse tells us that sacrifice is an act of exchange. When one makes sacrifice, one exchanges something dear, or something purchased with one's own money, in order to sustain personal happiness. Sacrifice involves human beings in a process of exchange or denial of oneself, or giving of one's time, forsaking one's pleasure, food, etc., in order to be at peace with both the benevolent and malevolent supernatural powers as well as to be at peace with one's neighbors, family, the entire environment and ultimately to be at peace with oneself.

Sacrifice is the principle of resolution of a would-be conflict, or cessation of a conflict which has already begun, therefore leading to a restoration of peace and reparation of whatever damage, real or imaginary, has already occurred. Below is the Yoruba version of the Ifa verse which is taken from *Osa Meji*, the tenth *Odu* of Ifa, and an attempt in English of a very difficult verse:

The old man who strolls gracefully like an elephant.
The old man who gallops like a buffalo.
When a wooden pestle falls on the ground,
    it makes the sound *ogbonrangandan*.
Help me catch my chicken with broken wings.
One room cannot adequately contain two sick people
    with different diseases.
Exchange-exchange, Ifa priest of the household of the
    king of *Epe*.
Ifa divination was performed for *Elepe*
When he was told to use an animal for sacrifice
As an exchange for his own life
Because of imminent death.
He listened to the prescription of sacrifice.
And he performed the sacrifice.
He was told to offer sacrifice to *Esu*
And he complied.
He then heard the Ifa priests tell him that his
    sacrifice was accepted.
He praised his Ifa priests,
And his Ifa priests praised Ifa.
Death then left *Elepe* untouched
But took away the head of the animal.
Exchange-exchange, Ifa priest of the household of *Elepe*.
Loss left *Elepe* untouched,
But took away the head of the animal.
Exchange-exchange, Ifa priest of the household of *Elepe*.
All evil spirits left *Elepe* untouched
But took away the head of the animal.
Exchange-exchange, Ifa priest of the household of *Elepe*.

In the following verse, *Olomo* (the mountain) was besieged by all
the *Ajogun*. *Olomo* was told by his Ifa priests to perform sacrifice with
yam-flour. After he had performed the sacrifice, *Esu*, the trickster
divinity, went ahead of the *Ajogun* to the front of *Olomo's* house.
Whenever the *Ajogun* tried to enter the house, *Esu* poured yam-flour
into their mouths knowing that it was forbidden for the *Ajogun* to
taste yam-flour. When they tasted yam-flour, some of the *Ajogun* died
and some of them were sick. As a result they could no longer affect
Olomo. He then started to sing in praise of his Ifa priests saying:

Death who boasted that he would kill the Ifa priest
Can no longer kill him.
Death has shifted away from the head of Ifa priest
Death does not eat yam-flour.
If Death attempts to eat yam-flour,
His mouth would be terribly shaken.
His mouth would be tightly compressed.

The full excerpt in translation which is taken from *Oyeku Meji*, the second *Odu* of Ifa, follows:

The Ifa priest known as *Atata tun-in tan-in*
Performed Ifa divination for *Olomo*, the mighty one.
All the *Ajogun* surrounded *Olomo*
In order to kill him.
He was told to perform sacrifice.
And he performed it.
It happened one day,
Death, Disease and Loss stood up,
And went to attack the house of *Olomo*.
They met *Esu* outside the house.
As they were trying to enter the house
Esu poured yam-flour into their mouths.
Since the *Ajogun* must not taste yam-flour,
Some of them died, and some became sick.
But none was able to enter the house of *Olomo*.
When *Olomo* became happy,
He started to chant the song of Ifa priests.
He said, "Death who boasted that he would kill Ifa priest
Can no longer kill him.
Death has shifted away from the head of Ifa priest.
Death does not eat yam-flour.
If Death attempts to eat yam-flour,
His mouth would be terribly shaken.
His mouth would be tightly compressed.
All the evil spirits who wanted to attack Ifa priest
Can no longer attack him.
Death does not eat yam-flour.
If death attempts to eat yam-flour,
His mouth would be terribly shaken.
His mouth would be tightly compressed."

In the following translated excerpt from *Obara Meji*, the seventh *Odu* of Ifa, *Agbigboniwonran*, a bird believed to be a messenger of the *Ajogun* and who is believed to be a carver of coffins because of the tuft of hair on his head, carried his coffin to the front of *Orunmila's* house. Since *Orunmila* had performed sacrifice, *Agbigbo* met *Esu* in front of the house. *Esu* asked *Agbigbo* the evil messenger of Death what he would take so that the life of *Orunmila* might be spared. *Agbigbo* said he would take a rat, a bird and an animal. *Esu* replied that all those things were included in *Orunmila's* sacrifice. *Esu* then brought those things out for *Agbigbo*, who gathered the materials hurriedly, lifted up his coffin, and went to another place.

> Water inside a spring cannot completely immerse
>   a water gourd.
> Ifa divination was performed for *Agbigboniwonran*,
> The carver of coffins.
> After *Agbigbo* had finished carving a coffin,
> He would go and place it outside a man's house.
> The result would be that that man would die.
> When *Agbigbo* finished carving a coffin,
> He carried it,
> And went to *Orunmila's* house.
> That night, *Orunmila* dreamt of death.
> He took his divination instruments,
> And inquired about his dream.
> Ifa warned *Orunmila* to perform sacrifice immediately.
> After he performed the sacrifice,
> He carried the sacrifice to the shrine of *Esu*.
> Before long, *Agbigbo* arrived in *Orunmila's* house
>   with his coffin.
> And he met *Esu* outside the house.
> *Esu* asked him what he intended to put inside
>   the coffin.
> And *Agbigbo* replied that *Orunmila* was the one.
> Then *Esu* inquired further from him
> What things he would like to have
> So that he would leave *Orunmila* untouched.
> He said that he would take a rat, a bird, and an animal.
> *Esu* replied that all those things
> Had been included in *Orunmila's* sacrifice.
> *Esu* then brought those things out for *Agbigbo*,

Who gathered the materials hurriedly,
Lifted up his coffin,
And went to another place.
When he was out of sight,
Esu issued a command that he should never be able to
    remove the coffin from his head.
Up till this day,
The coffin is still on *Agbigbo's* head.

Sometimes the *Orisa* themselves were the aggressors, attacking the *Ajogun*, their avowed enemies. Provided sacrifice was offered and accepted by *Esu* before the attack, the *Orisa* concerned would be victorious. In the following translation taken from *Ogunda Meji*, the ninth *Odu* of Ifa, *Orunmila* was frightened on his farm by an unknown thing. He therefore returned home to cast Ifa. His Ifa priests gave him three arrows to shoot about on his farm. One of the arrows hit Death on the chest, and he temporarily died or disappeared from the earth.

The Ifa priests known as *Pomu-pomu-sigi-sigi-sigi-pomu-pomu*,
Performed divination for *Orunmila*
When he shot an arrow and killed Death on his farm.
Something frightened *Orunmila* on his farm
He therefore returned home,
And inquired about it from his Ifa priests.
He was told to perform sacrifice,
And he performed it.
After he had performed sacrifice,
His Ifa priests gave him three arrows,
And asked him to shoot them all about his farm.
When one of the arrows was shot,
It hit Death.
It hit Death on the chest.
Death fell down with a loud noise,
And he temporarily went out of the earth.
It was from the farm that *Orunmila* danced homewards.
He said that was exactly what his Ifa priests predicted.
Oloniimoro shot an arrow
And killed Death on his farm
We praise *Pomu-pomu-sigi-sigi-sigi-pomu-pomu*.

The forgoing excerpts from verses of Ifa, the sacred literature of the Yoruba, present us with a clear picture of the nature of the conflict and resolution in the Yoruba cosmos. In the Yoruba belief system, conflict rather than peace is the order of the day. Resolution can only be achieved through the offering of sacrifice via the intervention of *Esu* who is at the same time an *Orisa* and a master of the *Ajogun*. But we must always remember that resolution is temporary. It is not unlike conflict, a permanent feature of the universe. Hence the need for constant divination leading always to the performance of sacrifice.

We, therefore, have a God and anti-god as a permanent feature of the world in which we live, leading to conflict between the forces of good and the forces of evil. It seems that to sustain the concept of God (or gods), there must always be an anti-God (or anti-gods). So, when humans created the idea of God, they also at the same time created its negator. God is responsible for the good while the anti-god is responsible for the evil. The one can hardly exist without the other. A well ordered universe or value system must have a sufficient trace of both ideas. The issue, therefore, is not whether evil is real but whether or not human beings in their thought systems, religions and societies can always resolve the inevitable conflict between good and evil. Such resolution alone can lead to peace, understanding, harmony, progress, community and civilization in the ideal and real world that human beings as individuals and societies have created and will always create for themselves.

NOTES

1. See Wande Abimbola, *Ifa: An Exposition of Ifa Literary Corpus* (Ibadan, Nigeria: Oxford University Press, 1976).·

2. The original language of this translation and others in this article, along with the long verses, can be found in this author's, "Gods Versus Anti-Gods: Conflict and Resolution in the Yoruba Cosmos," *Dialogue & Alliance*, Vol. 8, n. 2 (1994), pp. 75-87.

3. See Wande Abimbola, *Sixteen Great Poems of Ifa* (Zaria: UNESCO and Abimbola Publishers, 1975).

PART FOUR

Contemporary Responses

15

Prophecy and Contemplation:
The Language of Liberation Theology Against Evil

By Peter C. Phan

I f God is able but unwilling to prevent evil, God is malevolent; on the other hand, if God is willing but unable to do so, God is weak. In either case, God is not God. But if God is both omnipotent and benevolent, as believers say, whence is evil? Ever since Epicurus (341-270 B.C.) argued that it is not possible to uphold God's power and goodness simultaneously in the face of evil, an argument repeated by David Hume in the eighteenth century, philosophers and theologians have been busy devising a theodicy to defend both divine goodness and power.[1]

In general terms, this theodicy has taken three basic forms. The first explains evil in terms of its causes, either positing two independent principles of being, one good and the other evil, each responsible for the good and evil realities in the universe[2] or affirming only one creative being (the good God) and maintaining that evil is not being but a lack of being.[3] The second form explains evil in terms of the purposes it may serve such as character formation and spiritual development of the human person.[4] The third form redefines the notion of divine omnipotence in order to avoid

Epicurus's dilemma. Process theologians suggest that divine power is one of persuasion and attraction, not of coercion. God does not create the world *ex nihilo*; rather, God creates it out of pre-existent actualities, luring them into greater self-realizations. Evil, both physical and moral, is an unavoidable price for this process of self-actualization in response to the divine lure. We are assured that evil is ultimately not absurd because God, who is, in Whitehead's memorable words, "the fellow sufferer who understands," suffers along with us.[5]

These three strands of theodicy have been subjected to stringent criticism and have all been found wanting in one aspect or another.[6] Perhaps this is to be expected, since evil seems to be a surd defying rational explanation. In despair of ever finding a satisfactory account of the origin of evil, some suggest that instead of trying to understand evil, one should develop mechanisms to cope with it.[7] Others argue that evil is neither a problem susceptible of rational explanation nor simply a disaster to be coped with on an individual basis; rather it is something that must be faced and overcome collectively. Still others contend that theodicy as a discourse practice must be abandoned because it does not solve the problem of evil and itself creates evil.[8]

The intention of this essay is to examine how Latin American liberation theology approaches the problem of evil.[9] I will focus on Gustavo Gutierrez, both because he is widely regarded as the progenitor of liberation theology and because he has explicitly dealt with the problem of evil. I will first examine how liberation theology understands the nature of evil. Secondly, I will look at the strategies it proposes to speak of God in the midst of evil. Finally, I will attempt an assessment of the approach of liberation theology to the problem of evil as a whole.[10]

Evil as Poverty and Oppression

One searches in vain for a treatise in liberation theology which deals with the problem of evil in the terms framed by Epicurus and David Hume. Though fully conversant with the classical responses to these skeptics (e.g., the distinction between physical and moral evils, between God's causing and permitting evil), liberation theologians do not make use of them. The reason for this is that for liberation theologians these arguments were devised for an entirely different audience than the one they speak for and to. Traditional theodicy addresses nonbelievers; liberation theology addresses non-persons. Gutierrez points out the difference:

> Ever since the Enlightenment a large sector of modern theology has taken as its point of departure the challenge launched by the modern (often unbelieving) mind. . . . But in Latin America the challenge does not come first and foremost from nonbelievers but from non-persons—that is, those whom the prevailing social order does not acknowledge as persons: the poor, the exploited, those systematically and lawfully stripped of their human status, those who hardly know what a human being is. Nonpersons represent a challenge, not primarily to our religious world but to our economic, social, political, and cultural world; their existence is a call to a revolutionary transformation of the very foundations of our dehumanizing society.[11]

To put it differently, whereas traditional theodicy attempts to overcome the crisis of meaning produced by the first phase of the Enlightenment (Kant) by explaining and defending the orthodoxy of Christian belief in God's omnipotence and goodness, liberation theology, as Jon Sobrino has argued, takes up the challenge of the second phase of the Enlightenment (Marx) by transforming the sinful situation of exploitation and oppression and by emphasizing orthopraxis. This new task requires what Sobrino calls an epistemological break in theology, that is, instead of constructing a natural theology in which the God-question begins from what is positive in the world (by way of analogy), liberation theology answers the question of theodicy by starting from what is negative (by way of dialectic): How is the existence of God to be reconciled with the real wretchedness and evil in the world?

This different situation of Latin America effects a new approach to the problem of evil. Rather than using philosophical analysis to grasp the nature of evil, liberation theology, whose interest is sociopolitical and economic transformation, makes use of the social sciences to decipher its historical roots.[12] In liberation theology's social analysis, evil is seen not as the ontological *privatio boni*, or part of a good whole, or a necessary stage in the evolutionary process, or a penalty for sin. Rather it is regarded as the result of inhuman social structures. Evil is primarily the twin phenomena of poverty and oppression. Poverty is neither vice or ignorance to be remedied by alms-giving (the empirical explanation) nor backwardness to be reformed by means of economic development (the functional explanation). Rather it is the fruit of oppression, that is, the actual economic organization of society which exploits some (workers) and excludes others (the underemployed, the unemployed, and the whole mass of the marginalized) from the system of production (the dialectical explanation). This kind of poverty is rooted in the primacy of capital over labor and can be transformed only by an alternative social and economic system.

In this way liberation theology has redefined the notion of evil. First, the distinction between physical and moral evil, essential for traditional theodicy, is no longer operative. More precisely, there has been a shift in focus from moral to physical evil. The former is subsumed under the latter to which, however, a moral quality is attached. Indeed, for Augustine, Thomas Aquinas, C.S. Lewis, and John Hick, most of the world's evil is brought about by the sins (moral evils) of human beings themselves, and physical or natural evils (e.g., poverty, squalor, malnutrition, diseases, death, and ecological disasters) are acts of God for which humans are not directly responsible (except as punishment for their sins). On the contrary, for liberation theology, evil is primarily what is traditionally regarded as physical evil, that is, oppressive and exploitative structures. While not neglecting the personal dimension of sin, since "behind an unjust structure there is a responsible individual or collective will, a will to reject God and others,"[13] liberation theology emphasizes what has been called social sin or structural sin. It is evil as embodied in institutions, whether secular or ecclesiastical, in legal structures, in sociopolitical and economic systems that perpetrate what has been referred to as "institutionalized injustice."[14]

Secondly, physical evil is cast primarily in terms of suffering, especially when caused by poverty and oppression. Poverty becomes the comprehensive category for interpreting evil in general:

> Poverty means death. Death, in this case, is caused by hunger, sickness, or the oppressive methods used by those who see their privileges endangered by any and every effort to free the oppressed. It is physical death to which cultural death is added, because in a situation of oppression everything is destroyed that gives unity and strength to the dispossessed of this world.[15]

The emphasis on the socioeconomic aspect of oppression is, however, not exclusive. Other forms of oppression are also taken into account, such as those based on racial, ethnic, and gender discrimination. Nevertheless, socioeconomic oppression, which produces social classes and class conflicts, is, in liberation theologians' view, the more radical, infrastructural form of oppression of which the other forms are but superstructural expressions.

Having underscored the importance of unjust structures in liberation theology's understanding of evil, I find it imperative to point out at this point, lest we distort liberation theology entirely, that unjust structures are but one of three forms of evil. The other two are the power of fate and personal sin and guilt. By the power of fate is meant the sense that one's station in life is foreordained and that one should accept it as God's will. Under this power, oppressed people fail to see that the world they live in should not be the way it is and therefore must be changed. Liberation from poverty presupposes liberation from this fatalism. With the destruction of the evil of sin and guilt, liberation theology emphasizes the gratuitousness of grace and of God's kingdom, which no human work can ever produce but for which humans must prepare the way.[16] There is no contradiction between liberation from unjust structures and forgiveness of sin because acceptance of the gift of God's kingdom calls for a certain behavior, namely, commitment to work for other human beings, especially the poorest and most helpless.

The third way in which liberation theology recasts the problem of evil is to frame it in terms of innocent suffering. It is not evil as deserved suffering (the evil of guilt) that liberation is concerned with; rather it considers the challenge of what Gutierrez, following Adolphe Gesche, calls the evil of misfortune, that is, the evil suffered by the innocent. The prototype of the innocent sufferer is, in Gutierrez's judgment, Job, who refuses to curse God even in the depths of his suffering and who stubbornly maintains his innocence against the accusations of his friends. It is innocent suffering that poses the question of how to talk about God: "[T]he suffering of the innocent and the questions it leads them to ask are indeed key problems for theology—that is, for discourse about God. The theology of liberation tries to meet the challenge."[17]

Speaking to God in the Midst of Suffering

The problem of how to speak of God to nonpersons (not un-
believers) has been sharply formulated by Gutierrez:

> How are we to talk about a God who is revealed as love in a situation
> characterized by poverty and oppression? How are we to proclaim
> the God of life to men and women who die prematurely and un-
> justly? How are we to acknowledge that God makes us a free gift of
> love and justice when we have before us the suffering of the
> innocent? What words are we to use in telling those who are not
> even regarded as persons that they are daughters and sons of God?[18]

Speaking about God or God-talk in liberation theology is never just
verbal, whether oral or written. Antecedent and intrinsic to such talk
is an effective commitment to and solidarity with those who suffer
from poverty and oppression. Such a praxis for liberation, as has
been said above, is an essential component of theological method. As
Gutierrez repeatedly remarks, theology is only the second act which
reflects critically on praxis: "The Christian community professes a
'faith which works through charity.' It is—at least ought to be—real
charity, action, and commitment to the service of others. Theology
is reflection, a critical attitude. Theology *follows*; it is the second
step."[19]

With such a prior solidarity with the poor and the oppressed,
how does one proceed to speak of God in the midst of innocent
suffering? Gutierrez's answer to this question takes the form of a
commentary on the book of Job. It is not, strictly speaking, an
exegesis of the book of the Hebrew Bible, though the author's
knowledge of relevant biblical literature is extensive. Rather, it is a
theological interpretation in the context of massive innocent suffering in Latin America because "the innocence that Job vigorously
claims for himself helps us to understand the innocence of an
oppressed and believing people amid the situation of suffering and
death that has been forced upon it."[20]

Gutierrez suggests that the fundamental thrust of the book of Job
is to raise a wager: Can human beings have a disinterested faith in
God? Can they, in the midst of unjust suffering, continue to
maintain their faith in God and speak of God without looking for
rewards? Clearly Satan and those who have a barter conception of

religion deny that they are capable of doing so, whereas the biblical author affirms that they are and uses the experience of his hero to make his point. It would be instructive therefore to follow the story of Job and gather from his reactions to suffering hints on how to speak about God.

It is interesting to note that in the book of Job the wager is not between the existence or nonexistence of God, as is in Pascal's famous wager, but "between a religion based on the rights and obligations of human beings as moral agents, and a disinterested belief based on the gratuitousness of God's love."[21] In other words, whereas Pascal's wager is made to unbelievers, the book of Job's is made to non-persons, and is therefore appropriate to the suffering innocent.

One kind of God-talk that is excluded by Job is that based on the doctrine of retribution as expounded with conviction and vigor by his three friends, Eliphaz, Bildad, and Zophar. The core of this doctrine is that God punishes the wicked and rewards the upright. At the theoretical level, Job accepts the logic of this doctrine, but at the existential level, he knows that there must be something amiss with it, because he is deeply convinced of his innocence. Gutierrez carefully points out that in his resolute defense of his innocence, he does not make the mistake of considering himself sinless: "The question for Job is not whether or not he is a sinner; he knows well that as a human being he is indeed a sinner. The question rather is whether he deserves the torments he is suffering. His answer is unambiguous: no, he does not deserve them."[22]

Job's ambivalence toward the doctrine of retribution, Gutierrez suggests, is to be attributed to two different ways of doing theology. One starts from abstract principles, in this case God's justice, and applies them to concrete cases, in this case, Job's suffering. The other begins with concrete experiences, especially that of innocent suffering: "Over against the abstract theology of his friends he [Job] sets his own experience (and, as we shall see later on, the experience of others, especially the poor). On the basis of this experience, and motivated by the faith he has received from his forebears, he is trying to understand the action of God."[23] He rejects his friends' way of theologizing which does not take account of concrete situations, of the sufferings and hopes of human beings and forgets the gratuitous love and unbounded mercy of God. Gutierrez puts it tersely: "The friends believe in their theology rather than in the God of their theology."[24] Job knows that he is innocent and that his suffering is undeserved, but he refuses to follow the facile logic of his sorry comforters that says that his protestations of innocence would convict God of injustice. Instead of speaking ill of the God in whom he believes, he challenges the foundation of the prevailing theology. So the question remains: How should one speak of God in the midst of innocent suffering?

The Language of Prophecy

The answer to this question Gutierrez finds in Job's gradual shift from an individualist ethics to a social one: Job begins to see his suffering in relationship to other sufferers, especially the poor. As a result he realizes that relatedness to God implies relatedness to the poor:

> The question he asks of God ceases to be a purely personal one and takes concrete form in the suffering of the poor in this world. The answer he seeks will not come except through commitment to them and by following the road—which God alone knows—that leads to wisdom. Job begins to free himself from an ethic centered on personal rewards and to pass to another focused on the needs of one's neighbors.[25]

This speaking of God in the midst of innocent suffering by commitment to the poor and by doing justice Gutierrez calls the language of prophecy. In this language Job realizes that he is not the only one who suffers innocently and that "poverty and abandonment are not something fated but are caused by the wicked, who nonetheless live serene and satisfied lives."[26] In chapter 24:2-14, poverty is described not as the result of destiny or God's punishment but of the exploitation and oppression of the poor by the wicked. This realization forces Job to examine his past conduct and he affirms that he has always practiced justice and compassion: attention to the needs of the poor, guidance for the orphan, food for the hungry, counsel for the afflicted, clothing and shelter for the destitute, justice for the innocent (31:16-22).

At this point, the biblical author introduces a young man by the name of Elihu who delivers a speech in which, according to

Gutierrez, two major points are made: first, God is great and the human mind can never comprehend him; God can manifest himself in unexpected ways, even suffering can be a divine pedagogy by which one is disposed to hear and accept God's word. Secondly, and this is the prophetic language, in God's eyes, all human beings are equal but the poor are God's favorites; God makes no distinction between rich and poor but God favors the most helpless. "This relationship of God and the poor is the very heart of the prophetic message. The Lord is ever watchful and ready to hear the voice of the poor, even though attentiveness to them may at times take unobtrusive forms."[27]

The language about God in the midst of innocent suffering then must be a prophetic one. It is a language of both denunciation and annunciation. It denounces, by deed and word (in that order), every dehumanizing situation and every form of oppression. And it announces that God wants justice and favors the poor and the oppressed.[28] The prophetic language preserves the ethical dimension of the traditional doctrine of retribution, but places it in a new and different context, namely, that of solidarity with the poor. However, prophetic language is only the first step. It is necessary but still inadequate: "Job's thirst for understanding, which his trials have awakened and inflamed, is not satisfied. Gropingly, and resisting false images, he looks insatiably for a deeper insight into divine justice and an unlimited encounter with the God in whom he believes and hopes."[29]

The Language of Contemplation

Gutierrez notes that Job's theologian friends speak about God but not to God. Job feels the need to speak to God himself. His full encounter with God is a real spiritual struggle with God. Gutierrez summarizes Job's dramatic inner development as a three-stage movement:

From a nebulous request for the presence of an *arbiter* he has advanced to the need of a *witness* and thence finally to an expression of confidence in a *liberator* who will come to rescue him. Each affirmation of hope is immediately preceded by a renewed expression of angry complaint and protest. The spiritual struggle with himself, with his friends, and, above all, with God brings him to a conviction that for the time being amounts to no more than a cry of hope: that he will see, and with his own eyes, his liberator, his *go'el*, and be able to look upon him as a friend.[30]

When, finally, God comes face to face with Job and answers him "from the heart of the tempest," speaking of his plan and just government of the world, what does Job learn from the encounter? Gutierrez suggests the following. First, God's absolute freedom: "God will bring him to see that nothing, not even the world of justice, can shackle God."[31] This means that even if God has a plan, it is not one that the human mind can grasp so as to make calculations based on it and foresee and judge the divine action. God's freedom finds expression in the gratuitousness of divine love that refuses to be confined within a system of predictable rewards and punishments.

Secondly, human freedom: though human beings are insignificant and not the center of the universe, they are free. Their freedom is respected by God, and therefore the wicked cannot simply be destroyed with a glance:

> God wants justice indeed, and desires that divine judgment (*mishpat*) reign in the world; but God cannot impose it, for the nature of created beings must be respected. God's power is limited by human freedom; for without freedom God's justice would not be present within history. . . .The mystery of divine freedom leads to the mystery of human freedom and to respect for it.[32]

Thirdly, and most importantly, the true relationship between divine justice and divine gratuitousness:

> What is it that Job has understood? That justice does not reign in the world God has created? No. The truth that he has grasped and that has lifted him to the level of contemplation is that justice alone does not have the final say about how we are to speak of God. Only when we have come to realize that God's love is freely bestowed do we enter fully and definitively into the presence of the God of faith. Grace is not opposed to the quest of justice nor does it play it down; on the contrary, it gives it its full meaning. God's love, like all true love, operates in a world not of cause and effect but of freedom and gratuitousness.[33]

It is important to note that for Gutierrez the language of contemplation, in which God's freedom and gratuitousness is discovered, does not in any way diminish the language of prophecy. Rather it situates divine justice within the framework of divine gratuitous love, and in this way makes it possible to affirm God's predilection for the poor. The preference for the poor, now Job understands, is a key factor in authentic divine justice. Job's rejection of the theology of retribution does not free him from the necessity of practicing justice, but only from the temptation of imprisoning God in a narrow conception of justice. Gutierrez tantalizingly concludes: "The world of retribution—and not of temporal retribution only—is not where God dwells; at most God visits it."[34]

How does one speak of God in the midst of innocent suffering? By the language of prophecy and the language of contemplation. Both languages are necessary; they are mutually complementary and must be fused into one. The former is the language of deliverance, the latter the language of song. Mystical language expresses the gratuitousness of God's love; prophetic language expresses the demands this love makes on us.

Prophecy and Contemplation: Adequate Language?

A language is as good as its power to communicate what is intended. To assess liberation theologians' language of prophecy and contemplation fairly one must, of course, take into account their express purpose. It is important to recall here that they do not intend to defend the existence of God or God's attributes of omnipotence and goodness against unbelievers who reject these doctrines on account of evil. Rather they ask how they can talk meaningfully and convincingly about God to believing (in this case, Christian) nonpersons who suffer massive poverty and oppression unjustly. Presumably these people do not need to be convinced that God exists and that God is both good and powerful; they already accept these truths. Their question is not a philosophical one that demands rational arguments, namely, whether God exists and whether God is both powerful and good in the face of evil. Rather, theirs is a spiritual and pragmatic one: Why do we suffer unjustly? What can and should we do about poverty and oppression? And, as far as theologians are concerned, how can they speak of God amidst innocent suffering?

By taking Job as the prototype of the innocent sufferer and by
tracing his painful journey from a self-absorbing obsession with his
own suffering to altruistic actions to redress injustices on behalf of
his fellow innocent sufferers, from self-righteous protestations of his
innocence to a humbling encounter with the mysterious and free
God, from a demand for justice to a recognition of God's gratuitous
love, Gutierrez accomplishes several important things. First, he raises
the consciousness of the poor and oppressed about the innocent
character of their suffering.

Secondly, by insisting on the language of prophecy, he makes it
clear that God-talk amidst unjust suffering has no ring of truth and
no persuasive power unless it is accompanied by concrete deeds of
justice.

Thirdly, by requiring the use of the language of contemplation
Gutierrez prevents the struggle for social justice from being reduced
to being just that—social service. In this way he effectively refutes
the oft-repeated charge that liberation theology is nothing more
than secular or Marxist ideology couched in theological dress.[35]
More importantly, he prevents the language of prophecy from
degenerating into fanaticism and makes gratitude and hope central
virtues for those engaged in the struggle for justice, especially when
the going gets tough and concrete results are slow in coming. In this
way too he makes worship, prayer, and mysticism an integral part
of the struggle for justice.[36]

Finally, by making Job's argumentation against the traditional
theology of retribution a model for theologizing, Gutierrez indirectly
challenges the deductive approach to the problem of evil. Perhaps
this is Gutierrez's most significant contribution to the debate on evil.
What is wrong with most philosophical approaches to the problem
of evil (as illustrated in the Epicurus-Hume line of reasoning) is their
starting point: they begin with abstract principles about God's justice
and goodness on the one hand and evil on the other and then de-
duce their mutual incompatibility. What they fail to take into
account is the concrete ways in which God's justice and goodness are
embodied in history. Had they done so, they would have noticed
that God's justice is realized not in a rigid system of punishment and
reward (the philosophy of Job's theologian comforters) but in God's
preferential—not exclusive—love for the poor and oppressed (Job's
eventual realization). They would also have realized that God's

omnipotence is not arbitrary power but manifests itself in the help-lessness and powerlessness of the poor. This notion of preferential love does not, of course, resolve the problem of evil outright, but at least it makes the apparent contradiction between God's justice and goodness in the face of evil much less acute.

The problem, of course, remains: How do we speak of God to un-believers in the face of evil? Clues can be garnered from Gutierrez's writings on the language of prophecy and contemplation to reveal what liberation theologians think of traditional theodicies.

By appealing to the absolute freedom and mystery of God in his language of contemplation, Gutierrez effectively rules out the kinds of theodicy (e.g., Augustine's) that explain evil as punishment for sins. After all, he is speaking about innocent suffering. He does ac-knowledge that no human being, including Job, can say that he or she is not a sinner. The question, however, is not whether the poor are sinful or not, but whether their suffering is merited. Gutierrez's answer is no, or at least, he says one cannot be certain because God's plan is unfathomable. Those who say that suffering is God's punish-ment must claim that they can grasp God's design in history, a dubious pretension at best. There is another reason for Gutierrez's negative answer to the question of whether the poor's suffering is unmerited, and that is, it is caused by the exploitative and oppres-sive structures imposed by the powerful.

By invoking God's incomprehensible freedom Gutierrez also implicitly questions the time-honored distinction between God's causing and merely permitting evil (e.g., Thomas Aquinas). This dis-tinction, it may be recalled, serves to exonerate God of moral evil and to preserve human freedom.

It seems also that liberation theologians would look askance at what has been called the aesthetic theory of evil, according to which the world as a whole is good; even if its several parts may appear to fallible human minds as evils, in fact they are good either because they are means to good ends or parts of a good whole. Liberation theologians would argue that such a view, espoused by process philosophers among others, does not take seriously the reality of evil which is massive and overwhelming in Latin America.

There is, however, an aspect of process thought which liberation theologians would find congenial, namely, the notion that God's power is not absolute, at least as it is exercised in history. As has been pointed out above, for Gutierrez, God's power is limited by human freedom whose decisions God respects. God's limitation, however, is self-imposed because he freely and gratuitously creates human freedom.

Finally, liberation theology would not be averse to the theory that evil is the absence of a due good (Augustine's *privatio boni*). For them, the situation of poverty and oppression is something that ought not to be and ought to be changed. The theory of *privatio boni*, if understood not negatively but as a positive reminder of something that ought to be, can be a mobilizing factor propelling the poor toward utopia through the historical praxis of liberation. Poverty and oppression as *privatio boni* can be contrast experiences, to use Schillebeeckx's expression, which, by a sort of negative dialectics, point to their opposites of abundant life and freedom for all and ultimately to the reign of God.

For those who favor discovering ways to cope with evil rather than to understand it, liberation theology provides a fresh approach and a useful corrective to other predominantly individualist and psychological solutions. Indeed, it may be argued that the best way to overcome one's own suffering is by attempting to alleviate the suffering of others. Here the goal is not simply how to deal with suffering but to remove it. Like Job, innocent sufferers of our time must also vigorously denounce and protest against injustice, commit themselves to the poor and those who suffer unjustly, face up to the incomprehensible God, and discover God's gratuitous love for all, especially the poorest and weakest. In the long run, this is perhaps the most convincing answer to the challenge of evil.

NOTES

1. For a helpful survey of various theodicies, see Barry L. Whitney, *What Are They Saying about God and Evil?* (New York: Paulist Press, 1989) and Terrence W. Tilley, *The Evils of Theodicy* (Washington, D.C.: Georgetown University Press, 1991). For a survey of contemporary theologies of suffering, see Lucien Richard, *What Are They Saying about the Theology of Suffering?* (New York: Paulist, 1993).
2. The dualist teaching of Manes (c. 215-275) is a typical case in point.
3. Besides Augustine's well-known theory of *privatio boni*, others argue that divine goodness cannot be adequately represented by one grade of

perfection alone and therefore there must be created beings less perfect than others with the ability to fall from the good (Austin Farrer) or that the world as a whole is good while its individual parts may appear to limited human minds as evil in themselves (Jacques Maritain), or that God does not cause evil but only permits it (Thomas Aquinas), or that evil is God's punishment for our sins (many Christian theologians).

4. Proponents of this theory include Irenaeus, F. R. Tennant, Teihard de Chardin, Richard Swinburne, and John Hick.

5. See David Ray Griffin, *God, Power, and Evil* (Philadelphia: Westminster, 1976) and Charles Hartshorne, *Omnipotence and Other Theological Mistakes* (Albany: State University of New York Press, 1984).

6. For a succinct presentation of criticisms of these three types of theodicies, see Barry Whitney, *What Are They Saying about God and Evil?*

7. Brian Hebblethwaite discusses such coping strategies as the renunciation of the world, seeking mystical knowledge through a variety of meditation techniques, religious worship, performing morally valuable acts, and self-sacrifice. See his *Evil, Suffering, and Religion* (London: Sheldon Press, 1976).

8. See Terrence Tilley, *The Evils of Theodicy* (Washington: Georgetown University Press, 1991).

9. For an excellent comprehensive introduction to liberation theology, see Ignacio Ellacuria and Jon Sobrino, eds. *Mysterium Liberationis: Fundamental Concepts of Liberation Theology* (Maryknoll: Orbis, 1993); Marc H. Ellis and Otto Maduro, eds., *The Future of Liberation Theology: Essays in Honor of Gustavo Gutierrez* (Maryknoll: Orbis, 1989). For a survey of the most recent literature on liberation theology, see Peter C. Phan, "The Future of Liberation Theology," *The Living Light*, 28/3 (Spring 1992), pp. 252-71.

10. An extended version of this essay has been published in *Louvain Studies*, No. 20 (1995), pp. 3-20, under the title "Overcoming Poverty and Oppression: Liberation Theology and the Problem of Evil."

11. *The Truth Shall Make You Free: Confrontations*, trans. Matthew J. O'Connell (Maryknoll: Orbis, 1990), p. 7. See also his *The Power of the Poor in History*, trans. Robert Barr (Maryknoll: Orbis, 1983), pp. 56-58.

12. On the use of the social sciences by liberation theology, see Gustavo Gutierrez, "Theology and the Social Sciences," in his *The Truth Shall Make You Free*, pp. 53-84.

13. Gustavo Gutierrez, *The Truth Shall Make You Free*, p. 15. Also see, pp. 132-133.

14. Gustavo Gutierrez, *The Power of the Poor in History*, p. 132.

15. Gustavo Gutierrez, *The Truth Shall Make You Free*, pp. 9-10.

16. See Gustavo Gutierrez, *A Theology of Liberation*, trans. and ed. Caridad Inda and John Eagleson, revised edition with a new introduction (Maryknoll: Orbis, 1988), p. 104. In response to the charge of reductionism and horizontalism, Gutierrez repeatedly emphasizes the three dimensions of liberation: from socioeconomic and political oppression, from fatalism, and

from sin. See, for example, *The Truth Shall Make You Free*, pp. 13-14; 34-36; 127-40.

17. Gustavo Gutierrez, *On Job: God-Talk and the Suffering of the Innocent*, trans. Matthew J. O'Connell (Maryknoll: Orbis, 1987), p. xv.

18. Gustavo Gutierrez, *On Job*, p. xiv.

19. Gustavo Guitierrez, *A Theology of Liberation*, p. 9. See also chapter 7: "Theology from the Underside of History," in *The Power of the Poor*, pp. 169-221.

20. Gustavo Gutierrez, *On Job*, p. xviii.

21. *Ibid.*, p. 15.

22. *Ibid.*, p. 24.

23. *Ibid.*, p. 28.

24. *Ibid.*, p. 29.

25. *Ibid.*, p. 31.

26. *Ibid.*, p. 32.

27. *Ibid.*, p. 47.

28. See *A Theology of Liberation*, pp. 150-56. For Gutierrez's further elaboration of the God of justice and gratuitous love, see his *The God of Life*, trans. Matthew J. O'Connell (Maryknoll: Orbis, 1991).

29. Gustavo Gutierrez, *On Job*, p. 49.

30. *Ibid.*, p. 66.

31. *Ibid.*, p. 72.

32. *Ibid.*, pp. 77-78.

33. *Ibid.*, p. 87.

34. *Ibid.*, p. 88.

35. For these charges, see "Instruction on Certain Aspects of the 'Theology of Liberation,'" Congregation for the Doctrine of the Faith (August 6, 1984) in *Liberation Theology: A Documentary History*, ed. Alfred T. Hennelly (Maryknoll: Orbis, 1990), pp. 393-414. For an evaluation of the connection between Marxism and liberation theology, see Arthur McGovern, *Liberation Theology and Its Critics: Toward An Assessment* (Maryknoll: Orbis, 1989).

36. For a study of liberation spirituality, see Peter C. Phan, "Peacemaking in Latin American Theology," *Eglise et Theologie*, 24 (1993), pp. 25-41.

16

The Unification Understanding of the Problem of Evil

By Anthony J. Guerra

A s with other world scriptures, the *Divine Principle*[1] contains a number of striking, paradoxical and even radical statements. Take, for instance, the chapter entitled "The Fall of Man." In one statement it seems to affirm the revolutionary's call to insurrection:

> As man's volition for the restoration of freedom is cultivated, he naturally seeks to create the social circumstances in which he can realize freedom. Social revolution is unavoidable when the circumstances of the age cannot satisfy the desires of the men belonging to the age. The French Revolution in the 18th Century is a representative example. Revolution will continue until the freedom of the original nature of creation is restored completely.[2]

Then, in another statement it seems to propagate a conservative, loyalist view of citizenship obedient to the governing authorities: "Any act that is performed apart from one's own position and limit, out of an unrighteous desire, is without exception a manifestation of this original nature of the Fall. . . Human society was thrown out of order by those who left their positions and reversed their dominions."[3] Similarly, Jesus in the New Testament has been characterized by some as a militant and by others as a pacifist. Compare, for instance, Matthew 10:34, "Do not think that I have come to bring peace to the earth: I have not come to bring peace, but a sword," with Matthew 26:52, "Then Jesus said to him, 'Put your sword back into its place: for all who take the sword will perish by the sword.'" Although one may ask any question of a text, including scriptural texts, it is often less productive when such questions are tangential to the central concerns of the text under consideration.

The religious worldview finds the political perspective a partial one in that it does not perceive the fundamental reason for human misery and suffering. From the religious perspective, everyone is spiritually ill and in need of a path to perfection, achieving unity with God and self-realization. Unlike nationalistic or racist ideologies, a world religion provides a perspective which finds all humanity with the same basic need: salvation, enlightenment, and liberation. Such global religions often developed from particularistic origins and confronted hostile communities informed by tribal religious traditions. Thus, Islam's prophetic faith transformed the independent city states into larger coalitions, giving rise to more comprehensive regional societies. Beyond the expanded social and political collectives a world religion may generate, its worldview seeks to offer an explanation of the human condition, human nature, pertinent to every person. It is such a universalist worldview that gives a religion its global evangelical reach. Although a given religion may be dominant in one area, it may also appeal to individuals in another part of the globe as, for example, Buddhism in America.

For Judaism, Christianity, Islam and Unificationism, the symbols of Adam and Eve are significant vehicles by which these traditions articulate their understanding of the human condition. Although recent scientific theories about the origin of the human, specifically the "Mitochondrial Eve" hypothesis[4] would seem to affirm the possibility of a common ancestor for all human descendants, the religious significance of Adam and Eve cannot be exhausted by understanding an Eve and/or Adam as the progenitor of the human race, for their story is meant to reveal something about the potential as well as the experienced frustration of all humankind. However ambiguous the merits of the scientific rationale for affirming the monogenesis of the human, the ethical imperative for the position is unmistakable. The affirmation of common human ancestors makes preposterous racism, ultra-nationalism and other insidious and socially divisive ideologies. We should want conclusive scientific evidence if we abandon the notion of monogenesis, given its salutary social and ethical implications.

As with Judaism, Christianity, and Islam, the Unification discussion of the origin of evil or the human fall, is set within a wider revelatory and/or theological framework. This larger context is the creation, fall, salvation, history, and eschaton wherein the fall is the decisive moment which separates humanity from God; it also separates humanity from God's purpose of creation necessitating a providence of salvation in order to prepare for a final culminating moment in which the original purpose of creation is to be achieved. The fundamental theological affirmation is that God is an absolute being whose purpose of creation, although temporarily frustrated, shall ultimately be consummated. The fall is, indeed, the cause of the long-suffering and painful history of humanity. Further, God is also suffering: a divine passion caused essentially by the deep disappointment in not being able to share divine life and love with God's children.

The Problem

It may indeed be a cliche that the fundamental problem of humanity is the failure of love but it is also a profound theological dilemma. If, as the main Western religions, Judaism, Christianity and Islam affirm, God is the all-good, omnipotent creator, then the problem of human sinfulness appears to call into question one or the other of these divine attributes. The traditional recourse to free will in response to this problem is less than satisfying because it is not clear how something desired by a created being should be contrary to the will of its creator and in effect contrary to its own endowed nature. The founder of the Unification Church, Sun Myung Moon, confronted this question as he read the Genesis story of Adam and Eve which is known to Jews, Christians and in a somewhat modified form to Muslims.

In the context of the Genesis narrative, the abstract question just mentioned becomes, how is it that Adam and Eve, without a sinful heritage, came to disobey God's commandment? What is the nature and process of the fall of humankind? Partly as a reaction against the Marcionite dualistic conception of an evil creator God, the early Christians stressed that Adam and Eve were good, perfect beings. This understanding enhanced the problem in accounting for the wrongful act attributed to the first human ancestors. Irenaeus, the early Christian theologian, stands as an exception in proposing that Adam and Eve were created as infants and developed through natural stages to adulthood. According to Irenaeus, Jesus who was the antitype of Adam and Mary that of Eve, also had to be born and grow through stages of natural human growth. The view is consonant with the Unificationists' notion of restoration as a reversal course necessitating Adam and Eve type figures to trod the path of the original ancestors, indemnifying the mistakes of the original ancestors.[5]

The biblical text is not subtle in indicating that the original sin was a sexual act. As in several modern languages, ancient Semitic languages used the expression picking or eating fruit to refer to sexual intercourse as is also the case with the expression to "know" a woman. The Genesis narrative indicates that before the fall, Adam and Eve were naked and unashamed but after it they became aware of their nakedness and covered the lower parts of their body. Accordingly, the Genesis account narrates that Eve is to be punished by experiencing pain in childbearing. Interestingly, modern biblical criticism confirms the sexual nature of the fall adducing a number of extra-biblical parallels, including the Mesopotamian epic of Gilgamesh wherein the figure Enkidu is seduced by a prostitute. Following this act, Enkidu is forced to leave his wilderness paradise and puts on clothing for the first time.[6]

Although Gnosticism may be perfectly content with a sexual interpretation of the fall, as it seeks to deny the material world as entirely evil, for Judaism, Christianity and especially Unificationism, it presents a paradox. Namely, God is understood to have ordained marriage as a blessing to humankind as well as for the procreation of children. How then can the sexual relationship of the first human parents be the cause of the human fall? Reverend Moon's teachings emphasize that God is a being of love and the motivation for creation is to complete God's love by allowing God to have reciprocal relationships with God's children. It is this motive of divine love that explains God's risk-taking in creating beings who could thwart God's own desires. Love allows for the possibility of pain as well as happiness: "God is an absolute being, however, He needs to have a being which can become His object of love. God's object of love is man and woman."[7] God's own fulfillment of love, according to Unificationism, awaits the uniting of man and woman in true love: "Male was created for the sake of female, and female was created for the sake of male. God cannot dwell in places where one insists on his own being. But God dwells where one values the other."[8] Such love takes time to develop and the prohibition on sexual relationship between Adam and Eve was to assure the proper development of unselfish emotions which were to accompany their physical intimacy and also assure that they were capable of fulfilling their parental responsibility to offspring:

> If Adam and Eve had reached perfection without falling, they would have become perfect not only individually but also on a universal and historical level and they would have been able to start a new family centering on God's love. From this family, a society, tribe, nation and world would have been realized in which God could have dwelt.[9]

The significance of Adam and Eve and this first family becomes clear in Unification theology. It is the equivalent of the incarnation in Christianity coupled with a federal theology.[10] Adam and Eve should have formed their union centered on God and assumed the position of true parents reflective of God's loving heart towards humankind.

The Solution

Given the Unification understanding that original sin prevented the establishment of a true family, it follows that the central efforts of Reverend Moon and his movement have been devoted to the restoration of a God-centered, perfected family. Indeed, Reverend Moon teaches that God shall only be liberated from God's own suffering, disappointment and frustration—as a result of humankind's failure to achieve the purpose of creation—with the establishment of this family. Thus, the Unificationist attitude in prayer is first and foremost to comfort the suffering heart of God, believing that however deep the pain and suffering of humanity is, God's sorrow remains greater. Although Unificationists' prayer services may often be experienced as highly affective, including intense weeping, self pity is explicitly eschewed. We learn from the official biography of Reverend Moon that even when he was imprisoned in a Communist concentration camp, he prayed with the intention of relieving God's sorrow rather than pleading that his own burden be lifted. Unification spirituality seeks to reorient the center of emotional concern from the self towards the other and to ground this concern in divine love: "The most important subject is how we can reform our self-centered love, transforming it into a love for others. God absolutely does not have self-centered love. His love is only centered on others. If love is not for the sake of others, no matter what kind of love it is, it is not true love."[11] Reverend Moon's construal of the fall of humankind shapes not only his understanding of his own mission but also his reading of the ministry of Jesus. If, as the apostle Paul said, Jesus is the last Adam (I Cor. 15:45), then he should have accomplished that which God willed Adam to have achieved. Accordingly, Jesus, as the second Adam should have married a woman who would fulfill the role of second Eve. Following this pattern of a restoration course reversing the Adamic family fall, Reverend Moon teaches that representative Cain and Abel figures should have united in love, reversing the hateful history of the first siblings of the old Adamic family. Thus, John the Baptist and the official Jewish leadership should have united together and cooperated with Jesus. The failure to do so prevented Jesus from restoring the position of the first true husband and parent. Instead, Jesus undertook a secondary, alternative course in enduring the crucifixion and provided a partial salvation necessitating the return of the Lord of the second advent.

It should certainly be unsurprising that a central topic of Reverend Moon's spiritual guidance is marriage and family. He encourages individuals to transform the self-concern in approaching marriage so as to embrace the divine intention: "For what reason do we marry? It is in order to fulfill the ideal of creation, i.e., to realize the purpose of creation. Then, what purpose is this purpose of creation? Before it is the purpose of Adam, it is the purpose of God."[12] Accordingly, Unificationists refer to the marriage ceremony as the blessing because it represents God's original intention to provide the opportunity for Adam and Eve to realize the divine intention for true love. Self-sacrifice is essential: "You must believe that marriage is not for your sake, but for your partner. . .If you have understood the basic principle that people are to live for the sake of others, you should know that you will get married for the sake of your spouse."[13] Single members of the church are discouraged from pursuing romantic love marriages and instead are matched by Reverend and Mrs. Moon. Adam and Eve's disobedience is restored by obediently following the advice of the True Parents as to one's marriage partner. This creates a condition for centering the marriage relationship beyond self-concern and to make room for *agape*, sacrificial true love. Marriage is not an egoistic opportunity for self-gratification but the opportunity to exercise unselfish love and to recover our original identity as children reflecting the love of God. Reverend Moon's spiritual guidance concerning the sexual relationship challenges conventional wisdom. A recurrent motif in his sermons is that the wife is the owner of the husband's sexual organ and the husband of the wife's: "The sexual organs enable man and woman's bodies to unite and provide a path through which mind and body can unite completely centering on love. The sexual organ of man is not for the sake of man, and the sexual organ of woman is not for the sake of woman. You were not born for the sake of yourself."[14] Reverend Moon clearly seeks to sacralize the sexual relationship within the marital union: "Where is God's holy of holies? It is where love dwelt before the fall—the sexual organs of man and woman. This is the holy of holies of heaven."[15]

This intention to resacralize marriage grows out of Reverend Moon's understanding of his own mission and the providential significance of his acts. Because Jesus was not able to restore the old Adamic family by virtue of the failure of those surrounding him, the Lord of the second advent should establish the true family which will become God's mediator for dispensing a blessing on the rest of humanity. Thus, Reverend Moon understood, apparently from a very early stage in his ministry, that his own marriage would have messianic significance. For Unificationists, the marriage of Reverend Moon and Hak Jan Han in 1960 represents an eschatological moment in which God's purpose that should have been fulfilled at the beginning of human history by Adam and Eve is at last realized. It thus makes available in human history the God-centered love of true parents.

Soon after their blessing (wedding), the Reverend and Mrs. Moon initiated and officiated at the first of what was to be a continuing series of mass marriages. Each successive marriage has seen an increase in the number of participating couples; at the last such marriage in summer, 1995, 360,000 couples were in attendance. Reverend Moon provides a rationale for such mass marriages that refers back to the old Adamic family and the mission of Jesus:

> If the Blessing event had happened in the Garden of Eden, it would have been the big cosmic event. However, due to the human ancestors' fall, in order to indemnify the failure to accomplish the heavenly standard in the garden of Eden, we are holding the mass wedding ceremony. Jesus should have held such a marriage ceremony on the level of all the Israelites, at the least. However, no one was even concerned about Jesus' marriage.[16]

Reverend Moon has also given a two-fold explanation of the main mass wedding ceremonies pointing backwards to the primordial history to be restored and forward to the present and immediate providential missions of the participants. The first such mass marriage of the 36 couples in 1961 represented the restoration of the historical ancestors. The 36 couples consist of 3 groups of 12 couples based on their previous marital status and stand as the closest disciples of the True Parents (Reverend and Mrs. Moon), similar to the position of Jesus' 12 apostles. Likewise, the next blessing group was the 72 couples representing the restored Cain and Abel or the children of the first ancestors and also standing in the position of Jesus' 70 disciples. A third mass marriage consisted of 120 couples symbolizing the restoration of all nations of the world as well as the disciples of the post-resurrection Jesus.[17]

Successive blessings (mass marriages) of 430, 777, 1800, 2000, 6000, 30,000 and as already mentioned 360,000 couples were presided over by Reverend and Mrs. Moon. The participants in the 430 couples blessings as well as the earlier mass weddings were exclusively Korean.[18] The 430 couples blessing was understood as a national level condition to indemnify Korea whose legendary history is said to be 4300 years long. The 777 couples mass wedding involved peoples from several Eastern as well as Western nations and explicitly marked the moment when the blessing was made available to all humankind. Indeed, in this as well as all later marriages, there was a significant emphasis on international and interracial marriages encouraged by Reverend and Mrs. Moon as an important condition for unifying the world community.[19] The 1800 couples blessing that followed continued this focus on the Unificationist's world wide providential mission. Many participants from this blessing were sent as foreign missionaries to initiate the Unification Church in countries around the globe. Each blessing group (36, 72, 120, 430, etc.) has a sense of common purpose that results in the formation of Blessing Associations that not only provide spiritual support for individual couples in need but also promote the shared providential mission that allows individuals and families to transcend private concern and often to make heroic sacrifices for humanity and God.

In Unificationism marriage is the central sacrament and encompasses both a personal spiritual dimension as well as a universal providential significance. The blessing or marriage in Unificationism reverses the primordial fall of the first ancestors and creates a new history of families united in a spiritual and social quest to reform world society. For Unificationists, the blessing offers both deep personal meaning as well as a sense of historical and even cosmic significance to marriage and family.

Conclusion

In a religious worldview, one is looking for a comprehensive vision that is internally logical, consistent, and perhaps most importantly, elevates human life, offering a perspective enabling an individual and society to feel that life is meaningful. Moreover, such a religious worldview empowers those embracing it to transform their lives and the world around them, generating new cultures and civilizations. Intellectually, a religious worldview cannot transcend the hermeneutical circle, cannot be proven, but is a generative presupposition. Its first premise, as is the case with all human thought including skepticism, is not rationally deduced. The difference between philosophical schools and religious movements is that the latter have the capacity to radically transform society as well as individuals. Stoicism had its moments of prominence as in the time of Marcus Aurelius, but it was the mystery religions and later Christianity that moved the masses as well as the most influential and wealthy of the Roman Empire. In our present time, a plethora of new religions have emerged to satisfy a felt need for a new spiritual vision. For believers, Unificationism has the depth of spirituality and breadth of intellectual vision, in responding to evil, to generate the future global civilization.

NOTES

1. The *Divine Principle* contains the essential teachings of Reverend Sun Myung Moon and is considered also to be the Completed Testament or a part thereof. The English version of the same is: *Divine Principle* (New York: Holy Spirit Association for the Unification of World Christian ity, 1973).
2. *Divine Principle*, *op. cit.*, 1977 edition, p. 45.
3. *Ibid.*
4. For a concise summary of the pros and cons of the 'Mitochondrial Eve' hypothesis see, James Shreeve, "Argument Over a Woman," *Discover*, August, 1990, pp. 52-59.
5. Indemnity is a term used in the *Divine Principle* to refer to the process required of humankind to recover the original heart, attitude and relationships appropriate to children of God.
6. See Andrew Wilson, "The Sexual Interpretation of the Human Fall," in Anthony J. Guerra, *Unification Theology in Comparative Perspectives* (Barrytown: Unification Theological Seminary, 1988), pp. 51-70.
7. *Blessing and Ideal Family* (New York: Holy Spirit Association for the Unification of World Christianity, 1993), p. 7. This book also contains many basic teachings of Reverend Sun Myung Moon on the topic of marriage and family.
8. *Blessing and Ideal Family*, p. 35.
9. *Ibid*, p. 21.
10. For an insightful exploration of Unificationism as a federal theology, see Herbert W. Richardson, "A Brief Outline of Unification Theology," in M. Darral Bryant, *A Time for Consideration: A Scholarly Appraisal of the Unification Church* (N.Y.: The Edwin Mellen Press, 1978), pp. 133-140.
11. *Blessing and Ideal Family*, p. 88.
12. *Ibid.*, p. 56.
13. *Ibid.*
14. *Ibid.*, p. 36.
15. *Ibid.*, p. 43.
16. *Ibid.*, p. 223.
17. *Ibid.*, pp. 415-416.
18. A separate much smaller mass wedding of 43 couples including Japanese as well as Westerners was held shortly after the 430 couples mass wedding. It should be noted that except for Korea the movement was still young and

small in all countries in the 1960's when these first several mass marriages were taking place.

19. Indeed, one of the most significant factors in the widespread persecution of the Unification Church has been the disgruntlement of parents whose children married partners of an unacceptable race or nationality.

17

Ecological Evil and Interfaith Dialogue:
Caring for the Earth[1]

By M. Darrol Bryant

N o greater imperative faces us than that of the environmental or ecological crisis. It is a crisis that has revealed a particular face of evil in our time. Let us be clear about what this crisis means. There is nothing the matter with the planet earth; it unfolds in its own remarkable way following the evolutionary patterns, interactive processes and cycles that order the natural world. There is an ecological crisis today not because there is something wrong with the ecological order of planet earth or the cosmos. Rather, the ecological crisis is caused by a distinct form of human intervention and interaction with nature. This is not to say that the human is not part of nature. But human beings are a part of nature who can intervene in nature in ways that no other species can. In the course of human unfolding and history, there has emerged an attitude towards the natural world as well as sciences of mastery and technologies of intervention that are remarkable in their power but devastating in their impact upon the natural world. It shall be the burden of this essay to say something about the nature of the environmental crisis, the contributions to addressing that crisis that need to emerge from the dialogue between faiths, and to conclude with a plea.

The Crisis

The problematic human attitude that arose in Western society at the beginning of the modern era (or the end of the medieval world, if you prefer) has been described in many ways. The Canadian philosopher, George Grant, described it in a memorable phrase as mastery over nature.[2] This attitude was new. It replaced the attitudes toward nature that had preceded it: the magical (nature was something to be appeased), the contemplative (nature as something to contemplate for the sake of understanding its dynamics and patterns), and the enduring (nature is something we suffer and endure). It also implicitly rejected the attitudes towards nature that were found in traditional religious cosmologies East and West. Causally linked to this new attitude of mastery over nature were sciences that gave us control over nature and technologies of intervention that allowed us to intervene in nature and bend it to human will. The story of this attitude, the sciences of mastery, and these technologies of intervention is a long and complex one that I cannot recount here in detail.[3] But its unfolding has generated the predicament in which we now find ourselves. At a New Delhi conference on "Ecological Responsibility: A Dialogue with Buddhism" in 1993, Jose Lutzenberger, former Environmental Minister in the federal government of Brazil, put the predicament in this way: "The ecological crisis is a direct result of progress. This is the contradiction we must acknowledge."[4]

Though recounting the story of the emergence of the sciences of mastery and the technologies of intervention exceeds our purposes here, it is essential to understand two aspects of that progress. First, it is built on a perception of nature that regards the world, in vernacular terms, as mere stuff rather than as a living system. As dead matter, nature and all the things of the earth (including the human) need not be approached with respect for their intrinsic value or the integrity of their processes. Rather, they can be measured, quantified, and used for whatever purposes we desire. It is another example of what C. Badrinath calls the either/or mentality of modernity, in this case it is the either/or of living or non-living.[5] When the earth is made non-living, then it is removed from the sphere of those things that we have an ethical relation to and placed in the sphere of mere stuff. Secondly, this attitude has deprived us of a comprehensive vision of nature and our place within it. This point has been eloquently argued by the ecologist Thomas Berry in his book *The Dream of the Earth*. Berry observes that, "even the most primitive tribes have a larger vision of the universe, of our place and functioning within it, a vision that extends to celestial regions of space and to interior depths of the human in a manner far exceeding the parameters of our own world of technological confinement."[6]

From these developments has emerged a form of industrial-technological culture that has had a disastrous impact on nature. This merging of *techne* with *logos*, knowing as technique rather than contemplation, that emerged in the West has become the new universal of our time. It is enveloping the whole earth. In its onslaught, industrial-technological culture has overwhelmed more traditional cultures and civilizations West and East.[7] No culture seems able to either resist it or even to significantly qualify it. It is symbolized in the industrial smokestack that spews out its waste into the air, its effluents into the water, and endlessly transforms dwindling natural resources into products for consumption. It would be better to symbolize this development in the automobile: a mode of transportation that is much valued but is polluting the air we breathe to remarkable degrees and degrading the environment. While we all can generate opposition to smoke stacks, the automobile is another matter. The image of the automobile discloses the ambiguity of the resultant technology made possible by this new attitude towards and relationship with nature. In the past, humans had to either cooperate with horses, camels, bullocks or some other species in order to move across the landscape. With the new sciences of mastery, we learned how to transform iron ore into steel, oil into gasoline, rubber into tires. To create a machine that has captured the desire of humankind allows us to overcome space and time and the limits of interspecies cooperation. It grants us mastery and at the same time is polluting nature, including our own human nature in unprecedented ways. As Lutzenberger baldly and rightly remarked, "industrial culture is destructive of the earth."

The irony is that the ecological crisis, the destruction of the earth, is unintended. Lutzenberger called this destruction the contradiction at the heart of progress. No one has set out to despoil nature, to eradicate species, to pollute the water we drink and the air we breathe. These consequences simply flow from the nature of what has been created. This reveals the peculiar face of evil that we are confronted with in the ecological crisis. It is the evil, we might say, that arises in Augustine's terms from the absence of good. Evil, Augustine rightly saw, is often the consequence of an absence. In this case, it is the absence of the good of our relationship to the living earth. It also reveals the suprapersonal character of ecological evil: it is built into the very nature of industrial institutions and no one is responsible.

Chemical companies never intend to pollute the water; industries never intend to dump tons of toxic waste into the environment; logging operations never intend to destroy species. Environmental degradation is simply the unintended byproduct of pursuing our mastery over nature with the technologies of intervention that we have created. The whole enterprise is justified by products that enhance human life: healing chemicals, newsprint and books, bridges and automobiles, dams and hydroelectric power, and even, genetically programmed children free of defect.

The effect of this industrial-technological culture is a profound ecological crisis. We are now starting to understand its devastating impact on nature. We are destroying the ozone layer which protects human life from the damaging effects of ultraviolet light, effects which can create cancer. We have despoiled the earth's rain forests and continue to do so every day. We are devastating the forests of the world and have created barren and eroding mountain sides where life-giving forests used to stand. We are polluting the water we drink and the air we breathe with toxic chemicals inimical to human life. We are polluting the earth with pesticides, insecticides and fertilizers that enhance productivity but at the same time kill birds and animals and introduce toxins into the soil and the food chain.[8] Some of those chemicals are mutagenic and may alter the very genetic structures of a new generation. Edward O. Wilson, the noted Harvard biologist, observes that even if all further destruction of nature were to be halted today it "will take millions of years to correct. . .the loss of genetic and species diversity by the destruction of natural habitats."[9] It is this crisis and this evil that we must address. It is this crisis that has revealed a fundamental face of evil in our time.

Ecology and Religious Dialogue

I propose to relate the ecological crisis to the dialogue between religions. The primary aim of such dialogue is mutual respect and understanding in order to overcome the antagonism that has been with us far too long in the history of human religious life.[10] In the midst of dialogue towards mutuality, the religious traditions need to come together to address fundamental human, social, and ecological issues. It is not only a matter of respect for the diverse traditions, rituals and beliefs of various religious ways, but finding within these traditions the inspiration, insight, and wisdom that can address pressing human and world problems, especially the evils that confront us in life. Many of these are issues and problems that were not even on the distant horizon when the religious traditions emerged. First on that agenda, I believe, is the ecological crisis, or if I may speak in the language of Buddhism: the suffering earth.

The dialogue between religions can contribute, if they are to exercise their ecological responsibility, first, a critique of the mentality of mastery, the sciences of mastery and the technologies of intervention. To lay the blame for an industrial-technological mentality at the feet of any specific religious tradition, as Lynn White does, is not only profoundly misguided but nefarious as it deflects our attention from the real issues.[11] The mentality of mastery and the technologies of intervention are hostile to the traditional cosmologies of all religions and spiritual traditions East and West. The relationship of the religious traditions to the mentality and technology of mastery ranges from complicity (Christianity, as it contributed to the desacralization of the earth in the name of an excessive transcendentalism) to sheer incomprehension and silence (most religions). It is quite clear that no religion has truly stood in opposition to the mentality of mastery that has fueled the industrial-technological behemoth; nor has any religion effectively critiqued the sciences of mastery and the technologies of intervention. Religion cannot and should not reject sciences that seek to know and understand things, but it must reject the hubris that assumes that knowledge bestows the right and the necessity to intervene.

Secondly, the religious traditions must come to understand that the industrial-technological behemoth knows no boundaries. It is as present in the East as in the West. Where it is not yet fully present, it is sought and longed for and identified as progress and development. Industrial-technological culture belongs as much to Shinto-Buddhist Japan as it does to Evangelical Christian America, as much to the aspiration of contemporary communist China as to an increasingly post-Christian European Common Market. It is seen as the way out of poverty for the Third World and as the source of endless material benefits for the so-called First World. It has been enshrined in capitalist, communist, and socialist ideologies and championed by those who seek a mixed economy. Shinto may acknowledge the *kami* in every tree and brook and natural phenomenon, but this acknowledgement has not fundamentally altered the industrial-technological way in Japan. While some Muslims may abhor modernity and seek to create Islamic states, they still send their sons and daughters to be educated in the mentality of mastery and the technologies of intervention as doctors, engineers and scientists. Taoists have simply been overwhelmed as have the Confucian traditions.[12] Hindus may see the entire cosmos as sacred, but their view has not prevented their embracing of the mentality of mastery or the technologies of intervention. Witness that the most sacred rivers in India are among the most polluted in the world. Some Christians may have spoken against the new way, but they have been reduced to conspiratorial silence by the powerful products and proponents of mastery. It seems that Christianity is reluctant even now to say anything critical of science and technology. Religion is generally still portrayed as the opponent to science and thinking. People seem to be mesmerized by the very evil that is destroying the earth and possibly the very ecological processes on which life depends.[13]

In the industrial organizations of our industrial-technological culture we have embodied a face of evil that discloses what Walter Rauschenbusch, the nineteenth century American founder of the social gospel movement in Christianity,[14] might have called evil's suprapersonal character. It is evil embodied in industrial organizations that by their very character wreak havoc on the environment; yet no one is personally responsible. Thus we have the anomalous situation of widespread evil, yet a failure to take personal responsibility. It was, for example, a precedent setting judgment in the Canadian legal system when an owner of a local Elmira, Ontario, industry was found guilty and sent to jail for the ecological damage done by his company. Even here, when the case is examined more closely, one discovers that he is never really charged with harming the water or polluting the ground, but rather a failure to file certain papers in regard to the handling of toxic wastes. The question is whether nature—water, trees, air—has rights. Within a legal system, it is difficult to raise the issue of ecological evil. Evil in the ecological sense I am proposing here means simply the failure to respect the dignity or *dharma* of things. Could a legal system acknowledge this kind of evil as a legal wrong?

For the religious traditions to take seriously the ecological crisis, they must begin with a religiously inspired critical analysis of the roots of the ecological crisis. That analysis must not be content with an indictment of human grasping or greed, as important as it is to indict such desires. It must also seriously analyze the structures and dynamics of modern industrial-technological civilization which has enfolded us all. We cannot be content with the easy formula: Technology is neutral—it is only a matter of how we use it. Religious traditions must turn their intellectual and moral effort to the critique of modern industrial-technological culture. Such a critique must be grounded in a profound sense of the sacredness of our living planet, in compassion for all sentient beings, and in the best scientific information available on the devastating effects of industrial culture on the planet earth. It must face the evils that result from the absence of good—a relationship to the living earth, an awareness of the interdependent character of all things, respect for the inherent *dharma* (order) of all things—as well as the actuality of evil present in institutions and the devastation of species and the environment.

David Ross Kormito in an article "Madhyamika, Tantra, and 'Green Buddhism'" sees a "tremendous similarity between dharmic and ecological attitudes."[15] Specifically, he sees the theoretical connection to lie in dependent origination and selflessness, two profound Buddhist concepts of reality. Finding theoretical links between a religious tradition and ecological responsibility is typical of a religious tradition, if the issue is to be addressed. While there is some value to this approach, it is not adequate, as Kormito acknowledges, if it is not linked to transformative practice.[16] Nor is the approach adequate if it fails to identify the historical-cultural forms that have generated the crisis. To move from the philosophical to the psychological, a general religious tendency, while ignoring the social/institutional forms that embody the prob-lem, is also not adequate. Things do not move only from the inner to the outer. Rather, the outer social forms have themselves a life and a logic that we must grasp if we are to adequately respond to the crisis. We may also discover that our traditions do not have all the answers, theoretical or practical, to the crisis.

We can begin to act responsibly on the basis of an adequate analysis, one that both understands the social institutions and prac-tices that generate the problem and begins to rearticulate the wisdom of our respective traditions concerning the natural order. The religious traditions need to inspire us to think globally, but act locally to address the environmental crisis.[17] While we need to understand some of the larger philosophical issues and the cultural forces that have given rise to the ecological crisis, we need to act locally in relation to the suffering earth. It is not possible to redress the ecological crisis in general, but only in the specific places where we live. We cannot wish away our industrial-technological era nor can we wait to take action until we all become enlightened or liber-ated or saved. Rather, it is essential that now, in the name of this sacred earth, or the interdependence of all things, or the Tao, or Allah's creation, or whatever we name this remarkable earth, we act to preserve nature in all of its wondrous diversity and to reverse the process of destruction. That may mean, as it did in the case of our small town of Elmira, Ontario in Canada, that we have to do battle with a local chemical company that has polluted the water supply.[18] We must insist that the company simply not produce what pollutes and that it begin the process of cleaning up its own waste. In the Elmira case, this will mean 30 to 40 years of continuous effort to reverse the 50 years of continuous violation of water, air, and soil. But while this is going on, we continue to create hundreds of new chemical compounds each year and only a handful are tested for their effect on human and animal life, let alone there impact on air, water, and soil.

In these efforts we must also become literate in the language of science and know how to read its findings. It is, for example, pos-sible to have nonpolluting chemical plants or paints that are not full of lead. It is not necessary to destroy the remaining rain forests. There are alternatives to fluorocarbons that destroy the ozone layer.

We need not drive whales to extinction, nor dump tons of toxic waste into the atmosphere.

We must recover or develop alternative cosmologies that reject the mentalities and technologies of mastery. The religious traditions have failed to fulfill their ecological responsibility. Few within any of the traditions are even aware of the problems that confront the suffering planet. Traditional analyses will not be sufficient; we will have to find ways to formulate adequate directions, calling upon the deepest resources and insights of our respective traditions. For example, it will not be adequate for Christians simply to speak of stewardship but we must recognize and overcome our complicity in the emergence of the sciences and technologies of mastery and insist on the glory and integrity of creation. Nor will it be adequate for Buddhists to assert the interdependence of all things without finding ways to effectively act to preserve the integrity of the natural world. We must seek to inform our communities of faith of the crisis with which we are confronted, formulate effective acts of compassion for the suffering earth, and inculcate habits of ecological living that embody a sense of unity with all living things.

We must mount religiously inspired campaigns to preserve the ecological integrity of the planet. Different religious traditions have different languages for nature. For example, the theistic traditions speak of the earth as divine creation; the primal traditions speak of mother earth;[19] the non-theistic traditions speak of the interdependence of all things. These diverse languages should not be seen as mutually exclusive but as giving us diverse access to and aspects of what is. They should lead us to stand with the suffering earth against the onslaught of industrial-technological culture. Such a stand will inevitably be perceived as religion involved in politics. But it is a religious duty that emerges from the respective traditions as a love for the earth. It is a duty that exceeds politics; it is a matter of the future of the earth itself.

A Plea

Let me indulge in a moment of madness, a kind that I hope is touched by some wisdom. Wouldn't it be marvelous if His Holiness the Dalai Lama were to call Buddhists and men and women of other faiths to join him in nonviolent protest at the plants of the leading producers of fluorocarbons in the USA and Europe? Or Pope John

Paul II to call on Catholics in Latin America and people from other faiths to join him in a vigil at the edge of the Amazon rain forest until its destruction is halted? Or if the Grand Muftis of Syria and Saudi Arabia would call, in the name of Allah, the creator, on all Muslims and other believers to join them in protest against the destruction of the fragile ecology of the desert by the oil industry? Or, if the Head of the Grand Shrine at Ise (the foremost Shinto shrine in Japan) were to join hands with the Head of Eiheiji (one of the foremost Soto Zen Monasteries of Japan) to cry out on behalf of the earth, for an end to the pollution that daily envelopes the cities of Japan? Or, if Reverend Moon would invite leaders of other religious communities to join him in opposing dragnet industrial fishing in the oceans of the world, a practice that is not only destroying the spawning grounds of numerous species but is also resulting in the deaths of fish and mammals (dolphins and small whales) caught in the nets? M. Varadarajan suggested at Tibet House in New Delhi that it would even be better to have such acts initiated by an interreligious group of religious leaders. Such scenarios are not frivolous suggestions. They would awaken and enhance our consciousness to the evil of what we are doing to nature, inspire us to seek alternatives and begin to reverse a process that is destroying living things and the earth.

I have argued that we must see the ecological face of evil in our times. The roots of the ecological crisis and ecological evil lie in a particular human attitude towards and intervention in the natural world. That complex of attitudes, sciences, and technologies of mastery that I have here called industrial-technological culture is the primary source of the ecological crisis that has enveloped our planet. It is ecological evil. The consequence is a suffering planet.

I then urged the religious traditions in the context of the dialogue of faiths to confront the face of ecological evil and exercise their ecological responsibility through (1) a critique of the ways of mastery, (2) rearticulations of their visions of nature and the place of the human within it, (3) actions which think globally and act locally to redress the particular suffering that our place on the earth is currently undergoing, and (4) arm ourselves with the requisite spiritual disciplines[20] and scientific knowledge. Religious people must become effective actors in addressing the healing of our suffering planet.

NOTES

1. This essay has two sources. The first is my experience in a local environmental group dealing with environmental issues in Elmira (population 8,000), Ontario, Canada. In 1989, the citizens of Elmira learned that the water supply had been contaminated by chemicals from the local chemical company. Thus began my own awakening to environmental issues. Secondly, this essay grows out of a conference on ecological responsibility and a dialogue with Buddhism that was organized by the Venerable Doboom Tulku of Tibet House in New Delhi, September 30 to October 4, 1993, that I was able to attend. Thus, the essay is a contribution to matters raised in the New Delhi conference as part of my effort to understand the sources of the crisis that has presently emerged.

2. See George Grant, *Technology and Empire* (Toronto: Anansi Press, 1968), *Time as History* (Toronto: CBC Publications, 1972), and *Technology and Justice* (Toronto: Anansi Press, 1986).

3. See, for example, S. H. Nasr, *The Encounter of Man and Nature: The Spiritual Crisis of Modern Man* (London: George Allen and Unwin, 1968). This neglected gem by an Islamic philosopher is worth noting. More recently, see Phillip Sherrard, *The Rape of Man and Nature* (Ipswitch: Golgonotha Press, 1987), where he says that what "the building of our modern technological and economic order demonstrate is the triumph of precisely the view in which the world is seen as a self-contained entity, existing in its own right, apart from God, and consequently as something that man is quite entitled to explore, organize and exploit without any reference to the divine," p. 94. Sherrard also rightly notes the complicity of Christianity, especially Latin and Protestant Christianity, in the "desacralization of nature."

4. These quotes from Mr. Jose Lutzenberger are from my own notes taken during his address to the conference. "Progress" is here used ironically and, as Lutzenberger made clear, to mean the modern way of science, industry, and technology. There are now many studies that see the negative underside of industrial-technical culture and that chronicle the environmental crisis. I mention two further studies: Jonathan Schell, *The Fate of the Earth* (New York: Alfred A. Knopf, 1982), and William McKibben, *The End of Nature* (New York: Random House, 1989). One should also note Carl Sagan, "Preserving and Cherishing the Earth—an appeal for joint commitment in science and religion," *American Journal of Physics* (July, 1990). Sagan's appeal is moving but fails to address the problem of industrial culture, the sciences of mastery, and the technologies of domination.

5. See Chaturvedi Badrinath, *Dharma, India, and World Order* (Edinburgh: St. Andrews Press, 1993).

6. Thomas Berry, *The Dream of the Earth* (San Francisco: Sierra Club, 1990), p. 37.

7. Jacques Ellul already saw this in his still unheeded and important analysis called *Technological Society* (New York: Vintage, 1964). Ellul was one of the first to see the full meaning of "technique." Although it does not deal with the environmental crisis, it remains a book to read.

8. See Rachael Carson's classic, *Silent Spring* (Cambridge, MA: Riverside Press, 1962).

9. Edward O. Wilson, *Biophilia* (Cambridge, MA: Harvard University Press, 1984), p. 76. While the volume contains shocking information on our destruction of species, it is remarkable for its lack of awareness of the negative role played by science and industry and its naive view of human beings.

10. See M. Darrol Bryant and Frank Flinn, eds., *Interreligious Dialogue: Voices from a New Frontier* (New York: Paragon Press, 1985) and M. Darrol Bryant, *Religion in a New Key* (New Delhi: Wiley Eastern Ltd., 1992).

11. See Lynn White's often reprinted article, "The Historical Roots of our Ecological Crisis," *Science* (March, 1967), that lays the blame for the ecological crisis at the feet of Christianity even though he does acknowledge that St. Francis may be the appropriate ecological saint. What is especially appalling about White's proposal is the way it obscures the extent to which the industrial-technological culture is fundamentally contrary to all the religious traditions of humankind.

12. Taoism probably best illustrates the irony found throughout the religious traditions: a deep and profound sense of nature yet overwhelmed by the industrial-technical culture with nary a word of protest. For the relevance of Taoist wisdom to the ecological movement see Huston Smith's "Tao Now: An Ecological Testament," pp. 71-92 in *Huston Smith: Essays on World Religion*, edited by M. Darrol Bryant (New York: Paragon Press, 1992).

13. To see the ecological crisis in terms of the categories of good and evil is both helpful and problematic. The problem here is the "either/or" mentality of so much ethical thought in which labeling substitutes for analyzing. I hope to avoid that danger here. Also it is important to recognize the different aspects of evil. I agree with Augustine that ontologically evil is an absence, the absence of good. Many reject this view because it is felt to minimize historical evil. I think not. Ontological absence has historical reality; it has analogs to the notion of *maya* in the Hindu traditions.

14. See Walter Rauschenbusch, *A Theology for the Social Gospel* (New York: Macmillan, 1917), pp. 69ff.

15. See David Ross Komito, "Madhyamika, Tantra, and 'Green Buddhism,'" *Pacific World*, Institute of Buddhist Studies (Fall 1992), p. 48. This is an example of the growing literature that is now aware of ecological issues.

16. *Ibid.*, p. 49.

17. I think, for example, of the Chipko movement in India.

18. In 1989 a few citizens in Elmira founded APT Environment (Assuring

Protection for Tomorrow's Environment) and three months later found itself confronted with the Uniroyal crisis. We have been carrying on the efforts to address this local environmental issue ever since. For more information on our work, write to Susan Bryant, APT Environment, 5 Park Ave. West, Elmira, Ontario, N3B 1K9, Canada. See also Susan Bryant, "Confessions of an Unwitting Environmentalist," *Environments* (University of Waterloo, Spring, 1993), and M. Darrol Bryant, "Notes Towards an Eco-Spirituality" available from the author. Most of what I have said here is informed by our experience over the past five years.

19. See, for example, Ed McGaa, Eagle Man, *Mother Earth Spirituality, Native American Paths to Healing Ourselves and Our World* (San Francisco: Harper and Row, 1990).

20. I have not emphasized here the importance of spiritual disciplines for the inward transformation that is necessary to transform the heart and mind and develop the requisite virtues of compassion, love, and courage. I see this as essential, but I felt it was important in this essay to focus on the social/institutional forces that have given rise to the ecological crisis.

18

Divine Goodness
and Demonic Evil

By David Ray Griffin

Religion has to do primarily with the desire to overcome evil through proper relation to the supreme power of the universe. This characterization of religion reflects my own perspective, which is theistic, but I believe that it applies more broadly. To the extent that it does, religion in general presupposes belief in both worldly evil and divine goodness. In any case, in this essay I will suggest a solution to the theoretical problem of evil, including that form of evil that I call "demonic," from my perspective as a Protestant Christian process theologian, hoping that this suggestion will prove helpful to those within other traditions as well.

What is the (theoretical) problem of evil and why does it arise? The problem, in most general terms, is how to reconcile what we believe about the goodness and the power of the divine reality of the universe with the evil of our world. At one level of belief, there is no inconsistency: To be religious is to believe both in the reality of evil and in a divine reality that, because of its power and goodness, can and will provide salvation from this evil. Religious belief, in other words, presupposes that worldly evil is compatible with a divine reality.

However, attempts to provide more precise accounts, especially of divine power, often lead to difficulties. Not being content merely to affirm that the divine reality has power, at least sufficient power to save us from evil, devotees go on to speak of it as all-powerful, omnipotent. To some extent such a move is required by the very nature of religion, because religion, at least arguably, involves the desire to be in harmony with the supreme power of the universe. This religiously motivated move is supported, furthermore, by the fact that the idea of a supreme power of the universe arises also from another interest: the cosmological interest in understanding the existence of our world, the remarkable order of which seems to require assuming the existence of a cosmic power with vastly more power than any creature. If the term all-powerful (omnipotent) were taken to mean only this—that the divine reality is the supreme power of the universe and vastly more powerful than all others—an insoluble theoretical problem of evil would not necessarily result. The same is true even if one accepts a more stringent definition, according to which the divine reality has perfect power, meaning all the power that a supreme reality could conceivably have (with what is [consistently] conceivable not simply equated with what is verbally assertable). Quite often, however, the attribute of all-powerfulness has been taken to mean literally having all the power, at least essentially, so that any power possessed by creatures is merely on loan, as it were, so that it could be taken back or overridden at will. With this move, monotheism, the doctrine that there is ultimately only one power that is worthy of worship, turns into monism, which is the doctrine that there is essentially only one power.

Once this transition has been made, there is a contradiction between belief in worldly evil and divine goodness. If the divine reality essentially has all the power, there is, by definition, no power to resist it. There is, accordingly, no way satisfactorily to explain the existence of genuine evil, meaning things that not only appear to be evil at first glance but that really are evil, so that the universe as a whole would have been better had some other possibility occurred instead. There are only two ways to overcome the contradiction: Either deny that any of the *prima facie* evil is genuinely evil; or else say that the divine reality is not perfectly good. Neither of these solutions is, I believe, acceptable.

The denial of genuine evil, which has been the most prevalent solution accepted by traditional Christian theologians, is not one that I can accept. At the most basic level, I cannot but consider the idea obscene, that all cases of *prima facie* evil—from the Nazi holocaust to the rapes and murders of little children that occur every day—are somehow necessary to bring about a great good that would not have been possible without them, or at least that such things in no way detract from the overall goodness of the world. It is for me, in the strictest sense of the term, incredible.

In calling it incredible in the strictest sense, I have in mind what I call hard-core common sense beliefs. These are beliefs that we all presuppose in practice, even if we deny them verbally. To deny them verbally, therefore, involves one in contradictions with one's own presuppositions. I use the adjective hard-core to distinguish such beliefs, which are truly common to all people, from those beliefs that are often called commonsensical but are not truly universal and can, accordingly, be denied without necessarily contradicting any presuppositions of one's practice. Examples of soft-core common sense are the belief that the earth is flat and that molecules are wholly devoid of sentience and spontaneity. One example of hard-core common sense is the belief that there is a real world beyond our own experience: One can verbally claim to be a solipsist, but in the very act of making the claim, one shows that one does not really believe it. Belief that some events are genuinely evil belongs, I claim, in this class of beliefs: No one can in practice consistently live without presupposing that some events are genuinely evil. Without this presupposition, many of our most basic emotional reactions, such as remorse, guilt-feelings, blame, and gratitude (to those who have prevented what would have been genuine evils), would not make sense.

Besides not being able to accept solutions to the problem of evil that deny the ultimate reality of evil, I also cannot accept those that deny the perfect goodness of the divine reality. The whole point of a theodicy is to show that the evils of our world do not contradict the perfect goodness of the divine reality. To speak of the divine reality as beyond good and evil, or as having evil as well as good tendencies, is not to provide a theodicy but to say that none is possible. A pragmatic reason for rejecting this type of solution is my belief that religion involves the desire to be in harmony with the divine reality. If the divine reality is conceived to be evil as well as good, then religion sanctions our worst as well as our best impulses. In any case, as a Christian theologian I take the perfect goodness of

God, as pure unbounded love, not to be negotiable.

Having stated my beliefs about both evil and divine goodness, I need to explain what I mean by demonic evil in particular. With this term I point to evil that diametrically opposes divine power and does so with such strength as to destroy divine creations in a way that threatens divine purposes. Because this definition puts the demonic in direct opposition to divine power, fleshing out this purely formal definition requires a positive characterization of the divine power. And doing this requires that I anticipate the crucial aspect of my theodicy to be given below, which is the idea that divine power is strictly evocative, persuasive power, meaning that it is not power that can be used coercively and destructively. My threefold characterization of divine power is power that is (1) always employed persuasively and creatively, that is (2) always based on responsive love for the creatures, and that is, therefore, (3) always informed by creative love, which means that it always intends the good of those upon whom it is exerted. Given this idea of divine power, we can characterize the demonic as power that is (1) employed coercively and destructively (as well as perhaps persuasively and creatively), that is (2) based on hate and/or indifference towards at least some of those upon whom it is exercised, and that is, therefore, (3) not aimed at the good of all those upon whom it is exercised. This threefold characterization explains how demonic evil is diametrically opposed to divine power. The other condition for its being truly demonic is that it be strong enough to destroy divine creations in a way that threatens divine purposes.

The New Testament contained a realistic but mythical view of demonic evil. It must be considered mythical, because the demonic was portrayed in terms of an actual individual—Satan, the devil—who rivals God in cosmic scope, knowledge, and power, thereby having powers that no creature could have. This picture was realistic, however, in that it did justice to the extent to which the world seems to be under the sway of a demonic force. Rather than sanguinely regarding divine goodness as in control of all events, the New Testament speaks of the devil as "the ruler of this world" (John 14:30, 16:11) and "the god of this age" (II Cor. 4:4), says that "the whole world is in the power of the evil one" (I Jn. 5:19), and has the devil say that the kingdoms of the world are under his control (Luke 4:5-6). The battle between the divine and the demonic powers is regarded as a real battle, upon which the fate of the world depends.

To be sure, the New Testament also believed that "the present evil age" (Gal. 1:4) was coming to an end, thanks to the inbreaking of the rule of God in the life, death, and resurrection of Jesus. But, in whatever sense we may regard the divine reality's activity in Jesus as the beginning of the end of demonic control of our planet, it is empirically obvious that this was at most only the beginning of the end.

Indeed, demonic control of the planet has increased qualitatively during the intervening 2000 years, especially in the past four centuries, which we call the modern age. War in the 20th century has involved unprecedented slaughter of human beings. And this slaughter could have been much greater, thanks to the primary manifestation of demonic power in our century, the building of thousands of nuclear weapons, through which all human life and much of the rest of the planet's life could have been destroyed in hours—a threat that has by no means been removed. Furthermore, even if we do avoid nuclear holocaust, the present trajectory of civilization, with its increasing population, consumerism, and depleting-and-polluting technologies, promises unprecedented suffering through scarcity and climate change sometime in the 21st century. The projections based upon purely ecological matters are bad enough; when this growing scarcity of land, food, and other resources is combined with increasing ethnic and cultural animosities, the proliferation of nuclear weapons, and arms sales generally, any realistic picture of the future based on present trends is completely terrifying. We live in a world that is essentially good, created by divine power. But it is a world that is, even more fully than was the world in New Testament times, presently in the grip of demonic power.

To have a theology that is adequate to this reality, we need a way of formulating the New Testament's realistic portrayal of the demonic while discarding its mythology. We have not inherited such an account, however, because traditional theology did just the opposite: It retained the mythical aspect of the New Testament's portrayal of the demonic while giving up its realism.

In Augustine's theology, for example, Satan is an individual center of consciousness and will. Given Augustine's view of divine omnipotence as actually causing everything that occurs, however, he could not allow for any creaturely center of power that could truly act counter to the divine will. He says: "Nothing. . . happens unless the Omnipotent wills it to happen." Augustine does not flinch from applying this doctrine to sinful thoughts and actions, saying that God "does in the hearts of even wicked men whatsoever He wills." Augustine explicitly applies this doctrine to the devil. In speaking of the afflictions of Job and the temptations of Peter, he says: "God himself . . . did all things justly by the power he gave to the devil."[2] The battle between the divine and the demonic is, accordingly, a mock, not a real, battle. The demonic is entirely under the divine thumb. The realism of the New Testament image of the demonic is lost in the theology of Augustine and other classical theologians because of their monistic monotheism, according to which there is only one center of power.

The New Testament's view, by contrast, was what Jeffrey Russell has called "semidualistic monotheism."[3] Semidualism, in contrast with full-fledged dualism, does not hold that the demonic is fully autonomous from God and equal in cosmic scope and power. But it does allow some real autonomy to the demonic. We can express this semidualism by saying that the demonic is a creature and yet more than a creature. That is, the demonic, unlike the divine, does not exist eternally, but comes about only through the creative power of the divine. It is a creature. Once it has been created, however, it is not merely a creature, in the sense of being totally under control of the divine power. Rather, it can really oppose the divine power and threaten its purposes. The demonic has potentially deadly consequences.

What we need now is a way to formulate philosophically the New Testament's semidualistic monotheism. And we do now have a way to do this, thanks to one of Alfred North Whitehead's greatest gifts to theology, his distinction between God (the ultimate actuality) and creativity (the ultimate reality).[4] I will show how the distinction between God and creativity solves the problem of evil in general. I will be simply summarizing ideas that I have previously published.[5] However, I will develop the notion of demonic evil in particular. Finally, I will offer a suggestion as to how demonic evil came to dominance on our planet.

Creativity and the Problem of Evil

The distinction between creativity, as the ultimate reality embodied in all actualities, and God, as the ultimate actuality, provides the basis for a solution to the problem of evil that was impossible for classical theology, with its monistic monotheism. That kind of theism equated God with being itself, and thereby power itself, by saying that God was somehow both an individual being and yet also the being-ness of all things. Even some theologians who have rejected classical theism, such as Paul Tillich, have retained the identification of God with being itself, and thereby power itself. If all power is divine power, creatures cannot really oppose the divine reality. Whitehead, using the term creativity to point to what Tillich called being itself or the power of being, broke with this identification, saying that God is not simply creativity as such but the primordial embodiment of it. This distinction between power as such and divine power in particular allows us to understand how there can be evil in this world, even though it is God's creation.

Creativity involves two kinds of power: the power of self-determination and the power to influence others. The distinction between God and creativity means that this twofold power is necessarily embodied not only in God, but also in a plurality of finite beings. It is not the case, accordingly, that God can unilaterally bring about events in the world. God cannot, for example, determine when and where earthquakes will and will not happen, or when and where cells will and will not become cancerous. God cannot deflect a bullet heading toward a heart too young to die, or, for that matter, unilaterally convert the distorted heart of a person bent on sending millions to the gas chamber. The divine power is the power to evoke and to persuade, not the power to coerce and compel. The fact that the world is filled with evil, even unspeakably horrible evil, provides no evidence, therefore, against the perfect goodness of God.

According to this view, God did not create the universe *ex nihilo*, in the sense of absolute nothingness, as if God once existed all alone and thus as the sole embodiment of creative power. Rather, creation is creation of order out of chaos, a chaos of events with some creative power of their own. God is not essentially the sole power, but the soul of the universe, a power essentially in relation with other powers, even if their power at certain stages is extremely minimal.

One crucial implication of this denial of creation *ex nihilo* is that it removes the basis for assuming that all the basic principles of the universe were arbitrarily established by God. If what exists necessarily and eternally is not simply God, but God-and-a-world, then we should assume that there are some general principles that are metaphysical, being inherent in the very nature of things. Such principles would, like the fact that God exists and that God is loving, be beyond all decision, even God's. They would necessarily hold true of any world that God could create.

A most important example would be the principle that every increase in the capacity for good means a similar increase in the capacity for evil. This principle is certainly true of human society. For example, cities make possible all sorts of good that are not available in rural life; but they also greatly increase the possibilities of evil. The principle is also true of cultural evolution. For example, both modern transportation and communications systems have greatly increased the possibility for human enrichment; but they have also greatly increased the possibilities for evil, as they make possible world war and unprecedented invasions of privacy.

The principle that the possibilities for good and evil increase proportionately is also true of evolution in general, which is the main point here. The earth prior to the emergence of life was a much poorer world. Because there was experience, there was some intrinsic value, but it was trivial. The emergence of life, however, in bringing forth beings with greater intrinsic value, also brought with it the possibility of pain and thus the first significant evil. A similar increase in the possibilities for both good and evil occurred with the emergence of animals with central nervous systems, and then again with the emergence of primates. Surely the most dramatic example, however, is the rise of human existence. Prior to the appearance of human beings, there was, to be sure, much intrinsic value in the world, but it was all of a degree that is qualitatively different from the values that are distinctive of human life, such as the creation and enjoyment of great works of art, mathematics, and philosophy, the experience of religious ecstasy, the realization of moral beauty, and the enjoyment of human friendship and love. And yet, when we think of evil, especially really horrendous forms of evil, we realize that, if human beings did not exist to cause and suffer evil, most of the worst forms of evil would not exist. Human existence made possible qualitatively new forms of evil as well as good.

This principle, that every increase in the capacity for good brings with it an equal increase in the capacity for evil, is clearly an empirical fact. What is suggested by the distinction between God and creativity, and the correlative rejection of creation *ex nihilo*, is that it is not merely an empirical fact about our world. It is also a metaphysical principle, which necessarily holds of any world that God could have created. If this is so, we do not have to ask why God created the world so that it conforms to this principle. We do not have to ask, for example, why God created the world so that cancer and AIDS were possibilities; any world with animal life would have contained such risks. We do not have to ask why God created the world so that chemical and nuclear weapons were possible; any world God could have created would have contained such risks. We do not have to ask why God did not make human beings rational saints, meaning beings who would have our capacity for reason and yet would be guaranteed always to do good. Any beings with the capacity for human-like rationality would have had the capacity for human-like depravity.

Assuming that this principle is metaphysical in character is of utmost importance for the problem of evil. While the distinction between God and creativity explains why there should be some evil in the world, this additional principle explains why there is so much evil, especially now that human beings exist. God could not have created beings with our capacity for good who would not also have had our capacity for evil. Not all the evil that has in fact occurred was necessary, to be sure; but its possibility was necessary. The only way that God could have guaranteed the absence of the kind of evil that has occurred in human history would have been not to have brought forth human beings at all. Accordingly, we cannot indict God for the evils of this world, Auschwitz and all. These evils do not contradict God's perfect goodness and wisdom.

Creativity and the Possibility of Demonic Power

Having prepared the way by explaining how the distinction between creative power as such and divine power in particular provides the basis for a realistic theodicy, I now turn to my main concern, which is to develop a nonmythical but realistic idea of the demonic.

Demonic power became possible with the rise of human beings. Because of the human being's dual power to grasp things, both physically and conceptually, the rise of human beings meant the rise of a kind of creaturely power that could for the first time diametrically and strongly oppose the power of our creator. Because of our unprecedented power of self-determination, we can make decisions that run strongly counter to the divine influences upon us, which are always calling us to truth, beauty, and goodness. With humans, the power to know the difference between good and evil, and thereby the power of sin, entered the world. Because of our power to manipulate symbols with our minds and physical objects with out hands, we also have far more power to exert coercive power than do other creatures. Our power to sin is matched by an equally unprecedented power to dominate. Our unprecedented power of influence is not limited, however, to coercion: Our linguistic power has given us an unprecedented form of persuasive power as well, a form of power that was greatly augmented with the invention of writing. These unique abilities of human beings are necessary conditions for the rise of demonic power.

I had earlier characterized demonic power not merely in terms of its nature and strength, but also in terms of its being employed on the basis of hate or indifference, and therefore in a destructive way. This aspect of the possibility for the emergence of demonic power is rooted in our nature as creatures. Because we, unlike God, are local rather than all-inclusive beings, our sympathies tend to be very restricted. We can be indifferent about the welfare of most other creatures and positively antagonistic to the welfare of those whom we perceive to be threats to our own welfare. We do, to be sure, have the capacity to objectify ourselves, to realize thereby that we are simply one among many creatures, all of whom are creatures of the same creator, all of whom have feelings and interests. And we have the capacity to be aware of moral norms, such as the principle that equals should be treated equally, that we should do to others as we would have them do to us. But we, likewise, have the capacity to use our same intellectual capacities to ignore these norms when convenient, or so to qualify and circumscribe them that they become virtually inapplicable to all except those with whom we naturally sympathize. Rather than using these capacities to overcome our natural indifference or antagonism to others, in fact, we can use them to create a hostility towards others that greatly surpasses in intensity, extent, and duration anything found in the nonhuman world. It is our very humanity, in short, that creates the possibility for the emergence of demonic power.

I have indicated, in rejecting the mythical idea of the demonic as a devil, that the demonic is not an individual being. There is no evil soul alongside the divine soul of the universe. But the demonic is not, on the other hand, simply the aggregated power of individual human beings. It consists, instead, of what can be called a quasi-soul.

The Whiteheadian idea of creativity on which I am building provides a way to explicate what Walter Rauschenbusch, in giving a nonmythical account of original sin, called the suprapersonal power of evil.[6] Rauschenbusch described the structures and habits that promote sin, describing how people are seduced into sin, through the power of authority and imitation, long before they have reached the age of accountability. To all that Rauschenbusch says, we can add a form of influence that works at a presensory level and at a distance.

The science of psychical research, or parapsychology, has amply demonstrated that such influence occurs.[7] Evidence for telepathy and clairvoyance show that we have the capacity to receive causal influence at a distance. Evidence for psychokinesis shows that we have the capacity to exert this kind of causal influence. Modern science, philosophy, and theology have, however, largely ignored this evidence, because it did not fit with the reigning worldview. The early modern worldview, with its mechanistic view of nature and its sensationist view of perception, said that such influence cannot occur except through supernatural intervention. The late modern worldview, by retaining early modernity's view of nature and perception while rejecting its supernaturalism, has said that such influence cannot happen at all. This late modern worldview has made extra-sensory perception and psychokinetic influence seem all the more impossible by regarding the mind as epi-phenomenal, that is, as a mere byproduct of the brain without any autonomous power to exert power or to perceive. Modern theology, accepting the modern worldview's veto, has ignored parapsychology's offer of empirical evidence supporting the reality of spiritual influence.

A postmodern form of naturalism, however, allows for the reality of this spiritual influence at a distance. Because the world is made of events of creative experience, rather than bits of insentient matter, there is no reason to suppose that causal influence can be exerted only by contact and, therefore, only on contiguous things. Also, the idea that all individuals enjoy a nonsensory form of perception, so that sensory perception is derivative from this more primordial, nonsensory mode of perception, means that extrasensory perception, whether telepathic or clairvoyant, does not need to be regarded as a violation of the laws of nature. Reports of such occurrences need not, accordingly, be regarded as either fraudulent or as evidence of supernatural intervention. Rather, events in which people become aware of extrasensory perception can be regarded as simply the consciousness of a kind of nonsensory perception that is occurring all the time. What is exceptional about such perceptions is not that they involve nonsensory perception, but only that a form of perception that usually remains unconscious has risen to the conscious level of experience. Furthermore, this postmodern worldview, far from regarding the human mind or soul as impotent, regards it as the most powerful creature on the face of the earth. The parapsychological evidence that the human mind can directly exert far more influence on other things beyond its body, including other minds, than can other animals is, accordingly, what would be expected. Cases of reported psychokinesis can be regarded as merely conspicuous instances of a kind of pervasive psychic influence that is radiating from our minds all the time.

From this perspective, we can suppose that we are influencing each other directly, soul to soul, all the time. We can suppose that through the enormously complex web of psychic influence that results, we are born into a kind of quasi-soul, which shapes our souls for good or for ill, and to which we in turn contribute, thereby adding our influence, for good or for ill, to the psychic ether that will shape other souls.

This influence at a distance is, of course, usually quite weak in comparison with physically mediated influence. There is a factor, however, that somewhat balances out the power of these two kinds of influence on us. The distance over which this kind of influence operates can be temporal as well as spatial distance. Because of this influence over time, repetitions of a certain form of activity can have a cumulative effect. For example, if a certain image has been focused on by devotees of a particular religion for hundreds, perhaps thousands, of years, this image will be impressed upon the unconscious portion of the psyches of present-day individuals with considerable power. This, incidentally, is a way of explaining the reality and power of Jungian archetypes, a way that Jung himself sometimes employed.[8]

Through this idea, we can see how the demonic could be an even stronger power than Rauschenbusch thought. Everything he said about the power of the written word, pictures, patriotic songs, history books, examples, stereotypes, ideologies, and so on, would stand. To all this we can add the reinforcing power that comes from the hate and other violence-inducing attitudes, emotions, and images that have been repeated countless times down through human history. We are born into a kingdom of evil, a demonic quasi-soul, that not only influences us indirectly, through our sensory experience, but also directly, through spiritual influence.

The Demonic's Historical Rise to Ascendancy

My ideas in this section have been inspired primarily by Andrew Bard Schmookler's *The Parable of the Tribes*.[9] Schmookler's view of the central importance of the war-system in shaping the direction taken by civilization over the past 10,000 years has been reinforced by writings of William H. McNeill.[10] A position on the demonic similar to mine has been developed in Walter Wink's trilogy on the powers, especially the third volume, *Engaging the Powers*.[11] I know of no more important work on the contemporary theological scene.

The basic idea of this new perspective is that the war-system, along with the more general domination system (to use the term Wink has appropriated from Riane Eisler's *The Chalice and the Blade*), began within the past 10,000 years. It was occasioned by the rise of civilization, with its cities and agriculture. During the prior 40,000 years of the existence of *homo sapiens*, life was surely filled with evils of various sorts. Desires of revenge and other motives would have led tribes to carry out savage raids on each other from time to time. But the hunting-and-gathering mode of existence would have provided no motive for a war-system as such. For example, captives, who could not be entrusted to share in the hunt, would simply provide more mouths to feed. But the rise of civilization changed all this. Slaves could be assigned the drudge work involved in agriculture and the building of walls and water canals. Women captives could, besides working in the homes and the fields, bear children to build up the city's defensive and offensive capacity. The cities, their cultivated lands, and their domesticated herds also provided motives for attack. The rise of civilization brought the institutionalization of war.

Once the war-system began, everyone was forced to participate. Even if most societies wanted to be peaceful, any one society could force the rest to prepare for war or risk being subjugated or annihilated. As Schmookler says, "Nice guys are finished first."[12]

In this war-system, it is power, not morality, that determines the relations among the states. As stated in the Hobbesian analysis, the interstate realm is a state of anarchy: There is no superior power to declare and enforce any moral norms. Might rather literally makes right. The classic formulation is provided by Thucydides, who has the Athenian general limit the Meletans' choices to being taken over peacefully or violently, adding that if they had the superior power they would do the same to the Athenians. In this Hobbesian situation of the war of all against all—which means not that you actually fight against everyone else, but that every other society is at least potentially your enemy—war is not brought on only by the desire of one society's leaders for additional power, riches, and glory, but also by the fear that another society is amassing enough military power to attack them. Thucydides again provides the classic statement, having Alcibiades say, with regard to taking Sicily: "If we cease to rule others, we are in danger of being ruled ourselves."

In this anarchical state of civilization, coercive power inevitably grows. Each advance by any one state must be matched by advances by the others within striking distance. A move that may be intended defensively will often look offensive to others, evoking further efforts by them to increase their power. There is no stopping point. Although the development of nuclear weapons might have occurred either sooner or considerably later than it actually did, the fact that it did eventually occur was made virtually inevitable by the dynamics of the system.

The development of coercive power does not, however, involve only the development of new forms of weapons and defenses. The most obvious other element is military strategy and tactics. But a society's ability to wage war is also to a great extent a function of its political and economic systems. Any development (such as the rise of capitalism in the Italian city-states in the 14th century) that gives a society a temporary military edge will tend to spread to the neighboring societies.

The main point of this analysis is that the evolution of civilization in the state of anarchy is necessarily shaped in large part by a principle similar to that of survival of the fittest based on natural selection in Darwinian evolution. Schmookler calls this principle the "selection for power." This analysis is not reductionistic, as if the drive for power were at the root of all cultural developments. The point is, instead, that of those developments that do occur, those that increase a society's power vis-a-vis other societies will tend not only to survive but also to spread. In the long run, the direction of civilization is shaped most decisively by this selection for power. As civilization evolves, the need for power increasingly shapes every aspect of a society. In recent decades, for example, something like half of our nation's science has been devoted to military-related research. Anarchical civilization, with its war-system, results in a reign of power.

Implicit in this analysis is the idea that the reign of power in the interstate arena leads to the reign of power within each state. This is not to say that the rise of patriarchal, hierarchical, domination societies was motivated entirely or even primarily by the demands of the war-system. That interstate system did, however, provide the context in which hierarchical societies were virtually inevitable. As Gerda Lerner points out, non-hierarchical societies for the most part did not survive,[13] and it is hard to argue with the claim that survival must take priority over all other considerations. The argument from necessity in relation to external dangers has always, probably from the outset of the war-system, provided the excuse for the worst kinds of internal inequalities. The war-system has also provided an ever-increasing basis for the human domination of nature.

This is my suggestion as to how demonic power, which the rise of human existence made possible, actually came to dominance on our planet. Over the past 10,000 years, human civilizations have increasingly been oriented around the drive to increase human power, in the sense of the power to control, the power to destroy, the power to intimidate. Human beings in this context have wanted more power over nature in order to increase their power over other human groups in order to give them more power over nature. Civilization has been largely shaped by the drive to produce coercive power that would be used with hate or at least indifference—and this is our concept of the demonic. Civilization has increasingly been in its grip for the past 5,000 years.

The power of a society is determined not only by the size of its armies, its military technology, strategies, and tactics, and its political and economic systems. Undergirding all of these dimensions is the ideology of a society, its theology. (Any all-inclusive ideology is a theology insofar as it involves, at least implicitly, a notion of that which is holy or sacred.) Just as the selection for power operates with regard to all other dimensions, so too it operates in relation to ideologies.[14] We should expect, accordingly, that the history of anarchical civilization's theologies and philosophies will involve the gradual ascendancy of those ideologies that are most effective in producing a warrior-mentality and thereby a warrior-society. An effective ideology of power will, for example, make people unafraid to die in battle and may even lead them to desire such a death; it will lead them to believe that by being warriors they are obeying the will of, and even imitating the behavior of, the deity of the universe; it will lead them to hate, or at least be indifferent to the welfare of people in other societies; it will convince them that they are a chosen people, so that by subjugating others they are actually bringing about divine rule on earth. An effective ideology of power will also tend to promote political and economic systems that increase a society's military capacity; it will also tend to promote philosophies, sciences, and technologies through which nature can be effectively dominated. The growth of such ideologies of power has been an intricate part—in many ways the most important part—of the growth of demonic power over the past few thousand years.

By the demonic, I mean the whole complex of belief-systems, symbols, images, stories, habits, attitudes, emotions, sciences, technologies, institutions, webs of direct and indirect psychic influence, and everything else that is oriented around the production and deployment of destructive power, used with hate or indifference, to dominate and destroy fellow creatures of God. This demonic power is now, even more completely than in New Testament times, in effective control of the trajectory of civilization.

Although religion should seek to respond in various ways to evil, and should respond to evil in all its forms, its primary concern, I believe, should be to serve as an agency of the divine reality to overcome demonic evil. The above analysis of demonic evil implies that the effort by religious leaders to overcome demonic evil would have two primary foci: eliminating those aspects of our own religious traditions' theology that give support to the demonic, and working for the transcendence of global anarchy.

NOTES

1. See my "The 'Vision Thing,' the Presidency, and the Ecological Crisis, or the Greenhouse Effect and the 'White House Effect,'" in David Ray Griffin and Richard Falk, ed., *Postmodern Politics for a Planet in Crisis: Policy, Process, and Presidential Vision* (Albany: State University of New York, 1993), pp. 67-102.

2. These statements by Augustine are from the *Enchiridion* XIV: 96, XXIV:95, and *Grace and Free Will* XLII, which can be found in *Basic Writings of St. Augustine*, ed. Whitney J. Oates (New York: Random House, 1953).

3. Jeffrey Burton Russell, *The Devil: Perceptions of Evil from Antiquity to Primitive Christianity* (Ithaca: Cornell University Press, 1977), pp. 228, 248.

4. This distinction is made in John B. Cobb, Jr., *Beyond Dialogue: Toward a Mutual Transformation of Christianity and Buddhism* (Philadelphia: Fortress, 1982), pp. 110-14.

5. See *God, Power, and Evil: A Process Theodicy* (Philadelphia: Westminister Press, 1976; Lanham, Md: University Press of America, 1991 [reprint with new preface]); "Creation out of Chaos and the Problem of Evil," in Stephen T. Davis, ed., *Encountering Evil: Live Options in Theodicy* (Atlanta: John Knox, 1981); and *Evil Revisited: Responses and Reconsiderations* (Albany: State University of New York Press, 1991).

6. See Walter Rauschenbusch, *A Theology for the Social Gospel* (New York: Macmillan, 1918), especially the chapters on "The Super-Personal Forces of Evil" and "The Kingdom of Evil."

7. For excellent surveys of parapsychological studies, see Benjamin Wolman, ed., *Handbook of Parapsychology* (New York: Van Nostrand Reinhold, 1977); Hoyt L. Edge, Robert L. Morris, John Palmer, and Joseph H. Rush, *Foundations of Parapsychology* (Boston and London: Routledge and Kegan Paul, 1986); and the series, *Advances in Parapsychological Research*, ed. Stanley Krippner (New York: Plenum Press), especially Vol. I, *Psychokinesis* (1977) and Vol. II, *Extrasensory Perception* (1978). For evaluations of the evidence by capable philosophers, see *Essays on Psychical Research* in the

Harvard edition of the writings of William James, ed. by Robert McDermott, C.D. Broda, *Religion, Philosophy and Psychical Research* (London: Routledge and Kegan Paul, 1953; New York: Humanities Press, 1969); and Stephen Braude, *ESP and Psychokinesis: A Philosophical Examination* (Philadelphia: Temple University Press, 1978) and *The Limits of Influence: Psychokinesis and the Philosophy of Science* (New York and London: Routledge and Kegan Paul, 1986). See also my "Parapsychology and Philosophy: A Whiteheadian Postmodern Perspective," *The Journal of the American Society for Psychical Research* 87/3 (July 1993), pp. 217-88.

8. See my introduction to David Ray Griffin, ed., *Archetypal Process: Self and Divine in Whitehead, Jung, and Hillman* (Evanston: Northwestern University Press, 1989), esp. pp. 39-44.

9. Andrew Bard Schmookler, *The Parable of the Tribes: The Problem of Power in Social Evolution* (Boston: Houghton Mifflin, 1986).

10. See especially William H. McNeill, *The Rise of the West: A History of the Human Community* and *The Pursuit of Power: Technology, Armed Force, and Society since A.D. 1000* (Chicago: The University of Chicago Press, 1982).

11. Walter Wink, *Engaging the Powers: Discernment and Resistance in a World of Domination* (Minneapolis: Fortress Press, 1992).

12. Schmookler, *The Parable of the Tribes*, p. 45.

13. Gerda Lerner, *The Creation of Patriarchy* (New York: Oxford University Press, 1986), p. 35.

14. Schmookler suggests that the selection for power would have also operated with regard to religious ideologies (*The Parable of the Tribes*, pp. 73, 80), but he does not develop this idea at length.

19

Towards a
Global Theodicy

By Paul Badham

T heodicy is a technical Christian term, used to describe attempts to justify belief in the limitless goodness of God in the
face of the manifest suffering and evil in a world that God is
believed to have created. One theodicy frequently discussed in
western philosophy of religion is the soul-making theodicy classically
expounded in John Hick's early work, *Evil and the God of Love.*[1] More
recently Hick has championed the view known as religious pluralism, namely that all the great religions are culturally different
human responses to the one divine reality.[2] What I want to explore
here is whether the two strands in Hick's thinking can be brought
together. Has soul-making theodicy anything to say in a religiously
plural world? In particular can it relate to religious traditions that
have no concept of a creator God whose ways need justifying, and
that explicitly reject the idea of human persons having souls which
can be thought of as being made?

The fact that evil and suffering undoubtedly exist poses a challenge to the Christian supposition that this world was created by an
all-powerful, all-knowing, and all-benevolent God. Either God
cannot abolish evil in which case God is not all-powerful, or God
chooses not to, and cannot therefore be all-benevolent. Many
attempts have been made to meet this challenge. Process theology

suggests that God is not all-powerful. The Church of Christian Science sees evil as an illusion. Traditional theology explains evil as the product of the fall of the first man and woman. Popular piety suggests that though the problem cannot be resolved philosophically, it was resolved religiously in the crucifixion of Christ perceived as God incarnate, identifying with and sharing in the depths of human suffering. But serious problems face all these solutions. To deny either the competence of God to end suffering or to deny the existence of evil seem evasions of the issue. A historical fall is too much at variance with the discoveries of archaeology, anthropology and evolutionary history to be a live option. And I have never understood how the problem of evil is supposed to be helped by the notion that God also experiences it. We welcome the sympathy of friends whom we know are powerless to help us. But we would feel mocked by expressions of concern from those who had it comfortably in their power to save us but chose not to do so. The problem of evil is certainly not solved by saying that God chooses to suffer with us rather than rescue us from our plight.

Some philosophers have put forward the so-called free-will defense which argues that the possibility of evil and the existence of an objective world with stable laws of nature are necessary for the emergence of free and responsible agents. This view forms an important part of the soul-making theodicy and although it can to a certain extent stand on its own, I shall consider it simply as part of the wider thesis. For if the free responsible agents who are created through their interaction with the stable environment face a future terminated by suffering, disease, death and extinction, then the question of why God allows evil remains unanswered. Hence the free-will defense needs the wider perspective of the soul-making theodicy.

Soul-making Theodicy

The soul-making theodicy fully accepts that looking at life simply from within the transitory limits of human existence, the case against belief that the world was created by a wholly benevolent, all-powerful and all-knowing God is overwhelming. This world is not a hedonist's paradise. It is a struggle for existence where we earn our bread by the sweat of our brow. We face innumerable challenges, hardships and difficulties. Ultimately we will age and die, unless we experience premature death through accident, microbe or virus. But the Christian perspective is not confined to this life only. If it were so confined, Christians would, according to St. Paul be "of all people most to be pitied."[3] However, from its foundation Christianity has been a religion committed to belief in heaven, a divine kingdom in which sorrowing and sighing have no place and in which God becomes the most central feature of our experience. Yet Christians have always intuited that such a world could only be appreciated and experienced by fully formed persons. We have to become "fitted" for heaven by what we do here. Free responsible beings cannot simply be created by divine fiat. Rather we develop our characters and personalities through facing up to the difficulties and challenges of life and thereby becoming persons capable of an eternal relationship with God. John Hick expresses the principle behind this concept thus:

> Virtues formed within the agent as a hard-won deposit of his own right decisions in situations of challenge and temptation are intrinsically more valuable than virtues created within him ready made and without any effort on his part. . .If God's purpose was to create finite persons embodying the most valuable kind of moral goodness, he would have to create them, not as already perfect beings but rather as imperfect creatures who can then attain to the more valuable kind of goodness through their own free choices.[4]

This way of thinking was classically articulated by the poet John Keats when he wrote to his brother and sister in April 1819, "Do you not see how necessary a world of pains and troubles is to school an intelligence and make it a Soul?. . .Call the world if you please 'The vale of Soul-making.'"[5] In this schema we shape our personhood by the way we engage with the responsibilities and duties we face in the everyday tasks of life in a world subject to natural laws where what we do or fail to do has consequences. It is no part of the soul-making theodicy that suffering in itself is ennobling or character-forming, for there would be very strong evidence against so simplistic a view. But what this theodicy does say is that a real objective physical world, governed by regular physical laws, provides an environment more suited to the development of responsible agents than would an environment in which divine intervention saved humanity from the consequences of its folly, or from the heartache and challenge implicit in any finite and physical existence.

After personhood has been fully formed, then it may well be that life in a heaven of eternal rest, peace and bliss would become conceivable. But it could only be appreciated and experienced by those who have first undergone the person-forming experience available to them in this world. Moreover, it is likely that we may need to undergo further growth in a life after death. John Hick envisages many lives in many worlds[6] and this view has antecedents in earlier Christian writings. Within Catholicism there is the tradition of purgatory and many Protestants also talk of an intermediate state. Hence the soul-making theodicy does not require that the necessary growth is completed within this life. It merely claims that this life provides a good environment for spiritual growth which may well need further development beyond the grave as the person journeys into God.

It is integral to this view that our soul, character, or identity as persons is not innate. We shape our personhood by the way we live and in response to the challenges and stimuli of life. From a philosophical standpoint this view requires a concept of soul as an emergent property. Any view of the soul which takes serious note of modern genetics and neurophysiology has to accept that the soul is shaped and influenced by the way our brains and bodies develop and is molded by the experiences of life and our responses to them. Consequently, I see soul-making theodicy as literally descriptive language of how human identity is shaped. Such identity is clearly shaped in and through our bodily existence, but Christians believe that the ultimate destiny of the human subject will transcend this bodily form of existence. Keith Ward expresses this larger vision well:

> God is the true end of the soul, and in this sense, its goal, its proper purpose and true nature, lies beyond the physical universe. That is a strong reason for thinking that the subject which is embodied in this world may properly find other forms of experience and action, in contexts lying beyond this universe. . .Of course the soul depends on the brain. . .but the soul need not always depend on the brain, any more than a man need always depend on the womb which supported his life before birth.[7]

Soul-making in Judaism

The problem of evil, particularly in the form of the question, "Why do the righteous suffer?" has constantly been asked in Jewish history. Hebrew psalms and proverbs frequently raise the issue. One common response has been in the book of Job, namely that human beings have no right to question the ways of God, but must simply acknowledge God's divine wisdom.[8] But the inadequacy of such a response became apparent during the persecution of Antiochus Epiphanes, the first of the devastating persecutions to which the Jews have been subject throughout history when thousands of the most faithful perished. Faced with such a disaster the only way belief in God's love could remain at all credible was to affirm faith in the power of God to raise up the dead. In our day the Holocaust has had a comparable effect leading some Jews to feel that belief in God's goodness is no longer possible and that, to use Stendhal's epigram, "The only excuse for God is that he does not exist." But for those whose faith has held, a belief in a life after death has been reemphasized as an essential component of an intelligible faith. Rabbi Chon Sherbok writes: "The belief in the Hereafter has helped Jews make sense of the world as a creation of a good and all-powerful God and provided a source of great consolation for their travail on earth." Without such a belief Jews would "face great difficulties reconciling the belief in a providential God who watches over his chosen people with the terrible events of modern Jewish history."[9] A future hope is thus an essential component of an intelligible theism, due to both the problem of evil and for the fulfillment of the life of the righteous individual. As Cohn Sherbok makes clear, the "qualification for entrance to heaven (*Gan Eden*) is to lead a good life in accordance with God's laws."[10] Life, therefore, has meaning both for the individual and the community because it is directed towards the transcendent goal of the kingdom of God.

Theodicy in Islam

Islam shares with Judaism and Christianity the belief in an all-powerful, all-knowing, and all-compassionate creator God. From a philosophical standpoint the existence of evil is as much a challenge in Islam as in the other Abrahamic faiths. Religiously, however, the issue is far less pressing. A key requirement for one to be a good

Muslim is an attitude of submission (Islam) to what God has determined. Hence to question what God has done, or to feel a need to justify God in the face of evil indicates a non-submissive, non-Islamic attitude. If the problem is raised as an issue by a non-Muslim, a defense of God's ways can certainly be permitted. In constructing such a defense a Muslim would take for granted that the frame of reference would include the hereafter (*al-akhirah*). There is scarcely a chapter in the *Qur'an* which does not refer to the hereafter, and in the book as a whole there are no fewer than one-hundred and thirteen references to it. As Sulayman Nyang argues, "It is necessary to see the belief in a future life as integrally related to the total Islamic view of life in the sublunar world including man's role in this world and the significance of his faith."[11] The *Qur'an* makes clear that the human person was not created for sport but has a serious mission to undertake.[12]

In the Islamic tradition human life in the sublunar world is explicitly seen as a preparation for the hereafter. We will ultimately be accountable to Allah for the way we have lived; so what we do matters because it shapes the persons we become. The distinguished Islamic theologian Salih Tug expresses the matter thus:

> Just as from dust man has evolved, from the deeds he does the higher man is evolved. . .The human frame is only a vehicle by which the soul must develop itself. The soul has to evolve by its own effort from the crude form of simple consciousness to a certain stage of spiritual development. . .Our present life is a preparation. It is necessary to bring out our faculties and raise them to a certain stage of evolution during our earthly sojourn. Then alone shall we be fit for progress in the life after death. . .but we can enter that life only if we have made ourselves fit for it in our physical lifetime.[13]

This seems a clear expression of a soul-making theodicy.

Buddhist Responses to the Existence of Suffering

For Buddhism the existence of suffering does not constitute any kind of challenge. Rather the fact that the world is full of suffering is the essential starting point of all Buddhist thought and the essential presupposition of each of the Four Noble Truths from which the Buddhist philosophy of life derives. Buddhism does not believe in a creator God whose ways need to be justified, nor does Buddhism think in categories of a soul which needs to be developed. At first sight, therefore, to suggest that a soul-making theodicy might relate in any way to Buddhist insights seems perverse. However, I hope to suggest that if we look more deeply into the question we will see some striking parallels.

The Buddha was totally clear that to seek fulfillment through a materialistic or hedonistic approach to life was thoroughly misguided. Old-age, disease and death bring to naught all worldly hopes. The Buddha's primary response to the reality of suffering was to teach humans to overcome their fear of the unsatisfactoriness, suffering, or *duhkha* of life by recognizing the transience and impermanence or *anicca* of all things. He believed that if we really understood our situation, and achieved true enlightenment about the nature of reality, we would not attach a sense of identity or our search for meaning to anything as transitory and insubstantial as the present experience of selfhood or the fleeting desires which flow from sensory awareness in the present. Much of the Buddha's teaching is essentially concerned with helping people to cope with suffering in the here and now by gaining a truer insight into the reality of the human situation. This has led many to interpret the original Buddhist message as essentially practical and unconcerned about the nature of future life of which we can have no reliable knowledge. The Buddha urged his followers to avoid such speculation.

However, I think it is mistaken to suppose that the Buddha's thought was limited to this life alone. As Edward Conze points out in his preface to the section of his edition of Buddhist scriptures which deals with other worlds: "The horizon of Buddhism is not bounded by the limits of the sensory world, their true interests lie beyond it."[14] The Buddha himself saw human life within a cosmic perspective in which humans pass through a succession of lives on their journey towards enlightenment. The ultimate deathless state of *nirvana* will be reached only when we transcend the cycle of rebirth and finally rise above the self-centeredness of our present condition.

Anatta in Buddhism
and the Hindu Concept of Atman

One of the basic Buddhist understandings is the doctrine of
anatta, usually translated as the no-self doctrine and interpreted as
a total repudiation of the concept of the soul. However, every denial
has to be understood in relation to what is being denied. The
Buddha made it absolutely clear that what he opposed was the
Hindu notion of a soul or *atman* as an eternal, unchanging essence,
existing independently of others, unaffected by the traumas of life
and proceeding through a succession of lives. The *atman* should
ideally be unaffected by the claims of bodily nature. Ascetic practices
and an ideal of keeping apart from society have evolved to aid such
independence. This picture of an immortal changeless self at the
heart of our being was anathema to the Buddha. "The speculative
view that. . .I shall be *atman* after death, permanent, abiding, ever-
lasting, unchanging, and that I shall exist as such for eternity, is not
that wholly and completely foolish?"[15] It seems to me that the
Buddha was right in his denial. Modern philosophy of mind has
increasingly moved in the direction pioneered by the Buddha over
two thousand years. For example, Derek Parfit's influential work,
Reasons and Persons, concludes with a chapter on the Buddha's
views.[16] It has become increasingly clear that we cannot identify ourselves with an unchanging self. But as John Hick has pointed out, it
is not realistic to argue "no immutable, eternal, independent self,
therefore no self."[17] In the soul-making hypothesis it is axiomatic
that there is no unchanging soul, but rather that we are constantly
changing and developing as we respond to the challenges and
stimuli of life. Only a dynamic concept of selfhood does justice to
experience or empirical reality. It seems to me, therefore, that there
is no necessary clash between a soul-making theodicy and the no-self
doctrine when we examine the terminology of both theories
critically. Both repudiate an unchanging selfhood, and both affirm
that what we become is the product of what we do. Ironically,
therefore, I would argue that in real terms there are greater problems with fitting Hinduism into a soul-making theodicy than
Buddhism. Since Hinduism undoubtedly attaches great importance
to the soul, *atman*, the picture of it as an unchanging entity raises
fundamental problems. If we move on to consider the concept of

karma in both Hinduism and Buddhism, we may discover a resolution of this difficulty.

Theodicy and Karma

Neither Hindus nor Buddhists are concerned with theodicy in its classical form since justifying the ways of a creator God lies outside their frame of reference. Both are concerned with belief in a moral order underlying all things which finds expression in the doctrine of *karma*. The essence of the law of *karma* is that what we are is the product of what we have been, and what we shall be depends on what we do and think now. Historically this doctrine was shaped in a context of belief in rebirth or reincarnation leading through a succession of lives to the ultimate goal of being one with the ultimate (*moksha*) or entering the deathless state of *nirvana*. Hence, our behavior in this life has cosmic significance and meaning since it determines our future destiny. I suggest that this doctrine is in its practical effect analogous to soul-making theodicy. Both doctrines see life as having significance within a wider frame of reference than this life alone; and both possess a keen commitment to an underlying moral order so that what we do matters, whether to prepare us for heaven or to fulfil our karmic destiny. In each religion the ultimate goal which gives significance and meaning to human striving is a transcendent one. In Judaism, Christianity and Islam it is to find ultimate destiny in the hereafter with God. In Buddhism it is to achieve the deathless state of *nirvana*, and in Hinduism ultimately the hope is to achieve liberation or *moksha* from the cycle of rebirth. In all cases the ways in which humans respond to the challenges of life in this world are the means whereby they shape personhood or create and fulfil *karma* and hence grow more towards what they ought to be.

Affirming This World

It is frequently suggested that belief in a transcendent destiny leads people to despise this world or take it less seriously. This can sometimes happen; world renunciation is found in many religious traditions. But the central thrust of any soul-making theodicy or any doctrine of *karma* is to affirm the importance of what we do now. For although what the religions teach is directed towards the fulfillment of a transcendent destiny, what is actually prescribed as the means to that end is, at least for the lay-person, the conscientious fulfillment of the duties and obligations of everyday life. Saints in all three theistic traditions have warned against the idea that one ought to do good in order to win heaven. Rather, virtuous actions should be done for their own sake, because they are themselves good and contribute to the well-being of the individual and society in the here and now. If God is perceived to be a loving and good creator, one ought to be able to conclude that creation is for the benefit of the creature. Consequently, exploring what is natural to humanity becomes an appropriate basis for moral judgement, and attending to what can be shown empirically to enhance human fulfillment is, likewise, legitimate. Although there is often in practice a clash between the ethical thinking of ecclesiastical hierarchs and secular thinkers, in principle such clashes should not occur. As Grotius argued long ago, a true natural law ethic ought to be capable of being worked out *"etsi Deus non daretur"* (as if God were not a premise).[18] If we turn to Buddhism to exemplify the religious wisdom of the East, we note that the way the householder (as distinct from the monk) can obtain good *karma* is to follow the basic ethical principles of the *dharma* and fulfill one's obligations to family and society. In practical terms the behavior necessary for gaining heaven, or fulfilling one's *karma* is also the behavior best suited to the full realization of one's potential as a human person.

If we believe that what we do matters because it shapes what we become, we will have a positive attitude towards the challenges of life. These are the means by which we grow and develop. At different stages of life one seeks to throw oneself into the tasks and duties appropriate to any given stage. A conscientious person will take education seriously in youth, not simply in terms of academic achievement but hopefully the challenge of nurturing whatever talents one has. These may include the development of athletic, musical, aesthetic or organizational abilities as well as intellectual skills. Then one may move on to the tasks entailed by one's job or profession and perhaps also take on additional civic or social concerns. For many there will come family responsibilities and the cares and responsibilities of children and aged parents. For some there may be office in a voluntary society, cultural or political organization or church. These things provide people with a sense of meaning to their individual lives and give them their sense of worth and dignity. Such a positive attitude to life is a good in itself and from a humanist perspective might be self-chosen as a way to attribute meaning to one's daily activity. From a religious perspective the meaning is all the richer for being set in a cosmic framework, leading onwards to the fullness of life in a world beyond.

NOTES

1. John Hick, *Evil and the God of Love* (London: Macmillan, 1966).
2. John Hick, *An Interpretation of Religion* (London: Macmillan, 1989).
3. 1 Corinthians 15:19.
4. John Hick, "An Irenaean Theodicy," in Paul Badham, *A John Hick Reader* (London: Macmillan, 1991), p. 94.
5. M.B. Forman, *The Letters of John Keats* (London: Oxford University Press, 1952), p. 334-5.
6. John Hick, *Death and Eternal Life* (London: Macmillan, 1976), Part V.
7. Keith Ward, *The Battle for the Soul* (London: Hodder and Stoughton, 1985), pp. 149-50.
8. Job 42:1-5.
9. Dan Cohn Sherbok, "Death and Immortality in the Jewish Tradition," in P. and L. Badham, *Death and Immortality in the Religions of the World* (New York: Paragon House, 1987), p. 34.
10. Cohn Sherbok, p. 26.
11. Sulayman Nyang, "The Teaching of the Qur'an Concerning Life after Death," in P. and L. Badham, *Death and Immortality in the Religions of the World* (New York: Paragon House, 1987), p. 72.
12. Sulayman Nyang, p. 73, citing the *Qur'an*, 21:16-17.
13. Salih Tug, "Death and Immortality in Islamic Thought," in P. and L. Badham, *Death and Immortality in the Religions of the World, op. cit.*, pp. 87-88.
14. Edward Conze, *Buddhist Scriptures* (Harmondsworth: Penguin Classics, 1959), p. 221.
15. Cited in W. Rahula, *What the Buddha Taught* (New York: Group Press, 1959), p. 59.
16. Derek Parfit, *Reasons and Persons* (Oxford: Oxford University Press, 1986).
17. John Hick, "Response," in Stephen Davis, *Death and Afterlife* (London: Macmillan, 1989), p. 178.
18. Cited in F.C. Copleston, *History of Philosophy* (New York: Image Books, 1963), Vol. 3, Pt. 2, p. 145.

CONTRIBUTORS

Wande Abimbola: His Excellency Dr. Abimbola is a Paramount Chief and Priest in Nigeria. He is also President of the International Congress of Orisa Tradition and Culture. Under a previous government he was a senator in the Nigerian House of Representatives. He is author and translator of: *Ifa, An Exposition of Ifa Literary Corpus* and *Sixteen Great Poems of Ifa*. He has written many articles on traditional African religion. He has special concern for the Yoruba culture in the diaspora.

Muhammad Al-Ghazali: Dr. Al-Ghazali is Assistant Professor and heads the Department of Social Sciences at the Islamic Research Institute, International Islamic University, Islamabad, Pakistan. Recent publications include: "Islamic Philosophy of Dawah," *Journal of the International Islamic University* (1995); "Reason and Revelation - Conflict or Convergence," *Muslim Education Quarterly* (1944); a book *Socio-Political Thought of Shah Wali Ullah* is in production. He is presently working on a critique of methodology in the social sciences.

Paul Badham: The Reverend Professor Paul Badham is Dean of Theology and Religious Studies and Director of the Program in Death and Immortality at the University of Wales, Lampeter. He edited or authored the following books: *Christian Beliefs about Life and Death*; *Death and Immortality in the Religions of the World*; *Immortality or Extinction?*; *Ethics on the Frontiers of Human Existence*; and *A John Hick Reader*.

M. Darrol Bryant: Dr. Bryant is the Secretary General of the Inter-Religious Federation for World Peace. He is Professor of Religion and Culture, Renison College, University of Waterloo, Canada. He is author or editor of more than a dozen books, the most recent is *Jonathan Edward's Grammar of Time, Self, and Society*; other books include: *Religion in a New Key*; *Huston Smith: Essays on World Religions*; *Interreligious Dialogue: Voices from a New Frontier*; *The Many Faces of Religion and Society*; and *God: The Contemporary Discussion*. He is currently researching the notion of dialogue and a history of Christian thought.

William Cenkner: Dr. Cenkner is Professor of the History of Religions and former Dean of the School of Religious Studies, The Catholic University of America, Washington, D.C. His books include: *The Hindu Personality in Education: Tagore, Gandhi, Aurobindo*; *A Tradition of Teachers: Saṅkara and the Jagadgurus Today*; he is co-author and editor of *The Religious Quest* and editor of *Multicultural Experience in U.S. Church and Theology*. His current project is a book on Rabindranath Tagore.

Francis Xavier D'Sa: Professor D'Sa, S.J., is presently Director of the Institute for the Study of Religion, De Nobili College, Pune, India; he was also Director of the Department of Sanskrit and Symbolism at this institute. For many years Professor of Indian Religion and Theology at the Jesuit Jnana Deepa Vidyapeeth, he is author of *Gott, der Dreieine und der Allganze. Vorwort zur Begegnung zwischen Christentum und Hinduismus*; recent articles include "The Remembering of Text and Tradition: Some Reflections of Gerhard Oberhammer's Hermeneutics of Encounter," and "The Happening of Tradition: The Mimamsa's Vedapramanan," both in *Hermeneutics of Encounter: Essays in Honour of Gerhard Oberhammer*, ed. F. X. D'Sa and R. Mesquita. His research continues in the encounter of Mimamsa and contemporary hermeneutics.

David J. Goldberg: Rabbi Goldberg is Senior Rabbi at The Liberal Jewish Synagogue, Leo Baeck College, London. He is author of *The Jewish People* and his most recent book appearing in 1995 is *To the Promised Land*.

David Ray Griffin: Dr. Griffin is Professor of Philosophy of Religion and Theology, School of Theology at Claremont & Claremont Graduate School, California. He is also the Executive Director of the Center for Process Studies. Among his many books are: *God, Power, and Evil: A Process Theodicy*; *God and Religion in the Postmodern World*;

Evil Revisited; *Parapsychology, Philosophy and Spirituality*. He is co-author of: *Process Theology: An Introductory Exposition*; *Primordial Truth and Postmodern Theology*; *Varieties of Postmodern Theology*; *Founders of Constructive Postmodern Philosophy*. He has also edited a number of books, among which is *The Reenchantment of Science, Spirituality and Society*. He is now working on a project arguing the need for global governance to deal with security, and ecological and economic crises.

Anthony J. Guerra: Dr. Guerra is Vice Provost for Academic Development, University of Bridgeport, Connecticut. He is author of *Romans and the Apologetic Tradition: The Purpose, Genre, and Audience of Paul's Letter*. He is also editor of *Unification Theology in Comparative Perspectives*. He is presently working on a comparative study of the origins of various religions from ancient times to the modern period.

Riffat Hassan: Dr. Hassan is Professor of Islamic Studies, University of Louisville, Kentucky. She has done extensive development work in Pakistan among Muslim women.

Sheldon R. Isenberg: Dr. Isenberg is Associate Professor of Jewish studies in the Department of Religion and the Center for Jewish Studies, University of Florida, Gainsville. His recent writing includes: "Aging in Judaism," *The Handbook of Aging and the Humanities*, ed. by Thomas R. Cole; "The Post-Modern Return of the Metaphysically Repressed," *Aries* (1991-1992); "More Than We Can Say: Modern and Post-Modern in Perennialist Perspective," *Aries* (1990). He is now working on psychospiritual development from a comparative perspective.

Gene G. James: Dr. James is Professor of Philosophy, Department of Philosophy, The University of Memphis, Tennessee. He is author of numerous articles in philosophy of religion, social and political philosophy, ethics and related areas. He is also co-author of a textbook in logic and editor of several anthologies. He is currently working in environmental ethics and a book on evil in the world's religions.

Stephen Kaplan: Dr. Kaplan is a Professor in the Department of Religious Studies, Manhattan College, New York. He is author of *Hermeneutics, Holography and Indian Idealism: A Study of Protection and Gaudapada's Mandukhya Karika*. His recent articles include: "Yogacara Roots of Advaita Idealism?," *Journal of Indian Philosophy* (1992); "A Holographic Analysis of Religious Diversity: A Case Study of Hinduism and Christianity," *Journal of Religious Pluralism* (1993). His current project is the impact of orality and genre on interpretation of Indian philosophical texts.

E. O. Oyelade: Reverend Dr. Emmanuel Oguntoye Oyelade is Senior Lecturer, Department of Religious Studies, Obafemi Awolowo University, Ile-Ife, Nigeria. His recent articles include: "Religion, Politics, and Peace in Africa: A Study of Religious Pluralism and Islamic Fundamentalism," in *Religion and Peace in Multi-Faith Nigeria*, ed. J. K. Olupona; "The Creative Poems of Mu'azu Hadeja: An Aspect of Islam and Social Change in Northern Nigeria," in *Diversity of Creativity in Nigeria*, ed. Bolaji Campbell; "The Doctrine of Predestination: A Study of Religio-Cultural Interactions in Nigeria," in *IFE, Annuals of the Institute of Cultural Studies*, ed. Bade Ajuwon. His research project is Islam and Christian missions in contemporary Nigeria.

Peter C. Phan: Dr. Phan is Professor and former Chairperson in the Department of Theology, School of Religious Studies, The Catholic University of America, Washington, D.C. He is also former editor of the journal *Dialogue & Alliance*. Author of several books and many articles in theology, culture, and society, his book *Eternity in Time* is mentioned here with recent articles: "Contemporary Context and Issues in Eschatology," *Theological Studies* (1994); "Experience and Theology: An Asian Liberation Perspective," *Zeitscrift für Mission-swissenschaft und Religionswissenschaft* (1993). He is currently re-searching inculturation of theology in the Vietnamese society of the 17th century.

Mary Ann Stenger: Dr. Stenger is Visiting Associate Professor in Religious Studies, University of Louisville, Kentucky. Her recent articles include: "Tillich's Approach to Theology and Natural Sciences: Issues of Truth and Verification," *Natural Theology versus*

Theology of Nature?/Naturliche Theologie versus Theologies der Natur?, ed. by Gert Hummel; "Paul Tillich and the Feminist Critique of Roman Catholic Theology," *Paul Tillich: A New Catholic Assessment*, ed. by Raymond F. Bulman & Frederick J. Parella. Several articles on religious pluralism also appear in *Religious Pluralism and Truth: Essays on Cross-Cultural Philosophy of Religion*, ed. by Thomas Dean. She is currently working on a project to bring together pluralist and feminist critiques of Christian theology.

Medagama Vajiragnana: The Venerable Dr. Vajiragnana is Abbot of the London Buddhist Vihara, Bedford Park, London. He is author of three books: *Buddhist Meditation*; *Life of a Lay Buddhist*; *Parent and Child in Buddhism*; also two monographs, "Peace Through Buddhism," and "Health Through Buddhism." All were published in the 1980's in Malaysia and Singapore.

Chandra Wikramagamage: Dr. Wikramagamage is Professor of Pali and Buddhist Studies and Dean of the Faculty of Arts, University of Jayewardenepura, Nugegoda, Sri Lanka. His research publications include: *Galvihara, Polonnaruva*; *The Avukana Buddha*; *The Stupa*; *J. G. Smither's Architectural Remains, Anuradhapura* (Rev. Ed.); *First and Second Excavation Reports of Abhayagirivihara*; and *Buddhist Iconology*. He continues to research in Buddhist art and architecture.

Jane Mary Zwerner: Dr. Zwerner is author of *The Co-Existence of God and Evil*. Recent articles include: "Modalism Revisited," *Negation and Theology*, ed. by Robert Scharlemann; "Futility, Autonomy, and Informed Consent," *Health Progress* (March, 1994); "In the Patient's Best Interest," *Health Progress* (April, 1993); "Exclusively Male Imagery in Religious Language," *Worship* (July 1992). She was recently Vice President, Values Integration and Leadership Development, Allegany Health System, Florida. She is currently working on a textbook in ethics.